D1715869

Children and Animals

LIVES IN CONTEXT

Series Editor: Mihaly Csikszentmihalyi, University of Chicago

Perhaps the most important challenge for contemporary psychology is to apply its conceptual models and experimental findings to the explanation and understanding of individual lives lived in the complex world outside the laboratory. This task requires a more integrative, holistic, and socially and historically informed approach to the study of individual behavior than is usually practiced by psychologists. The *Lives in Context* series offers scholars an opportunity to take up the challenge, to publish their best work—work that combines empirical and theoretical rigor with an understanding of the whole person in natural settings.

Children and Animals

Social Development and Our Connections to Other Species

GENE MYERS

WestviewPress

A Division of HarperCollins*Publishers*

Lives in Context

Copyright © 1998 by Westview Press, A Division of HarperCollins Publishers, Inc.

Published in 1998 in the United States of America by Westview Press, 5500 Central Avenue, Boulder, Colorado 80301-2877, and in the United Kingdom by Westview Press, 12 Hid's Copse Road, Cum-nor Hill, Oxford OX2 9JJ

Library of Congress Cataloging-in-Publication Data
Myers, Jr., Olin Eugene
    Children and animals: social development and our connections to
other species / Gene Myers
        p.   cm.—(Lives in context)
    Includes bibliographical references and index
    ISBN 0-8133-3171-4 (hardcover)
    1. Children and animals.   2. Child development.   3. Child
psychology.   4. Human-animal relationships.   I. Title.   II. Series.
BF723.A45M94   1998
155.4'18—dc21

97-26350
CIP

The paper used in this publication meets the requirements of the American National Standard for Permanence of Paper for Printed Library Materials Z39.48-1984.

10   9   8   7   6   5   4   3   2   1

Contents

Preface

What transpires between a child and an animal when they interact is at once quite transparent and yet hard to fathom. Many a parent, educator, or interested adult has observed the plain delight, intense interest, and strong feelings animals evoke in young children. This phenomenon alone provokes curiosity. But beneath this sturdy fact, what is going on? What do animals mean in the context of children's blossoming capabilities of language, thought, and understanding of other minds together with broadening social abilities? Do animals provide something developmentally unique? What are the roots of our bonds with and antipathies toward other creatures? These questions initially motivated me to embark on a long study of this rather unexamined topic.

Unexamined—but not entirely; credit must go to a number of astute researchers whose work I review at appropriate places in this volume. Yet I felt a need to understand not just the general findings but the patchwork of patterns found in samples of children by researchers with differing viewpoints. After exploring such possibilities, I settled on an approach that let me learn to know some children deeply as individuals. What are the various meanings of animals for young children? I hope this book will convey some of the intriguing particularities of different children's approaches.

Sometimes, prolonged involvement with a small part of the world yields insights with broad application. As it turned out, my knowledge of the children in this book led to a new and wider picture. Consider the range of things children do with animals—touching, holding, feeding, imitating, talking to and about them. Hold in mind also all the ways animals differ, and how children do or do not accommodate themselves to the different qualities of animals. Is there any order unique to these arrangements or are they just the playing out of the children's early biases and predilections on fairly neutral others? Or are the children's behaviors just early expressions of their local culture? All these possibilities must be entertained and sorted out. Scrape the surface of everyday phenomena of home, classroom, zoo, pet shop, and the out of doors and a surprising complexity opens out. I believe there is a special pattern in what animals mean to children, and my main thrust in this book is to describe it.

Some readers may find it challenging even to accept such a pattern as a possibility. Animals are one of the most compelling, foreign yet familiar, and available aspects of nature, but there are reasons to look critically at attempts to understand children's relations with animals. I am aware that the topic is surrounded in popular culture with romanticism—and with skeptical dismissal in reaction to this very sentimentality. Animals are interpreted in many other ways in Western culture, too. I do not ignore these concerns. In fact, they provide a fascinating intellectual background to my subject.

But this book is certainly more than a history of children and animals in Western culture. I have sought to found my interpretations upon solid data and current understandings of child development. And I want to avoid underestimating children's abilities and contributions. Inevitably, however, such an enterprise has limitations. Many of my key findings are based on an intensive study of one group of preschoolers. I do not deal with all kinds of animal encounters—the book is not primarily about pets, animal-facilitated therapy, wild animals, zoo animals, or environmental education, although it has much to tell professionals in these areas. I chose to look rather at animals near human scale, representing a phylogenetic range and mostly found in the children's familiar school setting. I felt these conditions were optimal for the kind of pattern detection I wanted to attempt.

If this book accomplishes nothing else, it should show that children's relationships with animals deserve to be taken seriously. Before starting this project, I spent several years educating children about the natural environment. Stimulated by their responses, I sought to find out why it engaged them so much. To my surprise, I found existing traditions of developmental theory assigned little psychological importance to the natural environment in which we evolved. The reasons for this, pertaining specifically to animals, are part of the story in these chapters. More than a century after Darwin, we have yet to come to terms with our own animality, including the bonds it gives us, virtually ready made, to other species.

Although research on children and animals is young, there are many reasons to advance it. It turns out to be a key arena for studying developmental processes in which the characteristics of interactants might be expected to make a difference (for example, language; nonverbal communication; theory of mind; biological concepts; categories; social understanding; and, above all, the self). Surprisingly, it has not been exploited to a greater extent. But then, we (perhaps psychologists particularly) have tended to look at animals primarily as *lacking* in comparison to ourselves so that even such illuminating discrepancies have been largely ignored.

Other reasons to study children's relationships with animals have to do with what is at stake for the children developmentally. Here, the implications reach beyond animals to the ecosystems on which our community of life depends. Many have pleaded for a deeper understanding of the human processes that both tie us to, and alienate us from, our earthly matrix. If this book has one contribution to make in this area, it is toward understanding precisely how a sense of connection to animals, and by extension to a wider subjective ecology, may be a *telos*, or end, of normal development.

Thanks are owed to many who helped in the long process of creating this volume. Foremost among these are the members of my doctoral dissertation committee at the University of Chicago, where this work began. I want to thank Mihaly Csikszentmihalyi for his guidance and consistent support; one could not wish for a better mentor. Eugene T. Gendlin catalyzed, through his teaching and writings, important intellectual developments in myself. Daniel G. Freedman was always able to see both the details and the larger whole. All have contributed greatly as mentors, role models, and thinkers to my work.

Other important intellectual influences are John C. Miles and the late David E. Clarke of Huxley College, the late Richard S. Davis of College of the Atlantic, and J. Ronald Engel of the Meadville-Lombard Theological School. Much is owed to current and former faculty, students, and staff of the Committee on Human Development at the University of Chicago—an institution uniquely suited to such an interdisciplinary project. Their influences have been immensely rich, diverse, critical, and constructive. I would especially like to thank Betty Cawelti, Peggy Miller, Rick Shweder, Susan Stodolsky, Bert Cohler, Gil Herdt, Barb Glaessner Novak, Cindy Dell Clark, Daniel Messinger, and the members of the Person-Culture-Body Workshop. The Chicago Bateson Society, Almut Beringer, Rebecca Krantz, Carla Schafer, Dana and Rand Jack, and friends at the College of the Atlantic and Western Washington University all helped me formulate this project. Ken Shapiro also deserves thanks for his support. Portions of Chapter 4 appeared as "Child-animal interaction: Nonverbal dimensions" in *Society and Animals* (1996, vol. 4, no. 1, pp. 19–35), the journal he edits; they are reprinted here with permission. My appreciation goes also to the many child development and human-animal researchers and theorists whose ideas have influenced me.

And then there are others without whom this project would have literally been impossible. I owe thanks to the Chicago Community Trust and the Searle Foundation for fellowship support from 1985 to 1989 and to the

Spencer Foundation for a Dissertation-Year Fellowship in 1990–1991. Cathy Pusateri and Michelle Baxter of Westview Press guided this project through with stupendous grace, sensitivity, intelligence, and timing; their talents and those of their colleagues are deeply appreciated. Gloria Needlman offered the perfect setting and much enthusiasm for my project. And of course, without the graceful and open acceptance of the children who are featured in this book and the willing cooperation of their parents, little of it would have been possible. If it is worthy of them, it will stand as some sort of a testament to the possibility of a fine human home amid the earth's many other creatures.

Finally, my gratitude is greatest toward those closest to me. Mardi Solomon has supported me intellectually and emotionally throughout. And I wish to thank my parents for their endless generosity, unwavering faith, and love over the years this book has taken to come to fruition.

Gene Myers
Bellingham, Washington

1 Introduction: The Sense of Connection

ONE NOVEMBER MORNING, I sat on the floor of a nursery school classroom with two young boys, watching birds come to the feeder outside. Toby and Scott, each about three and a half, were two of the youngest in the class of twenty-five children whom I was to come to know during this school year. During that time, I shared many events with the children—usually in an avuncular sort of role: I was an adult who was very interested in their activities and thoughts but not inclined to discipline or correct them. Many aspects of life in this classroom were uncovered by my work as what might be called the resident ethnographer, but I focused especially, though not conspicuously, on episodes such as the one about to unfold—ones involving animals.

This nursery school, probably like many in North America, is inhabited by protean animal presences. There are storybook animals of several sorts. Others are animated by pretend—be they stuffed, plastic, or the transformed bodies of the children themselves. Curricular animals enhance preschool-level biology. And then there are living animals, outdoors and inside, constituting the locally available slice of the vast diversity of the animal kingdom. At times, the young child's world seems saturated by animal presences.

My task was no less than to understand what this entire mixed menagerie meant to these young children, to find and sort out its core importance, if any there was. Was this too sweeping a goal? Perhaps. In the previous list of kinds of "animals," some seem to spring solely from literary convention or children's television or toys. Animal pretend play is a subset of pretend generally and thus defined by considerations such as social interaction or the acting out of psychosocial issues. In the curriculum, animals are subservient to the child's cognitive development, and teachers know animals are useful in inculcating caring and responsible social behavior. Does such heterogeneity suggest there is no unitary phenomenon here to study? I do not think so.

1

The divisions of our habitual thinking cut across an underlying unity, a more primary level of our encounter with animals.

In his seminal essay "Why Look at Animals?" the sensitive cultural observer John Berger (1980) explained that it has become difficult if not impossible to "centralize" the animal. He meant that we have blurred the animal's distinctness by turning it into a reflection of ourselves—our family roles, our trivial traits. Our metaphors and our zoos reduce the animal to a spectacle and render it passive and marginal to our existence. Encounters are further foreclosed by the removal of animals from our environments and finally made impossible through the extinction of entire species. More and more, our world is dominated by and—we believe—constructed by our own species.

It should come as no surprise that it seems far-fetched to speak of all the animal presences of early childhood in one breath, since we also marginalize them in our understanding of ourselves and of child development. In this book, I explore these underlying obstacles, but I also offer a response, a different construal. Partly because we do not see animals as fundamentally important to human life, we have dispersed them to the official domains of child psychology—here in conceptual development, a bat that is not a bird; over there in psychoanalysis, the horse that is the father. Encounter is mediated, indirect, because some more important human feature intervenes. But in the actual lives of children, the animal is a whole and compelling presence. We can recover that animal by identifying the biases that have led us to marginalize other creatures and, most important, by going directly to the source—to children and their experience of animals. Thus, not coincidentally, the response this book offers centralizes animals in human development in exactly the way young children themselves centralize the animal other. Here, then, is a key case of how the natural world plays a unique and vital role in human development—a role that could be freshly recognized and cultivated by society in general and by psychology in particular.

That November morning, there were ten to twenty small birds and several pigeons on or near the feeder, which stood near our ground-level double glass doors. I asked Toby and Scott if they could see the birds, and Toby quickly replied, "Yes," adding that one was on the plants. In a tone of great awe, Toby declared he was "amazed." We talked about how many birds there were; the number impressed the boys. Then Toby said in wonder, "You funny birds . . . (pause) you funny birds . . . you funny birds."

Toby continued, "One flew on top [of the feeder]." We were close to a cage containing two diamond doves, recently brought to the class by the teacher, Mrs. Ray. Toby heard the doves, pointed to them, and noted they were making sounds. Meanwhile, Scott left and came back with scotch tape around his fingertips; he threatened to "cut" us with his fingers thus armored. Mrs. Ray intervened (just as well, since as ethnographer I avoided sanctioning the children lest they hide behaviors from me). But Scott's tape had given Toby an idea. Toby fetched the tape and put some around the tip of his index finger. He came back to the doves and moved this finger along a small area of the wires of the cage. Then he told me, "I cut the cage open." "Why?" I asked. Toby explained, "I'm pretending." " Why?" Toby: "So they can go out there and be with the other birds." Then, with his taped finger, he "cut" a small square in the glass on the door next to the cage. Satisfied, he left to take up another activity.

This sort of episode leads us deep into the significance living animals—even ones with which only simple interaction or merely observation are possible—have for children. In Toby's remark, "You funny birds," there is not primarily a psychosocial projection or an unrealized potential for more rational thought or a partly internalized cultural concept. Instead, there is a young child somehow recognizing and captivated by the nearly ineffable sameness-and-difference of another living animal.

If we were to follow one of those other developmental interpretations, we might find ourselves concluding that whatever sense of awe and connection Toby feels is something that he will, and even should, outgrow with maturity. Perhaps, he will. But something of great importance would be lost. Although I observed these children for only a year, the pattern I discerned in their relations to animals may offer its own developmental potential. What is that pattern and what is its potential? What about an animal—and what about a child—causes the child to experience the animal as a vivid and different subjective other? What dynamics of development cause the child's sense of self to arise in relation to the animal, not just to the animal's symbolic cultural meaning or some other factor? What are the wider implications for our understanding of children's relationships and of human development generally? These are the focal questions of this book.

My approach to answering these questions centers on the relational nature of the self, as it arises from interactions. Theorists from several schools of research into the child's sense of self agree that the self arises in relationships (patterns of interactions over time); some researchers have even examined animals as "others." But this book is different in taking a comprehensive view of interactive capacities and their implications for self. This will allow us to view the relational self in the context of the child's actual interactions with other species.

The pattern that we find is this: Young children demonstrate finely attuned sensitivities to certain basic and somewhat variable qualities of animals as interactants, even as the children also show certain biases as inter-subjective and linguistic young humans. We repeatedly find a small set of core traits of animals (including humans) uniting a whole range of animal-related activities of children. I label these traits *agency* (the animal moves on its own and can do things like bite, crawl, look around, and so on), *coherence* (the animal is easily experienced as an organized whole), *affectivity* (the animal shows emotions—or, better, patterns of excitement, relaxation, and many different qualities of feeling), and *continuity* (with repeated experiences an animal becomes a familiar individual). These qualities underlie Toby's responsiveness to the birds. And, crucially, they are qualities that form the child's sense of self and other, beginning at a very early age.

The questions I raise in this book about the patterns and potentials of the child's relations to animals take on a sharper edge in view of the later part of the example of Toby and the doves. The birds' capacity for flight—for agency or autonomy—and for subjective well-being mattered to Toby. They mattered enough for him to concoct a fantasy of liberating the doves. In this responsiveness to the doves' condition, we see the early stirring of a moral attitude toward living things. Research into early child development leads us to expect an emerging moral attitude toward other people, which some-times might generalize to animals. But the pattern I found indicates a some-what different explanation: The same interactive dynamics underlie early moral attitudes toward both humans and animals. Toby's moral concern could be a generalization from human to animal, but it contains more than that since the birds' exact animate needs are his focus. These needs of the animal as an agentic subject are closely related to the core traits I referred to previously, traits that apply equally to humans and animals. When these core traits are evident in an interactant, children are likely to feel a morally relevant sense of concern toward the other.

This explanation entails a developmental dynamic with broad implications for our understanding of several different aspects of children; indeed, it goes to the roots of a persistent problem in our psychological theories. This problem is that we see the animal body as simple, reflexive, and en-tirely different from the complex and autonomous traits of mind that make us human. It is no wonder we marginalize animals in human life and devel-opment. The dichotomy of mind and body resides within the person, too, and leads to theoretical quandaries about moral, cognitive, and social devel-opment. We are just beginning to learn how our knowledge is grounded in sensuous activity.[1]

Study of the child's relation with the animal adds to this growing under-standing because it shows how embodied interaction is at the root of the self, moral feeling, and other mental phenomena. For example, moral feeling toward animals bears the marks of its origins—the child's response to the core properties of animals. Morality is not, as some hold, merely an external social construction children are taught. Nor is it a byproduct of an isolated egocentric self. But culture and language certainly do affect moral development. Children's relations with animals tell us culture and language can foster continuity or discontinuity with embodied experience and feeling. In other areas of development also, this subject sheds new light on some old problems.

Finally, the findings I report here unavoidably resonate with concerns about one context of self and society—the ecological context, of which animals are members. We are more likely to act positively toward something if we perceive it to be indispensable to the well-being of the self. This book raises the strong possibility that our formalized understandings—our theories—of the self and its context have systematically obscured the importance of other species in our development. Greater recognition and cultivation of this developmental potential is an essential challenge for every human group. But it cannot be undertaken without an adequate understanding.

This book is about the obstacles to seeing the importance of animals to ourselves—specifically, to young children—and about the wider problems these obstacles illustrate. And it is about the solutions—solutions that often hinge on finding a new pattern among common but remarkable events. In this introductory chapter, I trace the main outlines of these problems and solutions. The book as a whole offers an interpretive framework that draws on a wide range of literatures and discourses—small parts of history, anthropology, and philosophy and larger parts of social and developmental psychology, both general and very specialized. At issue are matters of the body and interaction; language and culture; knowing other "minds" and the self-in-relationship; our evolutionary past and our evaluation of the ties it brings; continuities and discontinuities in development; and, ultimately, the scope of the human sciences.

Although this book tackles an interpretive and theory-building task, the interactions and experiences of the children I observed are a crucial empirical element in the whole project. This subject is also inherently interesting in its own right and, unfortunately, little studied. Most of the examples in the book come from Toby, Scott, and their twenty-three classmates. Since we are already getting to know them, a brief introduction to the children is overdue. About half were girls and half boys. The youngest were three and a half years old at the start of the school year, the oldest just six the following

June (this wide range resulted from it being a two-year program, after completion of which the children entered kindergarten). The children came from a variety of backgrounds, but all spent their days at this Midwestern university-affiliated nursery school, in the care of Mrs. Ray and her two assistants, Ms. Wick and Mrs. Tanner. And of course, there are other important personages to mention: Toad, who was frequently fed bugs the children found outside; Snowflake, the class guinea pig (generally to be found in her cage, or being fed on a child's lap); some goldfish; and two diamond doves in a large cage. Outside were urban "wildlife" such as gray squirrels, rock doves (pigeons), house sparrows, and other species that gathered near the bird feeder. In addition, I arranged for separate half-day visits by a wide spectrum of animals: Pogo, a dog accompanied by Mr. Grier; two box turtles brought by a herpetologist, Mr. Lloyd; two ferrets with Ms. Collins; two tarantulas and a spider monkey named Koko belonging to Ms. and Mr. Dean; and two ball pythons raised by Ms. Nol. In the chapters that follow, I frequently include portions of transcripts of videotapes of these visits to explore the children's relations with animals. Other examples come from my field notes, observations, and interviews (please see the appendix for more details on the children and my methods). The lessons I learned in this rich setting were fecund for the tasks of constructing and testing ideas and for conveying a sense of the children's varied experiences with animals.

Child and Animal, Self and Other

Living animals are central presences to young children, as shown by several kinds of episodes. Once, after running and playing in a nearby field, the class returned along the sidewalk, when, according to my field notes:

> At the entrance steps into the adjoining building, we pass a quiet dog, apparently waiting for its owner. Several children are interested, and Joe and Toby walk up to the top-step level where it is sitting. Mrs. Ray mentions it's a very nice dog, but that the children need to go on back. Nonetheless, Toby, Joe, Yasmin, Laura, Benson, and Katra wait longer and watch it quietly and intently.

No obvious interaction was happening, but the recently rambunctious children watched the dog silently until they had to go and looked back as they went. What accounts for such power of animals to hold children's attention? Different examples show children interacting intently with animals, expressing concern about animals' well-being, or finding special symbolic significance in something about an animal. The story about Toby and the doves is illustrative.

All these examples—and we will examine many more—relate to the child's self, which can be conceived of in functional (or goal-oriented) terms or in terms of the experience of having or being a self. The self can be seen as the child's system of goals, from self-survival to the continuity of others in relationship to whom the self is defined. In Chapter 3, I examine in detail how the child's self functionally incorporates the animal. The data clearly show the young child's self includes the animal in the sense of caring for it, wanting to continue interacting with it, and finding similarities to it. The problem these data pose for theory is how to understand the development and potential of this kind of self-in-relation to other species.

Animals are evidently vital in the child's sense of the important things in the world and thus should register in the child's *experience* of self. As traditionally defined in social psychology, two experiential senses of self—the subjective and the objective—can be distinguished. We all have the experience of being an acting, knowing, subjective "I." Here, the animal would be experienced as a dynamically interactive and subjective other, with whom the "I" is affirmed in its selfhood. This "I" is traditionally regarded as difficult to study because it is relatively inaccessible to self-reflection. The "me," or objective self, however, has often been studied in the form of a person's explicit self-concepts. Its ontogeny also seems simpler to grasp because its contents are linguistically conveyed in the ways we typify each other and ourselves. Although this self is easier to study, it has a shortcoming from the standpoint of this book. Although many now accept the idea of a socially generated sense of self, theories that stress the linguistic mediation of the self rule out animals as direct members of the community in which the self takes its bearings because they do not speak. Animals might contribute to the self in a secondary manner—as cultural symbols, for example. But this ignores their centrality to the young children. The task posed by my findings is to trace just how animals contribute immediately to the self. We need a way think about what animals mean to the child's developing subjective self.

An alternative tradition exists that can help us. The pioneering interpersonal psychologist Harry Stack Sullivan, the infancy researcher Daniel Stern, and others argue that the dimensions of the self relate to the structure of relationships—to patterns of interaction over time. The basic contours of the subjective self can thus be inferred from a close study of interactions. Here, I build especially on Stern's work, extending it in the new direction of interaction between young humans and other species.

Child-Animal Interaction: An Analysis

My claim that animals are directly important in the child's formation of a sense of self is bound to provoke those who hold several traditional notions about children or development. Some, influenced by psychoanalytic traditions, will argue that the child's interactions with the animal are actually projective episodes, in which some intrapsychic conflict is acted out on the animal, with indifference to its distinct being. Others are likely to object that the child's cognitive apparatus is too egocentric to differentiate the animal as a nonanthropomorphic other; instead, the child assimilates the animal to the human pattern. Still others, as noted previously, hold that language and culture are determinative over all else and that the meanings of the animal to the child are explained by such human-generated sources. Obviously, there are truths—or at least Western traditions—behind each objection. But when we carefully unfold interactions between child and animal, none of these objections holds absolutely. Indeed, a more fundamental pattern is evident in ordinary child development. Preverbal, intersubjective, and language abilities all contribute.

Preverbal Aspects

On one occasion, when a small group was with the large snake, Ms. Nol, its presenter, suggested the children were acting afraid of the snake just to get my interested response. This seemed an astute interpretation and fits well with the bias that animals are secondary to the human world in shaping children's experience. But as we will see later in examining this episode, closer analysis showed it was only when the snake pointed its head toward the children that they reacted. And they did this when I was absent, too. Something about the snake's behavior was meaningful to the children. To detect such telling cases requires a close look at interaction.

This book makes a new contribution to the field of human-animal relations because it provides a comprehensive and developmental analysis of such interactions. In Chapter 4, the positive and negative aspects of the human-animal bond are reviewed, as are the shortcomings of this concept. To start a new analysis of the differences and similarities of human-human versus human-animal relations, I will begin at the beginning—infancy—and organize an understanding of the structure of child-animal interactions around early emerging and enduring bases of the self.

Many a parent has undoubtedly noticed something recently discovered by researchers: Infants take a special interest in animals. The infant's pattern of responses to animals is not identical to that toward other humans, but not entirely unlike it either. This discovery invites us to ask in more detail about very early social abilities: How might they allow the differentiation of the animal as a special kind of interactant?

When we look into recent infancy research, a very different being emerges to greet us than the isolated and egocentric infant assumed by psychoanalysis or the "blank slate" supposed by empiricist positions. The infant comes prepared to integrate sense experience as a whole and to respond to invariant features of its world—including especially the patterns of its own bodily experience and the actions of other persons. Four particular invariants of self and other underlie the experience of the early "I," or sense of the self as a subject, and the corresponding subjective other. In quite specific kinds of interactions that infants can be observed to undertake, agency, coherence, affectivity, and continuity of self and other are distinct and do not vary across different contexts and actions. From this structure, we can infer the basis of a sense of "I" in relation to the other.

When we look at actual interactions, we can detect precisely how these properties are foremost. Together, they constitute the child's feeling of "core" or "animate" relatedness to the animal and form the basis for the child's sense of being a human self among an interspecies community of other subjective presences. Children announce these experiences, for example, in comments about what was memorable about the animals. About feeding the monkey, Laura explained, "I liked when he scratched my hand," reporting on her direct and tactile experience of the monkey's subjective agency. The importance of animate properties is evident in children's actions and responses. This becomes obvious when we observe that they respond with detailed appropriateness to the differences in various kinds of animals' coherence, affect, and agency. Similarly, continuity is revealed as an important dimension of self-other relatedness with animals by comparing the relations with the guinea pig of children in their first versus their second year in the classroom.

Such sensitive interactive responsiveness by children casts doubt on the idea that children are entirely egocentric and projective or entirely anthropomorphic in their approach to animals. In contrast to the anthropomorphism in what young children are able to report verbally (which has shaped previous major interpretations), their ability to distinguish animals as unique others in interaction is a further growth built on the infant's early skill and perceptiveness. Indeed, animals appear to be optimally discrepant social others by the time of early childhood, offering just the right amount of similarity to and difference from the human pattern and other animal patterns to engage the child. Crucially, animals are social others not as if they were simply behaving inanimates, but rather because they display the hallmarks of being truly subjective others. Such *animacy* is the precondition for another to serve psychological functions such as those ascribed by psychoanalysts and others. And, although many activities with animals are framed by cultural practices such as naming and petting, these frames cannot explain the fine features of children's actions. In fact, cultural interactive scripts are dependent on the immediate give-and-take of animate relatedness to be possible. Finally, animals are symbolic for the child not in the sense that their meanings are imposed by social or psychic factors (although I do not deny this occurs), but in the sense of confirming the child's own uniquely human self and representing and furthering the living, feeling self in a more vivid form than can other kinds of carriers of meaning.

Attention, Feelings, and Intentions

Core or animate relatedness is the earliest basis of self and other. What becomes of agency and so on as first the ability to nonverbally share feelings and later the use of language come into full bloom, as happens in early childhood? A comprehensive analysis of interaction must address this problem or risk missing important events and, more crucially, making it impossible to specify or assess the claim that linguistic constructions are in some sense secondary to animate relatedness. My solution follows the principle that the structure of interactions affects their meanings to participants. If so, then agency, coherence, affect, and continuity will remain important ever after their earliest emergence because they remain as constants in all interactions. We each put this insight into practice intuitively whenever we note meaning in discrepancies between another's (or our own) nonverbal and verbal expressions. The earlier nonverbal modes of person perception remain active. Thus, we might now ask how to characterize the forms of relatedness that emerge later and how to specify how these different domains themselves interact. In Chapter 5, I address these problems, building on Stern's (1985) efforts to trace the developing senses of self, on the work of researchers concerned with the child's theory of mind, and on analyses of the pragmatic foundations of language.

The sharing of certain subjective states creates a nonverbal form (or domain) of relatedness that applies between children and animals, but with special qualifications. In general, I found no *confirmed* sharing of affect, attention, or intention such as is possible between caregiver and infant; child and child; and, very rarely, person and animal. But what I did find strengthens the interpretation that the child differentiates the animal as a special kind of subjective other. The different characteristic vitality affects of different species—the lethargic slowness of the snake, the quick unpredictability of the monkey, the perky playfulness of the dog—were registered by the children and sometimes I observed a phenomenon like mood contagion.

Although marked sharing is rare, implicit attention and intentions of animals are conveyed by gaze and action. Some children's most profound experiences occurred when the child was the object of an animal's attention. Significantly, children are biased by their experiences with people to read some gaze and affect cues in certain ways, but they do not necessarily just assimilate encounters with animals to their usual expectations. Animals do not use affect alignment or attunement the way socialization agents such as parents do. As a consequence, animals may be experienced as sharing certain subjective experiences of the child to a greater degree than do adults and as providing a special interactive realm free of socialization pressures. This was humorously suggested by some children's admiration of animals' freedom from "mommies" and from the requirement to go to school.

Shared attention and intention have interactive developmental bases but also depend on the child's theory of mind, since both concern types of mental state. Four-year-olds attribute mental states to animals in ways consistent with findings of current research. Some children show signs of a further kind of concept not anticipated by a strictly cognitive approach: concepts about other minds that bear a close relation to the interactive qualities of the other, in this case the other animal. For example, children do attribute basic states of mind to animals, but one girl showed she grasped that the monkey did not understand her intention to play give-and-take. She scaled back her goal to simply establishing eye contact. The monkey provided the optimal difference for her to experience a sense of relatedness to a divergent other being and to form at least an implicit idea about interactive differences between species.

Animals Through the Lenses of Language

In the course of human development, linguistic communication is continuous with interintentionality. The recipient must understand that a meaning is intended by an utterance. This capacity first arises in infancy through the conveying of intentions by gestures. Built on such intended communicative actions are the conventional or negotiated meanings of words. Words are thus like "labels" of meanings that may be nonverbal in nature—the "contents" of the "file" labeled by the word. But if this were all there was to the system it would not work, because words do not correspond one to one with meanings. The system must additionally depend on certain assumptions language users routinely make and on their ability to read the social context to discern the precise intended meaning. This analysis helps us understand the consequences for the structure of interactions with animals of the fact that young children are linguistic beings .

Younger children in particular talked to animals as if they expected words to work as conventional gestures—that is, as if the animal interprets them as communicative. And in their attempts to understand an animal's actions, the children sometimes "put words in the mouth" of the animal, for instance, providing narration for an animal's exploratory activities. But although language is the implicit model, at least one older child expressed awareness that animals' communication, although like language, must be different in some respects. Animals thus provided a fascinating window on children's conceptions of language.

Children's status as language users has other effects on interactions also, concerning their assumptions that behavior may be "cooperative" and "communicative." The most important result is that children are interested in and concerned about the meanings implicit in core or animate-level interaction and behavior. If they were not language users, children (and people generally) could not wonder and care about animals' experience. The ironic and very underplayed conclusion is that language does not set us apart from animals but engages us with them.

Nonetheless, there is evidence that animals' divergences from human response patterns are not lost on children. Indeed, that the animal is outside the child's linguistic community has important consequences that we can identify. The animal is not part of the impersonal, role-structured, abstractly organized world created by language; again, it offers a special domain of interaction.

Self-Reflection, Pretend, and Continuity

It is certainly interesting to see the fine texture of child-animal interactions, and the material prior to Chapter 6 might well stand alone. Yet, my analysis of interactions with animals raises a curious dilemma: If animals are so important to the child's sense of being a subjective self, what about the sense of the "me"—the objective self with traits usually thought to be conveyed only in linguistic interchange? Children's often entertaining episodes at pretending to be animals, I will argue in Chapter 6, provide a key to this problem. But, really, the problem is deeper than the formulation I just suggested, for it concerns the relation between the nonverbal domains ("animate" and "intersubjective" I have called them), and the verbal domain and its products—the personal and cultural meanings conveyed by language. It comes as no surprise that an inquiry into human-animal interaction must confront this problem, and, indeed, this study represents a special opportunity to shed light on a host of related issues of broad importance. Some social constructionists would say objective and reflective meanings about the self are just imposed by others' words and by self-talk. But I ask, does preverbal animate relatedness constrain the meanings of culture in some sense? Is there continuity between the experience of preverbal and verbal meanings—and if so, what are its sources and its vulnerabilities? As society struggles to appreciate the significance of cultural diversity, cross-species interactive diversity steps in with an unexpected contribution! Within the constraints of our subject, I will suggest some of these wider implications.

In the tradition of social psychology founded by George Herbert Mead, it is often held that a self-aware sense of self, of the self as an "object," can arise only among the community of language users. This would suggest that animals are relevant only secondarily to the sense of being a human self—for example, as culturally constructed symbols. But if we find—as I do—that this analysis does not square well with what we observe, we might well seek another account. Indeed, there are also independent reasons to question Mead's tradition, having to do with the limits of words by themselves to objectify the self and with the integrity of the body, which Mead discounted but which is upheld by infancy research. Following the philosopher Karen Hansen (1986), sensitivity to social context, plus imagination—founded on the ability to find pattern, coherence, or invariants in experience—are prerequisites for language to produce self-awareness. But by the same token, other patterns of action besides verbal ones can do so also. And this is exactly what occurs in children's deliberate imitation of, and pretending to be, animals.

The child must self-consciously differentiate the self from the other to typify it in play. Thus many actions in animal-role pretend play reveal the child's concepts of animal other and human self—or rather, in the moment, of animal self and human other! Three such concepts stand out—human/animal differences in the orientation to the social world, the use of language, and the translation of the human body into the animal's. All of these preserve the otherness of the animal, and all confirm my interpretations of the interactively generated meanings of the animal to the child. Children accommodate their bodies in fine detail (as much as possible) to the animals they "become," showing the simultaneous closeness and clarity of the child-animal relationship.

But these results, informative as they are about an area of play that has not received careful study until now, also reveal an important continuity in experience. Self-awareness is not at all divorced from the preverbal realm. This is especially obvious in how the child "embodies" the pretended animal, as shown in this transcription of a videotaped episode:

> Ivy shows what it would be like to be a dog. Mr. Grier, the dog owner: "And what would you use to get [the ball]? . . . Why wouldn't you use your hand?" . . . Ivy: "Because you can't hold—dogs can't hold it up." Ivy holds both arms extended to the floor in front of her, partially lifting her straightened right arm three times.

The fidelity of the words "dogs can't hold it up" in communicating Ivy's meaning pales in comparison to her imitation, which conveyed exactly the sense of the dog's limited motion. A thorough verbal description would be awkward and even less adequate. As we look at many examples, the familiar animate categories of agency and coherence (both evident in the example), and affect and continuity stand out as what is salient and represented by the children pretending to be or imitating animals.

Here is a shining instance of a crucial form of continuity between the preverbal and the self-conscious, the embodied and the mindful. Pretending, translating the body into the animal's form, explains how the animal remains a vibrant subjective other—indeed, how it increases in this status once the child can self-reflectively realize the nuanced similarities and differences between self and animal.

Yet, there are many terms for the dichotomy language is presumed to create between these same domains: intentions-in-action versus prior intentions, natural versus nonnatural meanings, and so on. Why is there this exclusive emphasis on language in our self-understanding, in our theories? We need not negate the importance of language, but we can trace another parallel strand in social theory that emphasizes how action and interaction can be immediately meaningful. Other evidence from creative arts sheds further light on the underlying unity of experience—a unity that evidently can be disrupted but also offers important developmental potentials.

Language appears to pose a particular challenge for the developing mind—and often for the adult one, too. It offers the potential for the confusion of word with meaning—the reification of meanings or, in a sense, the forgetting that the word is a "label" for a "file" of meanings. Normally, these labels can be compared across files in metaphor and figurative language. But in some cases, meanings are captured by feeling or thought and made rigid, turning the idea into a thing. I suggest, with the psychologist Patrick de Gramont (1990), that this is one important mechanism underlying the discontinuity of preverbal meaning and verbal grasp. Interestingly, there are special cases—some rare, others common—where reification applies to "human" and "animal" as categories of identity.

The Animal in Moral, Cognitive, and Social Development: Continuities of Concern, Interest, and Community

How can moral, cognitive, and social development further the sense of connection to nonhuman animals? Pretend play and the self-reflective self provide a model by which we can identify similar patterns of continuity and discontinuity in other areas of development. In Chapter 7, we examine how cultural meaning and practice necessarily work within the prepotent animate or core domain—how children's responses to cultural inputs are channeled by their feeling of immediate responsiveness of self and other with the animal. Morality is clearly shaped by cultural inputs, and in the case of our treatment of animals we can point to many moral lessons taught by speech and deed. But these are conflicting lessons and do not explain children's concerned responses to animals' perils. I suggest to the contrary that certain adult cultural practices are called out by children's responsiveness. Some practices protect it; others allow it to be subverted by cultivating a sense of distance. None of these practices are arbitrary cultural conventions, I argue, but rather they reflect universal patterns of moral psychology. The roots of morality are fully present at this tender age and are an irreplaceable ingredient of further development. The message is that young children's moral feelings involving animals, equally as those involving humans, must be respected.

Animals intersect with cognitive development in a number of ways. Chapters 4 and 5 include discussions of new work on the child's biological knowledge and theory of mind. But my focus here is on the continuity of intellectual interest in the animal other—the optimally discrepant features of which make it intrinsically engaging to the young child. Again, cultural practices do not just create out of whole cloth (or fail to create) wonder at animals. Rather, such practices encourage or distort a process already functioning in its own way in the child. Cultural styles of objectifying and subjectifying animals are evident in the classroom and matter greatly for the child's potential to grow up with an interest in the life worlds of other species. So also do recognition and cultivation of the particular ways (artistic ones, for example) in which we understand and represent our knowledge of other animals.

The ultimate shape of the human self is a cultural matter, but given the compelling qualities of animate relatedness, we expect the axis of human-nonhuman is not likely to be neutral. At least in Western culture, it is a hotly contested question where the boundaries between our species and others lie. This is even true in the nursery school, and young children are active participants. And it is in them that identities are being formed. Just as with gender, race, and other categories, children are also learning what it means to be human. Based on what we have learned so far, we know that young children, both in immediate interaction and in self-reflection, experience continuity between human self and animal other. They are by no means oblivious to the differences; these differences are, indeed, what let children locate the human self as one among a community of diverse living others. But to be human can come to mean to emphatically *not* be animal. This is the ordinary reification of "human" and "animal"—the discontinuity I hypothesized earlier. There is evidence of this reification in some individuals' patterns of identification with animals—of averring that they would "like to be" this or that other creature. Some girls—especially older ones—consistently said "no" when I asked if they would like to be the animals that visited the classroom. What led to this interesting discrepancy? I argue there were factors motivating a reification of human identity. Here, again, culture is not operating on a neutral, formless psyche. The nursery school is replete with boundary disputes, evaluations of the "wild" or the "animal" body, and with rigid distinctions, sometimes motivated out of a need to put at a distance that which is morally disturbing.

Conclusion

The role of the human-animal boundary in the self has far-reaching consequences, since what is experienced as self or as vital to the self determines one's spontaneous "field of care." In this book, I argue that the natural world plays a unique and vital role in human development—that humans have a developmental potential for a sense of connection to the animal world and by extension to a wider "ecology of subjects."[2] This potential is evident in ordinary early childhood development; thus it demands greater theoretical and empirical attention from a wide range of psychologists, social scientists, educators, and others responsible for the growth of young humans.

But if we are to cultivate this potential, we must first understand it. One reason the social sciences dismiss connection to the natural world generally, and animal-human interactions in particular, is the lack of an adequate empirical description and theoretical framework for thinking about them. Indeed, we live in a world dominated by other humans. It is easy to believe that our sense of connection to other humans and their influences on us are real and important. Other people are compellingly present to us, and they influence us through many shared modes of interaction: bodily presence and gesture, as well as language with all its characteristics, such as vocabulary, dialect, and prosody, and its power to constitute. These modalities and others allow us to create and confirm intersubjective understandings with others. So powerful indeed do these modes—and our social scientific analyses of them—seem that anything less seems unimportant. This has resulted in a strong bias that the only social factors in development that matter are the human ones, those of which we are most conscious and that we fancy we control most completely!

But as this chapter shows in review and the following chapters tell in detail, children's relations to animals tap processes that lie deep in our own human animality and that bind us not only to each other but also to other species. The preverbal meanings of self-initiated motion, of unitary coherence, of displayed affects, and of sharing a past can transcend species boundaries for us. Children show this clearly, and the substance of their pretend play confirms these as the core of their apprehension of animals. In the intersubjective realm, children again show they distinguish animals as a *different* order of other, even as they use their humanly acquired abilities to read cues of affect, attention, and intentions. In linguistic relatedness, too, children distinguish animals as different. Their language abilities bias them to read meanings into animal behavior, providing a basis for further learning and making us a species that may be unique in our ability to *include* other species in our sense of who we are. My studies of children's pretend play expand the importance of the animate realm, for they reveal a pattern of continuity between preverbal embodied experience and self-consciousness. This pattern is reflected in other areas of development also, uniting the child-animal relation with other great issues in development and philosophy of mind.

The evidence in this book is essential in correcting the perception that the human world is of sole and paramount importance in child development. Yet, we place human interactive processes foremost in our theories of human development not only because they seem empirically compelling.

The underlying reason is that our intellectual forebears handed down to us a peculiar anthropocentrism and dualism in our manners of thinking about what it means to be human, and this has shaped our theories and thereby our attention.

The absence of attention to our connection with other species and the nature of the relationship between the body and our higher mental capacities are two coupled problems. Both stem from the divorce between what are thought of as a simple animal body and a transcendent human mind. Here is the broadest philosophical and historical context for understanding the problems of this book. It reaches into many areas of our culture and psyche: into ideas of social order, into popular conceptions of commonalities between children and animals, into theories of development, and into what we feel ourselves to be. In comparative perspective, it is by no means obvious that our manners of thinking and living out our human animality are the only or the best options. I end this introduction with these anticipations of Chapter 2, in which I clarify the import of this book for our common and our formalized understandings of what it means to be human. Change in such collective self-conceptions is the greatest possible contribution of this book.

2 Childhood Animality and Development: Child and Animal in Culture and Theory

I T SEEMS VERY NATURAL TO ASSOCIATE children and animals in our minds. The reasons are various. Many families with children also have pets; we take children to the zoo; and animals are very common children's toys. Not only do children and animals seem to have an affinity, but more abstractly, they seem similar—perhaps they might both be perceived as unruly or dependent. But despite these readily available associations, we should be cautious about accepting them uncritically. Interestingly, concealed in such everyday beliefs about childhood are roots reaching back into our culture's particular history of philosophical, political, and psychological thought. One prominent example will demonstrate this.

Writing shortly after the turn of the century, Freud (1913/1950) expressed a sentiment that continues to echo in our culture:

> Children show no trace of the arrogance which urges modern adult civilized men to draw a hard-and-fast line between their own nature and that of all other animals. Children have no scruples over allowing animals to rank as their full equals. Uninhibited as they are in the avowal of their bodily needs, they no doubt feel themselves more akin to animals than to their elders, who may well be a puzzle to them. (pp. 126–127)

This passage strikes so many familiar chords that it invites examination as an article of faith. Indeed, words to almost exactly this effect have been repeated by several contemporary authors. Interwoven with the child-animal theme in this passage are mixed feelings about maturity and distrust of bodily instincts, perhaps betraying an anxiety about a fragile social order.

We need to excavate some layers of our cultural history to grasp the nuances of Freud's quote, but it is evident that our response to it may contain several unexamined themes about childhood, maturity, animals, and animality. What roles are played by ideas—Freud's and those of others—that associate children with animals in our culture? Answering that question will take us to the heart of what is at stake in our notions of humanity and animality. Like people in many other cultures, we define humanity in relation to the animal condition and use animals as metaphors in evaluating different human characteristics.

The stakes involve not only children but also our formalized conceptions of ourselves and our development. The implications of these self-conceptions extend to our role in earthly ecosystems. Perhaps, it should not be surprising to find that to understand children's relations with animals we must first examine our inherited ideas about both children and animals; nor should we find it astonishing that this question sends out tendrils to a wide field of concerns about the meaning of human existence. But what may be surprising is that even though we easily associate children and animals, there are deep biases in our thought against granting the nonhuman an important role in human life and development.

Animals and the Symbolic Order

Exactly *which* qualities children and animals share appears to be largely a matter of culture, convention, and figures of speech. Cultures use animals in symbolically ordering human worlds, making comparisons between specific groups of people and certain animals. Child-animal juxtapositions are just a special case of the process[1] the historian Keith Thomas (1983) described: "The brute creation provided the most readily-available point of reference for the continuous process of human self-definition. Neither the same as humans, nor wholly dissimilar, the animals offered an almost inexhaustible fund of symbolic meaning" (p. 40).

A key feature of animal metaphors in human self-definition is their evaluative nature. As Aristotle said, in metaphor a name that usually belongs to one thing is applied to a new subject, and depending on what sort of comparison one wants to draw one's metaphor can be favorable to one's subject or not: To adorn, "take your metaphor from something better . . . to disparage, from something worse." (1984, p. 2240). Accordingly, animals may be used in two sorts of evaluative metaphors that contribute to the symbolic definition and division of humanity. On one hand, animals can be used positively as "exemplars" to show that what "we"—the social in-group—"are like" is natural and good. Simple examples would be the use of animals as sporting icons, national symbols, and the like. On the other hand, animals can be used negatively as "bad examples" to illustrate what "we are *not* like," thus making "our" virtues clearer for those who have yet to acquire them. Common cases would be referring to immoral behavior as beastly, epithets such as "swine," and so forth.

Fascinating examples of both patterns are provided by medieval European beliefs. On the positive side, the historian Esther Cohen (1994) discussed the use of animal *exempla* in how a preacher used a tale of storks as an index of piety: They "deserted their nest on top of an excommunicated man's house, returning only when the excommunication was lifted (p. 62)." Popular bestiaries, or books of animals, were full of Biblical and folklore meanings of real and fabulous animals as allegories of virtue and vice.

In a more sweeping sense, animals symbolized negative qualities. Theological writers of the Middle Ages clearly distinguished humans as above animals in the spiritual hierarchy. The human estate lay at as great a distance from animals as possible. Thus, animal antiheroes were common. "Lowly" animals were occasionally hanged along with criminals to emphasize the moral abasement of the latter. Animals were tried in lay courts for certain offenses, especially homicide, according to the historian Hampton Carson (1917). Some animal trials can be traced to the statement by St. Thomas Aquinas that animals are satellites of Satan and "instigate by the powers of hell and [are] proper to be cursed" (Aquinas, quoted by the theologian Reverend Andrew Linzey, 1990, p. 12).

As these examples show, certain groups, at certain times and places or performing certain acts, have been regarded as problematic animal-like humans. In other cases, praise is conveyed by animal metaphor or comparison. These two symbolic evaluative strategies have special expressions in discourses connecting children and animals.

Ideologies of Childhood Animality

Conceptions of human-animal difference are most tenuous and crucial where animals appear most "like" us. Just as our ideas about apes are highly contested today because they are where we now believe "nature" comes closest to "humanity,"[2] so, conversely, are our ideas comparing children to animals loaded with valuational meanings.

We can examine these junctures to discover the underlying meanings and motivations. Animality and affinity with animals are elements in our cultural beliefs or ideologies of childhood, which in turn are connected to political theory and philosophy. This is very evident in the fascination with "wild children," most notably the wild boy of Aveyron, discovered in 1798 and cared for and studied by Jean Marc Gaspard Itard (Malson & Itard, 1799/ 1964/1972). Dispute surrounds this and many other reported cases of wild children, but the impression left is that children would naturally be as wild as animals, save for parental socialization.[3] Let us examine three interwoven historical discourses in which animals and children are associated because both are "natural" in comparison with a civilized condition.

The Untamed Child

> "'What is an infant,' asked a Jacobean writer, 'but a brute beast in the shape of a man? And what is a young youth but (as it were) a wild un- tamed ass-colt unbridled?' . . . Young men, being still unable to con- trol their passions, were only a little better. They were 'like wild asses and wild heifers,' said George Fox; like young colts, thought Gerrard Winstanley."
>
> **—Keith Thomas (1983, p. 43)**

The sentiments expressed in the epigraph use animals symbolically as "bad ex- amples" in contrast to what is valued. The quality shared by children and ani- mals is original wildness, and culture is valued over such disorderly nature. Children must become "not like" the negatively valued "animal" condition. This theme has a venerable past in our culture, as well as recent expressions.

Although there were ancient expressions of a "bestial" version of human nature, John Calvin and Thomas Hobbes and their followers amplified it greatly. Both employed comparisons of animals to the human "state of na- ture." For Calvin, the acquisition of religion was necessary, for otherwise "men are in no wise superior to brute beasts, but are in many respects far more miserable. Subject, then, to so many forms of wickedness, they drag out their lives in ceaseless tumult and disquiet" (quoted by the historian Richard Ashcraft, 1972, p. 145).

Hobbes did not insist human nature was wicked, but merely that it was dangerous. Thus, in his famous "state of nature," life was "solitary, poore, nasty, brutish and short" (1651/1965, p. 96). Hobbes's living illustrations were of American Indians, especially evidence, new at the time, of their hostilities. He extended this conception to "our ancestors," universalizing his anthropology (Ashcraft, 1972). Although in Hobbes's *Leviathan,* his po- litical treatise of 1651, the "state of nature" was an analytical construct motivating consent to a sovereign with absolute power, it was interpreted more literally by others.

The precivilized condition was easily generalized to children. Hobbes held that the capacities distinguishing humans from animals had to be learned by instruction and discipline, implying they are not natural to the child. The parallel to acceptance of absolute power in the domain of child raising is socialization-as-taming. The psychologist Eleanor Maccoby (1980) summarized the development this ancient idea had reached around 1700: "Many contemporary writings compared the training of children to the training of horses, hawks, or dogs. And just as there were disagreements about whether horses ought to be broken or gentled, there were disagreements about the most effective approach to training children" (pp. 7–8). So strong was the parallel that some even felt that if animals would only live long enough they too would be capable of social elevation (K. Thomas, 1983, pp. 131–132).

Psychoanalytic thought features turn-of-the-century avatars of the untamed child. Throughout Freud's various formulations, the id was an anachronistic, animalistic part of the psyche. It primarily sought gratification of its strong consummatory, sexual, or libidinous, and destructive impulses. The brutish nature of the five-year-old is shown by "the propensity towards cruelty and violence which is a constituent of human nature" (Freud, 1909/1955, p. 270). Just as for Hobbes humans are selfish by nature, for Freud selfishness is never modified at its roots. Consequently, the adult's dreams reveal the child's mind: "Dreaming is a piece of infantile mental life that has been superseded" (Freud, 1900/1965, p. 606). In dreams, animals redundantly represent these atavistic impulses: "Wild beasts are as a rule employed by the dream-work to represent passionate impulses of which the dreamer is afraid. . . . It might be said that the wild beasts are used to represent the libido, a force dreaded by the ego and combated by means of repression" (p. 445).

How does infantile selfishness end up being repressed? The child seeks to gratify its wishes through others but to succeed must conform to their desires. Thus, the "reality principle" gradually supplants the "pleasure principle." Rational thought and "civilized" life are thereby possible, but the pleasures of civilization are dubious. Coexistence of animal-like id wishes with obedience to the dictates of civil conduct means a divided person. But this is the price to be paid to avoid a nasty and brutish emotional life—a sort of Hobbesian politics internalized.

This short summary merely suggests the outlines and persistence of this theme in our culture. Animals have been used symbolically (and without good ethological basis) to represent the innateness of antisocial tendencies in the child. The imposition of a civilized state is necessary, even though the animal within remains unmodified and frustrated. Clearly, this theme is related to many other Western attitudes to children but stems especially from old polarities in political and religious thought. In political thought, there is the tension between social control versus freedom. Christian doctrine also expresses an ambivalence between sin and innocence as humans' original state. Indeed, the positive poles of these dichotomies have also been expressed by animal analogy.

The Child of Nature

The second cultural story contrasts the "natural" with the "civilized" state in a manner diametrically opposite to that just considered. A recent incident at a U.S. zoo in which a child fell into the gorilla area and was carried to the enclosure door by a gorilla garnered interpretations along these lines: Virtuous ape recognizes and helps kindred innocent child. A coincident news item revealed the possible depravity awaiting the youth: With the complicity of adult leaders, a group of adolescents stoned a bear cub to death. Our minds close around such news with familiarity—they tell an old cultural tale.

Here, animality and childhood are conceived of as realms of relative goodness and innocence, whereas civilization is frequently viewed as the corruption of this condition. Thinkers of the Romantic period popularized this view, which, perhaps more than the "wildness" motif, influences contemporary thinking. Animals, like the "noble savage," are apt to be viewed as enviable or even superior beings untroubled by the division that afflicts humanity. Thus, we have the metaphorical animal as exemplar. The "child of nature," according to the cultural historian Peter Thorslev (1972), is like the animal in that both still exist somewhat apart from the fallen world of civilized adults and are thus superior.

A key figure in this strand of thought, Jean-Jacques Rousseau, in his *Emile* (1762/1979), agreed with Hobbes that "all our natural movements relate in the first instance to our preservation and our well-being" (p. 97). But Rousseau also protested that "Hobbes called the wicked man a robust child" (p. 67). Native self-love, for Rousseau, was not bad—his self-loving "savage" was independent, happy, and good in the state of "nature." His savage was not a beastly person but the "savage within": "Rousseau's rediscovery of the Wild Man was the uncovering and rehabilitation of the realm of feeling, which he instinctively felt was essential to an understanding of man and society, and without which social life could not be tolerable or fulfilling," argued the historian Geoffrey Symcox (1972, pp. 233–234).

Indeed, the passion of self-love is the basis of freedom, and showing the way to its preservation was an essential aim of Rousseau's political theory. Before society, there would have been no confrontation with others' wills, and thus no competition or need to please them. But history has placed us in a civil context, and there our selfish tendencies lead us to define and seek what we want through others. This leads to resentment, vanity, self-deceit, inequality, and excesses of pride. Enslaved both by such inner division and striving and by external laws imposed to curtail outright struggle, the civilized adult has lost the natural harmony of savage, animal, or child of nature.

Rousseau took as his task to show how society and person might be rebuilt aright on natural provisions—essentially to harmonize the child of nature with the needs of society as much as possible. To take only one related theme in Rousseau's thought, in his *Discourse on the Origins of Inequality* (1755/1986) he suggested that part of the natural goodness of humans is a capacity for pity—"an innate repugnance to see his kind suffer" (p. 160). He even argued that pity was "so Natural that the Beasts sometimes show evident signs of it" (p. 160). But this simple unreflective pity merely tempers our selfishness and cannot withstand the development of society and vanity. Thus, "reason is subsequently forced to reestablish [pity] on different foundations when, by its successive developments, it has succeeded in smothering Nature" (pp. 132–133).

In this story, although an initial positive commonality (and even sympathy) exists between children and animals, it is ultimately incompatible with civilization. Innocent, natural, and good, the animal-like child easily falls prey to the vanity and corruption of society; only carefully calculated child rearing such as Rousseau outlined in *Emile* can avoid it. In ordinary socialization, innocence, independence, vitality, and natural acuity of mind are lost, and the person comes to be ruled by the opinions of others and divided between inclination and duty.

For Rousseau, child development and social order required the intervention of a tutor or legislator. But later Romantic idealizations held that the child was inherently good and its inclinations should be unrestrained, according to the historian of psychology Lloyd Borstelmann (1983, p. 24). Thus, stronger versions of the favorable comparison of animals and children echo through much of the culture. In 1896, the psychologist James Sully mused: "In a sense a child may be said to belong to the animal community. . . . Has he not, indeed, at first more in common with the dog and cat, the pet rabbit or dormouse, than with that grown-up human community which is apt to be so preoccupied with things beyond his understanding, and in many cases, at least, to wear so unfriendly a mien?" (p. 247).

Assumptions of goodness and innocence may have contributed to the elevation of the moral status of both animals and children. For example, humane laws were applied to both. In 1874, the New York Society for the Prevention of Cruelty to Animals defended an abused child on the basis of an animal protection statute. Societies for the prevention of cruelty to children subsequently set up in New York and Great Britain were described by the philosopher Peter Singer (1975, p. 212).

In recent times, the theme of the child of nature has blended with what Borstelmann (1983) identified as the "child as future redeemer" (p. 30). Today, the corruption from which children may save society is environmental degradation. As in the earlier versions of the theme, society is problematic—only now in the thoroughgoing sense of destroying its own biophysical preconditions. Children themselves did not create this fallen condition and are not held responsible for it; in this they are seen to be like the animals of natural ecosystems. Both animals and children now need protection from environmental pollution and other dangers. The animal-child relationship becomes a paradise lost retrospective, as well as a hoped-for ecological Eden prospective. But at the same time, other agendas continue apace: The child must be ready to survive in the competitive economic world and so on. Too great an attachment to animals might hinder these goals, so interest in animals is seen as a passing stage.

Childhood Animality as a Stage in Evolution Reenacted

The question of stages invokes a key notion of the third discourse. The two themes in modern thought discussed so far link animals and children in the service of ideological evaluations of human qualities and prescriptions for society—especially the need for social control and for the encouragement of freedom. In the third discourse, additional elements lead beyond metaphor to the assertion of a literal child-animal similarity. Actual contact between children and animals is valued—but only at a particular phase of development. Again, an underlying theme is the suitability of the child to a particular society.

The history of ideas about childhood shows scant evidence of interest in children for their own sake. The first careful observational account of a child's development was published in 1787 by the German historian of philosophy Dietrich Tiedemann (1787–1927). But the work of Darwin brought the study of humanity firmly into the domain of natural science. It is thus ironic but expectable that when the scientific study of the child was vigorously undertaken by the American psychologist G. Stanley Hall and his followers at the turn of the century, it came with heavy evolutionary presuppositions. Indeed, in *The Descent of Man and Selection in Relation to Sex* (1871/1874), Darwin tried to reduce the gap between animals and humans by showing that animals had the rudiments of qualities most highly prized in humans—emotions and mental faculties: "The difference in mind between man and the higher animals, great as it is, certainly is one of degree and not of kind" (p. 126). In *The Expression of Emotion in Man and Animals* (1872/1965), he made the complementary case that humans demonstrate many remnants of animality and showed the adaptive roots of facial expressions and their analogues in other animals.

But although Darwin was cautious in his assertions, others assimilated his ideas to evidence from embryology: The stages of fetal growth retrace the steps of evolution. The similarity of animal and child represents this trend carried on postpartum. Borstelmann (1983) notes, "In the late 1800s, parallels between animals and children, primitive societies and the early history of humans were rampant. 'Ontogeny recapitulates phylogeny' became a slogan of the times" (p. 34). The newfound biological continuity of humans with other species suggested a developmental series common to both animals and young children. The Harvard historian of psychology Sheldon White (1983) notes that no less a psychologist than George John Romanes offered a single ordering of mental activities across phyla and across maturation. The child transcends the animal condition only upon becoming self-conscious at about age three. "What is the nature of the child?" people now asked of comparative anatomy and evolutionary history. According to the evolutionary biologist Stephen J. Gould (1977), "Recapitulation supplied the obvious answer: we understand children only when we recognize that their behavior replays a phyletic past. . . . Since a human embryo repeats the physical stages of remote ancestors, the child must replay the mental history of more recent forebears" (pp. 135–136).

This perspective underlay and confirmed the conclusions of the Child Study movement. Turn-of-the-century baby diaries and studies based on them concluded that babies go through a quadruped, "prearboreal" stage, as evidenced by a few babies who ambulate on feet and hands. One diarist noted "a curious resemblance between babies and monkeys. . . . Babies sit like monkeys, with the soles of their feet facing each other" (quoted in Gould, 1977, p. 137).

A major promoter of recapitulation was G. S. Hall, who suggested, for example, that children's fears of water "originated somewhere since the time when our remote ancestors left the sea, ceased to be amphibious and made the land their home" (1897, p. 169). Hall extended the idea to encompass the entire span of child and adolescent development, considering

the later stages to reflect cultural epochs in the development of civilization—the young child as primitive (and vice versa).[4] He held that these
stages must be passed in their predetermined sequence. His ideas had other
influential exponents, including for a time John Dewey. They were applied
in school practice in the United States, and they are reflected in authors of
the time such as Sully and Freud.

Consistent with his theory, Hall felt that the demands of schooling were
inappropriate before a certain age. Hall and his collaborator at Clark University, C. E. Browne, wrote in 1904 that part of the need for the natural world
is a need for association with animals. Thus, not only are children like animals, they need them. M. A. Kaylor (1909), another psychologist at Clark,
quotes "Dr. Hall" as having said, "Love of animals is inborn. The child that has
had no pets is to be pitied" (p. 206). He then cites a 1902 work by C. F.
Hodge, an educational expert, who is even more explicit: "The pet animal is
thus for the child, as it was for the race, the key to the door into knowledge
and dominion over all animal life. . . . Its fundamental character and value
for education are evinced in the passion of children for pets; and as in the
race, so in the life of the child, it should be made the most of as a step toward
civilization" (p. 206). All of this served to justify Kaylor's own investigations,
in which he found children prefer animals suitable to the stage of culture
they have thus far recapitulated. By the time children reach age sixteen, the
horse—integral to the achievement of human civilization—is most frequently their favorite. Kaylor concluded: "The acquisition of dominion over
animals was of fundamental importance to the development of the race. If
the child is to epitomize the race's experiences, the pet becomes the cardinal
factor at a certain stage in the child's development . . . to deprive a child of
association with animals is to deprive him of his phyletic inheritance" (1909,
pp. 236–237). What is strikingly evident in this passage is how this theme
served the progressive vision of the time while also preserving the Romantic
vision of the child as possessing natural goodness, the unfolding—now of an
ontogenetic kind—of which must not be obstructed.

Although the strictly recapitulationist stance was discredited in child psychology, it has had lasting consequences.[5] Perhaps one of these is the widespread notion that animals are a good "training ground" for the child's sense
of responsibility, morality, and nurturance. Other echoes occur in psychological research. Noting the similarity of methods used to study infants and
animals, the Yale psychologist William Kessen (1965) comments,

> The idea of animal-child parallels has been subtly transmuted to remain one of the
> central postulates of child study. . . . The animal and the child are imperfect adults for
> the associationist and imperfect in a critically important way. They can be assumed to
> have fewer, or more simple, units of behavior than does the full man, and their appar-

ent simplicity may permit finding the beginning of the thread that is woven into the in-explicably complicated pattern of adult human behavior. (pp. 113, 116)

Yet it is increasingly clear that child development is not a matter of the simple growing complex nor of a mere unfolding. The child is not like a completed animal or even an incomplete adult. Rather, development is a dynamic process we are just beginning to explore, an intricate dance of biological provision and cultural context. And the culture children encounter is shaped in part by assumptions about human-animal relations.

In all three "stories," we have seen the interplay of conceptions of nature with conceptions of humanity. The types of natural order are different, but in each animal's index the qualities deemed innate in humans, and the relation of child to animal, echoes and evaluates crucial issues of individual and society. Hobbesian "state of nature" conflict is shown in animal imagery—transmuted to childhood animal phobias in Freud; Rousseauian pity is shared by animals, bonding them with children; the inevitable ascendance of industrial humanity over nature is etched over the child's early "animal phase." By consensus, child development implicitly moves from a natural or animalistic state toward one that is distinctively human, regardless of how the initial and final states are evaluated.

Rhetorically, these transformations rationalize the type of person required by associated theories of society. Thus, the themes—or, widely speaking, the metaphors or stories—we have examined are parts of much broader discussions of human existence and development. In dealing with the foundational question of humanity's boundary with the animal realm, however, they constitute a special genre, which might be called "ideologies of childhood animality." Feminists, anthropologists, historians studying mental illness, and others have discerned other patterns of association between animalities and specific categories of persons. Animal-child associations are central to our particular "intentional world," our linguistically generated way of ordering and categorizing our experience. Indeed, as we shall see, our own traditions of child psychology are no exception to the use of animals in the cultural process of human self-definition observed by anthropologists.

Human-Animal Distinctions and Developmental Theories

We have been tracing themes of Western thought that took unsocialized children to be problematic and symbolized key societal concerns such as authority and freedom with metaphors of childhood animality. Interestingly, these ideas implied that the closeness of child to animal—whether based on wildness, innocence, or ontogeny—is, or must be, outgrown. Perhaps, some of this can be written off as mere moves in political theory construction. But in their outlines, such cultural discourses betray a more telling urge. Most of the themes sketched are from the modern period. Yet, if we look back to the earlier discussion of the medieval view of humans and animals, the clues stand out clearly. A rigid and peculiarly Western manner of defining the human-animal boundary is evident. It may underlie both the tenet that the child-animal association must be outgrown and also the pervasive assumption in psychology that animals are of marginal significance in human development. To grasp this manner of constructing the human-animal boundary, some comparisons may help highlight the pattern running through classical, medieval, and—in the guise of developmental theory—modern thought.

The Human-Animal Distinction

Human distinctness from other animals does not appear problematic in our contemporary view of life. Biological species, we think, differ in their appearance, habitats, and so on, but especially in their underlying essences encoded in their DNA and produced though organic evolution. Thus, humans are a distinct species within the zoological domain. But just how distinct? Actually, a number of doubts have been raised about our biological classification. The physiologist and writer Jared Diamond asked how the 2.9 percent genetic difference between two kinds of vireos or the 2.2 percent difference between two gibbons make for different species, whereas only 1.6 percent separates us from chimpanzees, but merits a separate genus (*Homo* versus *Pan*) (1992, p. 23). The linguist George Lakoff (1987) argued that Linnaeus's system of biological classification was inevitably relative to human perceptual and cognitive biases. In biology, the historical rather than factual bases of the classic typological notion of essences underlying species have been revealed. Today, definitions of the species concept abound, many holding that species are fuzzy biological lineages. By such biological or population genetics criteria, we are a unique species, but one with important continuities with other species and with our evolutionary ancestors. Yet, even a century and a half after Darwin we have been inclined to minimize the fuzziness.

The elements of subjectivity in our biological classification of ourselves point to another way in which we understand the idea of "human." Besides denoting our membership in the zoological kingdom, the term also refers to the "human condition," in contrast to mere animality (see the work of the anthropologist Tim Ingold, 1988a). Other societies also use animals in defining the human, but their human-animal distinctions diverge instructively from our own.

Not all humans everywhere and at all times have believed humans and animals and gods are simply distinct. The anthropological and historical literatures are replete with examples of continuity and blurred boundaries. For example, the Barasana people of northwestern Amazonia believe the human status of their souls is precarious. According to a myth about Yeba, the first man, people originally were animal-people. Some were turned unequivocally into animals when they were drunk at a party—they became jungle birds and tapirs and other game animals; some even became garden plants. But in the Barasana "Sõri Masa" myth, humans' souls are taken to the animal spirit house, where they become reincarnated in the bodies of game animals. That such transformations occurred in mythic times is taken as evidence that the same could happen today, according to the anthropologist Thomas Langdon (1975). Consequently, shamans are needed to mediate between these worlds, and special observances surround hunting.

To take a Southeast Asian example, although certain Thai villagers have a separate verbal category for humans, the Cambridge anthropologist S. J. Tambiah (1969) explains why monkeys are not considered food—they are semihuman: "A woman with twelve children . . . was too poor to support and feed them. The children therefore had to go into the forest in search of food, and they ate the wild fruits there. In the course of time hair grew on their bodies and they became monkeys" (p. 441). For Koyukans of interior Alaska, reports the anthropologist Richard K. Nelson (1983), present human-animal spiritual continuities derive from a distant past when animals were human and spoke human language before changing into the present forms—humans being created by a raven.

Many Australian Aboriginal cultures hold that such past time is still present in a sense. Inhering in the sensible world is another preexisting, continuing, and generative one known via "the Dreaming." From it, animal spirit entities can take human form. Thus, as reported by the anthropologist M. F. Ashley-Montagu (1937), the Aruntas believe that reproduction is not effected by intercourse but by a child-spirit or *Kuruna* of a particular totem animal entering a woman. For example, a woman might see a kangaroo suddenly disappear and then notice she feels pregnant (pp. 56, 77). The Nuer of Africa illustrate another kind of blurring the human and animal. *Teknonymy* is the cultural practice of giving a name to an adult that reflects his or her child's name. Tellingly, among the Nuer, people are named after their favorite livestock, around which their entire cultural system revolves, according to another English anthropologist, E. E. Evans-Pritchard (1940).

These other cultures illustrate how the human-animal boundary is intellectually malleable and not necessarily absolute. And they seem comfortable with a degree of "fuzziness." In contrast, we moderns tend to think of humans and animals as categorically distinct; differences have been overemphasized even in post-Darwinian biological thought. For us, the "human condition" is defined in opposition to the animal condition.

Medieval European thinkers especially were confident in the separate status of humanity. As noted earlier, humans held a special place above animals in the spiritual hierarchy. This idea had roots in the ancient philosophies of Plato and Aristotle. Plato's thought contributed the great dualism of the material world and the sensing body versus the otherworldly realm of ideal forms. If, according to Plato's reasoning in the *Timaeus*, God was "good," this dualism necessitated another principle, that of "plenitude": The entire range of ideally conceivable kinds of things must be represented in nature. From Aristotle, later thinkers took the idea of a single continuum or "scale of nature." The historian of ideas Arthur O. Lovejoy (1936/1961) described the combined result, which was vastly influential up to the late eighteenth century: the idea of creation as a "Great Chain of Being," "composed of an immense, or . . . infinite, number of links ranging in hierarchical order from the meagerest kind of existents, which barely escape nonexistence, through 'every possible' grade up to the *ens perfectissimum*—or . . . the highest possible kind of creature, between which and the Absolute Being the disparity was assumed to be infinite" (p. 59).

In this system, degree of "soul" determined closeness to perfection and thus to God. Just as humans were debased angels, so monkeys were vastly demoted below ourselves. Thus it went, all the way on down to lower forms and even, according to Aquinas, to things deficient in "good" and therefore evil (Lovejoy, 1936/1961 pp. 77–78); as we saw, Aquinas felt animals might well serve the devil.

But within this hierarchical continuity, humans possessed a characteristic distinguishing them from all other living things: an immortal soul. This idea also originated with the Greeks. Plato's dualism hinged on the mind's ability to conceive of the true objects of rational knowledge. These were the "immutable essences of things—of circles and all figures, of all bodies, of all living creatures . . . of the good and the fair and the just" (Lovejoy, 1936/1961, p. 34). A soul with the capacity for knowledge of eternal essences is transcendent.

Aristotle, Plato's pupil, was also struck by the capacity of the mind to discern eternal forms, and through him the idea of a transcendent soul was passed on to Christian thought. Indeed, his long-influential manner of essentialist definition exemplified the mind's presumed ability to perceive unchanging forms. For him, a class of objects was defined by the inhering characteristics that are shared by every member of that class and only by members of that class. Thus, when he came to consider living things in his *De Anima* (*On the Soul*), he discussed the different grades of "soul" evident in the abilities of plants and animals. Although these were not transcendent souls, they were the immaterial organizational principles that explained the living body—self-nutrition, sensation, and movement—and consciousness and volition. Humans shared the lower grades of soul but were set apart as the only being with a soul capable of reason, which was in turn was pivotal to Aristotle's *Politics*.

The idea of human-animal difference thus stemming from the Greeks possessed an immense influence through the Middle Ages; elements of it fit well with the version of creation presented in Genesis. Objects in creation each possessed distinctive inhering characteristics; humans stood in this array of creation, but our unique essence derived from a transcendent spiritual principle. The idea funded conceptions of human life centered on rationality and the idea of an immortal albeit fallen soul.

Of course, to cite only these major landmarks simplifies a complex history that has been examined in great detail elsewhere, but the elements presented are vital to understanding the problem of this book. We must examine one more historical step to link this discussion with the problem of children and animals. At the dawn of the modern era, the philosopher René Descartes radically revised elements of the Christianized Aristotelian view of living things but kept the idea of human specialness. He challenged the idea of an animating principle or soul within the living creature. Partly mechanistic analyses of the body had been invented by the Greek physician Galen (circa A.D. 130–200), the English physician and anatomist William Harvey (1578–1657), and Galileo, but in his *Treatise of Man* Descartes (1632/1972) extended such analyses to explain fully ten bodily functions. These included nutrition, sensation, and movement—the very capacities of Aristotle's three simpler grades of soul. Descartes argued that these functions

> follow naturally in this machine entirely from the disposition of the organs—no more nor less than do the movements of a clock or other automaton, from the arrangement of its counterweights and wheels. Wherefore it is not necessary, on their account, to conceive of any vegetative or sensitive soul or any other principle of movement and life than its blood and its spirits, agitated by the heat of the fire which burns continually in its heart and which is of no other nature than all those fires that occur in inanimate bodies. (p. 113)

In effect, his argument convincingly eliminated the role of the old concepts of the vegetative and animal souls, replacing them with what he supposed were the movements of fluids, of filaments in the nerves, and of other material cause-effect processes.

But Descartes stopped short of assigning rational thought a mechanistic origin. His own experience with doubt and volition and his ability to conceive of ideas such as "perfection," and geometrical proofs (all recounted in his *Discourse on Method,* 1637/1971) convinced him of the unquestionable reality of the rational soul. He believed this soul interacted with the body (at the pineal gland) but stood in contrast to its simple mechanistic nature.

The general effects of Descartes's skepticism, however, were corrosive on humans' exceptional status in creation. John Locke, for example, agreed with Descartes's physics and physiology but rejected the idea of a soul possessed of innate ideas. *All* knowledge comes from experience, he insisted. Hobbes reasoned that men's equality (he ignored women, since his concern was with political rights, which at that time were usually exclusively allowed only to men) derived not from rationality or divine status but from their ability to kill each other, which critics complained made men more barbarous than beasts (Ashcraft, 1972, pp. 150–151).

The dividing line between humans and animals fell more in doubt and contention. In response to the breakdown of the old order, people tried to strengthen the traditional distinctions where they seemed most problematic, for example, I suggest, in the themes of childhood animality. If humans were no longer automatically assured of special status and the basis it provided for social order or salvation, civilized status might still be *acquired*, and animals were apt analogies for those humans who had yet to acquire it. If hope was to be preserved, that similarity to animals had to be outgrown. Even the Darwinian view of humanity was co-opted into this pattern by those positing a cultural evolution through which the child ontogenetically progressed. But any attribution to animals of consciousness, reason, and other traits thought to make humans unique was contested: Animals have only the mechanistic, instinctual body. Thus, Western culture clung tenaciously to a clear distinction between humans and animals and at the same time conceded more and more continuity, partly by the device of a childhood animality that was to be transcended. This pattern has carried over, as we shall see, to the domain of theories of human development.

Animals and Human Development

We come now to the traditional and still-dominant perspectives on children—and thus on children and animals. The foregoing overview of the history of ideas about humanity and animality will help put psychological theories in perspective. "Human development" is conceived of in a number of ways. Some theories focus on changes that vary within context. Other times, development means maturation, especially in the case of changes that appear to be fairly invariant across different environments and thus are probably genetically driven. In reality, development is multidimensional and includes both of these kinds of change. Development often implies directionality and progress. Many theorists conceptualize it in terms of some goal or end point—some valued vision of maturity toward which development does or may proceed.

Which end points are thus enshrined in our theories of development? They are the features of humans that Western philosophy has chosen as most unique and thus essential to humans—rationality, self-consciousness, and related notions. Such features were classically seen as transcendent of the animal body. Thus, psychologists formalized old philosophical doctrines when they answered the question, "What distinguishes the mature person?" with one of these capacities. At the same time, they also participated in a culturally specific form of using animals in defining the human being—a form that assumes a value-laden difference. The result is a certain sort of anthropocentrism in our formalized psychological ideas about ourselves.

Of course, to view growing up as the realization of categorical human differences that allow creative and responsible autonomy is not in itself misguided. Examples we will examine shortly include development conceived of as psychological adjustment to social reality, as the attainment of rationality, and as the exclusively linguistic mediation of the self-in-society. Despite the fact that these concepts have led to many important understandings of ourselves, when children's relations with animals are viewed through one of these theories, a familiar pattern repeats itself: The child is seen to have some commonality with the animal (perhaps providing some form of closeness to it), but such connection to nonhuman animals is usually seen as secondary or even false in light of an especially human capacity that develops with maturity. As we might expect given the origins of these end points of development, not only relations with animals but also bodies are marginalized in modern theories of development.

Psychological Adjustment to Society.

As we saw, in Freud's conception, the id evokes a strong child-animal parallel; it is infantile and instinctual, animalistic and selfish, even destructive. The psychoanalytic tradition posed the end of development as the optimal psychological adjustment of this selfish core to the demands of society. This is inevitably a compromise, and a difficult one. The necessity of accepting realistic partial fulfillment of id wishes gradually gives rise to the ego. The ego is essentially oriented toward the human world, and it must channel instinctual urges away from awareness and direct expression. Thus, in general outlines, psychoanalytic theory assumes a biologically based commonality with animals, but this is normally expected to be transcended with development.

This attitude about animals has characterized psychoanalytic thought since its inception. One of Freud's prime cases of how animals represent repressed material was Little Hans (1909/1955), a young boy who expressed his fear of his father in a phobia of horses. The horse was his vehicle for Oedipal anxiety. In dreams and jokes, animal material also revealed the id—and a lapse of ego functions. Freud, like many others of the time, interpreted severe mental illness as regression to earlier animalistic phases.

Many other psychoanalysts have followed Freud's interest in animal symbols, if not his exact ideas. Carl Jung saw hostile animal images as the projection of the "shadow" side of the self (1971, p. 147). Other writers have held that interest in animals reveals unconscious motives; animal phobias betray sexual anxieties (though fears of animals may be of a more ordinary sort); real or stuffed animals may serve as "transitional objects," in the young toddler's creation of a stable world of symbols; and animals may symbolize security or authority figures. Recently, therapy techniques calling for identification with real or inner animals have emerged. The mythologist Heinrich Zimmer (1960) anticipated this trend: "The interior animal asks to be accepted, permitted to live with us, as [a] somewhat queer, often puzzling companion" (p. 129). And all this omits the now-widespread use of animals in psychotherapies not derived from Freud.

All these examples reflect the attention and importance given to animality by the psychoanalysts. But as noted earlier, these are largely negative animal metaphors; animal images relate to a temporary phase of immaturity, antisocial urges, psychic stress, or ill health. And ultimately, if they are important at all, animals are merely symbolic and projective. In therapy, they are but a means toward a mature social—that is to say, human—ego. Notably, psychoanalysis also holds that mind and body coexist uneasily. Occasionally, the mind or ego fails and some forbidden content disconcertingly breaks free from repression, but normally the mind governs over the animal body.

The child's early similarity and connection to animals is based on an inferior form of functioning, one that is outmoded with social adjustment and maturity. We see here a circularity also found in other schools of thought: Humanity, in the Western mind, is defined by what makes us unique; what is unique in humans is valued. And since development is the realization of a valued human capacity, maturity is the actualization of difference from other species. In this manner, any central importance of animals in human life is dismissed by the very assumptions of the theory.

Maturity as Rationality.

Not surprisingly, given the history of Western thought about human nature, rationality is considered a marker of humanity and maturity. Freud said the ego obeyed the reality principle, but this is only one expression of the idea. Rationality has meant instrumental or practical reason—the ability to coordinate means to reach a predetermined end. Rationality also may mean discursive or critical reason, dialogue to clarify knowledge and purposes, as well as means. In Karl Marx's celebrated comparison of the architect and the bee, both construct elaborate buildings, but only the human does so from a deliberate plan. In the guise of scientific thought, criticism of knowledge was wedded to instrumental ingenuity. The result inspired a distinctively modern vision of development.

Jean Piaget, the great child psychologist, brilliantly examined the mental development of the child from the point of view of an ideal of scientific knowledge. The end point he posited, "hypothetical-deductive reasoning," envisioned the child thinking in increasingly adequate patterns of logic while mastering the physical world. For Piaget, activity and cognition were the origin and cause of development, including of language. On the one hand, this does not necessarily imply a drastic split from animals: Neither instrumental thought nor possibly innate sources of it are necessarily restricted to humans. Piaget looked at knowledge from an organismic standpoint. But on the other hand, no particular closeness with animals is implied either. Piaget's standard for rationality is high—some of the child's thought is animistic and anthropomorphic and therefore inferior.

Piaget called attention to the infant's impressive bodily or "sensori-motor" intelligence but showed that later the young child's thinking is quite deficient in understanding physical causality and the actions of living things. The child "animistically" projects intentionality onto inert events (see Piaget 1929/1975). More recently, the psychologist Susan Carey (1985) has argued that the young child judges whether an unknown object has animal properties by mentally comparing it with a human model. In either case, the child anthropomorphizes animals (and other things). But this tendency is outgrown. Such errors are corrected, for Piaget by a gradual process of decentering; for Carey by differentiating three domains of objects: inanimates, living beings, and people.

I do not deny the importance of insights generated by cognitive researchers, but theories in this tradition have tended to regard thinking about animals mostly as just instances of some more basic thought process not of interest in its own right. Again, the importance of animals in human development is assumed away at the outset. One exception is a new focus on the child's "biological knowledge," which we will discuss later.[6] But at this point, it is worth briefly noting fundamental problems with the elevation of rationality as the end of development.

The prizing of rationality as the point of development seems hardly contestable. Our science has flourished with the realization of this potential. Perhaps more important, the objective quality of moral judgments of fairness and justice depends crucially on discursive rationality. Yet, an exclusive focus on rationality has been vigorously criticized for the distortions it can encourage in our thinking. Philosophers going back at least to John Dewey emphasized the unity of cognition with emotional and bodily aspects of activity. But the epistemology of science holds that such subjective processes are not directly observable. Even though the scientist could observe them in herself or himself, felt bodily processes (ironically including aspects of creative thought) cannot appear in the world of constructs through which the cognitive scientist observes other beings.

Thus, the experienced bodily complexity of lived interactions shows up neither in our science nor in the conception of thought we derive from our own scientific activity. It is therefore omitted from our account of child development. Without asking about the possible value of the child's naive sense of psychic "participation" in nature, it is assumed the child must develop away from this incorrect apprehension.

Language and the Human Self-in-Society.

A third unique attainment of the growing person is membership in human community and culture—unquestionably of great value and deserving of status as a telos, or end of development. Cultural systems are supraindividual since they are reproduced in successive generations of persons. Thus, symbolic media must somehow impose their patterns on individuals, and language is thought to be the principle medium. Membership in the human community is thus a matter of coming to share linguistic meanings, and many cultural anthropologists assume no development is needed, just mere acquisition. Yet, even very domesticated nonhuman animals cannot participate in language as proficiently as even the least socialized humans.

Thus, this theory assumes a drastic gulf between humans and nonhumans. We allow that cultures may appropriate nature for symbolic purposes, but we hold, as the English structuralist anthropologist Mary Douglas (1975) bluntly stated, "In the last most inclusive set of categories, nature represents the outsider" (p. 289). Indeed, thus far we have been viewing the construction of animality and humanity as a culturally malleable affair, in which nature has no voice. But we can invert this perspective, stepping into the shoes of other cultures, as hinted in Tim Ingold's remark: "If humans everywhere and at all times have engaged in the activity of world-making, perhaps the difference between Western and other cultures is that the world-view of the former incorporates the idea of man as maker . . . whereas those of the latter incorporate a denial of human authorship" (1988a, pp. 11–12). Only a few anthropologists have followed up by taking other cultures' insights seriously.

The perspective enshrining the human self-in-society as the defining unique quality of humans is founded upon a basic—and important—distinction between the human and the nonhuman animal. Language is important not only because it allows the transmission of knowledge and meanings but because it allows self-reflective thought. Descartes and his latter-day followers set the criteria of rationality very high: "Thought" means reflective self-awareness. Hegel voiced the idealist version of this widespread consensus: "What distinguishes man from the beasts is the faculty of Thought manifested and first laid down in . . . human Language" (quoted by the philosopher Richard Routley, 1981, p. 412, n. 2).

The same bias is clearly repeated in George Herbert Mead's (1934/1962) influential theory of social interaction: "Man's behavior is such in his social group that he is able to become an object to himself, a fact which constitutes him a more advanced product of evolutionary development than are the lower animals" (p. 37, n. 1). Mead explicitly replaced the Aristotelian and Cartesian markers of human difference—"soul" or "mind" with a secularized version—language behavior. The "verbal gesture," enables self-reflectiveness, the only means by which the person integrates the various perspectives of others. Thus, selfhood is only attained in the context of a society of other language users, in which animals are not participants.

This perspective reduces the significance of animals to symbolic meanings, assumes linguistic processes override others in which the animal is a more equal participant, and generally regards other humans as the significant environment of the person. To be sure, animals have meant widely different things to people at different places and times. But many studies inappropriately subsume the animal in the mesh of human meaning and social interaction. In an otherwise path-breaking book, the ethnographer of childhood William Corsaro (1985) sampled episodes of children's animal pretend play only to the extent human social roles were enacted. The anthropologist James Fernandez (1986) watched older children attain human "mastery" roles over younger children's subservient animal roles in pretend play in a northern Spanish village, commenting "They fully become subjects, that is, themselves, by becoming masters of animals" (p. 35). It is as if he saw the children recapitulate the "linguistic" human origin story told by cultural anthropologists. The child acquires knowledge of the meanings of the animal through words; any role of the real animal is secondary and subject to interpretation, usually as structured by adult discourse. Again, we see the circularity by which animals possess no fundamental importance to us, since what is essentially human eventually sets us apart.

The sociolinguist Harvey Sarles (1977) has criticized the use of language as a species boundary marker in social theory. Although language is described via numerous abstractions (grammar, meaning, sound, lexicon, structure), it is typified as *not* being other things—emotion, paralanguage, analogue; "and whatever language is, animals don't have it!" (p. 62). As Sarles indicates, this perspective can also be criticized for splitting aspects of the person, as if meaning exists on a separate plane from action. Curiously, Mead (1934/1962) eliminated the body as a source of the sense of self, because "We cannot get an experience of our whole body" (p. 136). As the philosopher Karen Hanson (1986) observes, Mead's "denial of . . . the body's reflexivity verges on a denial of the body's integrity" (p. 72). But proprioceptive capacities and evidence of infants' amodal perception reported by Stern (1985) suggest a more central role of the body in meaning and the sense of self. The phenomenological philosopher Maurice Merleau-Ponty (1945/1962) objected to "linguocentrism." He rejected the isolation of the inner subject who must construct the world from externally transmitted meanings and held that we discover ourselves already in the world. He rejected the solipsism of an opaque nonmeaningful outer world of others who can be known only as they tell about themselves. That view required that animals be known only in a very secondary way since they do not reveal themselves in speech.

As before, we find the familiar circularity, but it is time to amplify the parallel theme we have been tracing alongside children and animals—the separation of animal body from "higher" human faculties.

The Self-Organizing Human Animal Body

At this point, our line of thinking has linked the seemingly simple topic of children and animals to cultural history, to major theories of development, and to philosophies of mind. A fuller exploration of these topics demands book-length treatment, but this survey is sufficient to illuminate the broader significance of this book. In particular, two negative consequences are evident from our review of the history of developmental theories and how they treat our relations with animals.

First, such theories marginalize the importance of other animals since maturity sets us apart from them. When our social scientists have looked at our relations with animals, they have unavoidably done so through the lenses of their theories, and these, embedded in Western philosophical traditions, define human nature and virtue in ways that hinge on what makes us unique. Humans and animals are split by the very assumptions of the theories, whether at the outset or with the development of special capacities. These premises invisibly marginalize relations with animals. Thus, when children's (or adults') interest in animals comes up, the animals end up being secondary. Despite the growing attention of a small community of researchers, relations with animals are not regarded as central developmental issues.

The second negative consequence is much broader—it is the implied dichotomy in the person's functioning. The theories posit, on the one hand, a simple and mechanistic body with either primitive instinctual order or no inherent pattern at all; and on the other, a conceptual order imposed by an impersonal logic of the mind, society, or culture. Since the body is simple and unreflective, our knowledge necessarily derives from the latter—from some interposed percept, concept, or schema, placed there psychodynamically, by the ascendancy of rational thought, or by linguistic symbolism.

The underlying theory requires there to be no inherent relation between embodied knowledge and what we think as cultural beings. The body becomes socialized but offers no order of its own that can help determine the outcome. We build up our world from the objects of perception and cognition, such that animal or human can be known only as an object. The subjective self falls out of the legitimate subject matter of psychology. Theories embracing this epistemology must conclude that a sense of connection or intersubjectivity is epiphenomenal or secondary.

As we can see from repeated previous encounters, there is a link between the perceived lack of value in relations with other species and the problem of the relationship between the body and our cognitive, ego, or linguistic capacities. Both arise from the assumed divorce in our theories of a simple animal body from a transcendent intellect, today most often identified with language—the most structural, mindful, and independent form of behavior. This divorce is questionable from the standpoint of our evolution, which took place in an interspecies context, and wherein language grew in already highly social bodies. The divorce is also subject to a developmental critique. Evidence of how interaction and language are united in the human animal body would address this dual quandary. Research of many sorts is now examining the coupling of body and language in precise detail. Indeed, in our explorations of child-animal interaction we will find just such evidence.

Our culture has labored under the impression that we are an isolated species, alone in lofty (or anxious) detachment from this-worldly bonds. In the old account, the child's understanding of animals comes from egocentric projection, anthropomorphic reasoning, or cultural meanings. But if children and animals interact directly on a bodily level, then the meanings children make about animals derive from the experience of interaction. Simply put, animals may be directly meaningful to us. Perhaps, our language is even a factor that unites us with other creatures.

But not if our language (or other cognitive order) first divides our very person. This book also addresses this schism. If children's meanings about animals demonstrate a fine sensitivity to the differences animals present as interactants, this would be no inferior grade of ability to be overcome by imposed verbal order. Instead, this would show that children's embodied understanding is capable of being carried forward in more than a single or projected human pattern (although we may find the familiar—psychodynamic and so forth—patterns also). We may even further see how these interactive meanings work within and after language—that is, if children's meanings about animals do not just stop at those imposed by language, this would be evidence for how the human animal body is self-organizing in a way that includes and surpasses simple linguistic orderings.[7]

Of course, abstract conceptual thought and language are marvelous human achievements, but we may have been mistaken in assuming they are what make us *most* human. Rather, children's relations with animals show that what is most human is something deeper and older in us—indeed, something that connects us with other animals. Language and mind can make us yet *more* human only if that older connection is not lost.

Conclusion

Cultures—perhaps universally—define the human in comparison to nonhuman animals. But Western culture may be exceptional in positing categorical human/nonhuman *contrasts*. Being human means *not* being an animal! This view has permeated our thinking about social categories, including the category of childhood. Ironically, even psychology has affirmed that as children grow, they become less like animals. This kind of self-conception fosters alienation from other living things, and it also exacerbates our ongoing confusion about how "mind" and "body" relate.

Now that I have introduced the full depth of the problems motivating this book, I will focus on children's interactions with animals. This primary subject—intrinsically interesting in itself and relatively uncharted—will lead us to insights and suggestions of broader importance by the end. I begin by showing that children do indeed incorporate a fine-grained appreciation of animals in their sense of self. Contained therein are clues to the sources of this self in direct interaction. What are the bases of such interaction, and what are its full implications? Not only will I show how animals are an inevitably and uniquely important part of the world in which children take their bearings as persons, but I will also suggest how interactive "bodily" knowledge intricately reflects interaction. It both forms an essential basis for adjustment, thought, and language and determines and surpasses the paths these more "human" abilities take with development.

3 An Ecology of Subjects: Animals and the Child's Self

A YOUNG BOY VENTURES OUT onto the Florida beach "monster hunting"—spending his days watching the intertidal life, waiting for the shadow of a passing giant stingray below the dock, and listening for the messages of the wildlife around him. This could have been many a child. But the story comes from *Naturalist,* the autobiography of Edward O. Wilson (1994), one of the century's premier students of biology and originator of the term *biophilia* for the possibly innate human tendency to take an interest in living things. Wilson's career demonstrates the developmental potential for engagement with other species. He narrowed his focus to one group of insects, the ants, and become the world authority on them; but he also applied biological insights to humans; made key contributions to ecology; and, turning interest in life into concern for it, is now a leader in the fight to save biological diversity.

Of course, Wilson's life story shows the many circumstances that came together to produce such an exceptional biologist. But it also hints that the roots, the earliest beginnings, of the lifelong love affair with the world of other creatures may be the heritage of every child. Indeed, it is especially appropriate to introduce this chapter with Wilson because he has also promoted the study of biophilia—the idea that we humans are genetically inclined to take an interest in living things. Perhaps, he is right. Yet, even if we have biologically programmed "learning rules" for biophilia, we need to account for this potential in the context of our full human capacities. Especially, biophilia may mean interest in the *subjective* side of other creatures; we may be the species that locates itself in an ecology of subjects.

If our past thinking about animals and children has been biased by our ambivalent evaluations of the "animal," the body, and other matters or if the topic has simply languished from a lack of interest, that does not prevent us from looking at it freshly. We are somewhat freer today to acknowledge our biological continuity with other organisms and certainly aware it would be wise to respect our interdependence. Not every aspect of our relations with nature can be revealed through children's time with animals, but it is an area calling for new visions. The neglect of animals in child research does not fit kids' behavior.

Indeed, we can look at the child's relations to animals as a subject in its own right and search for structure in what we find. My year in the nursery school produced a wealth of episodes, stories, observations, and recorded interactions that showed striking patterns. And several of these, we shall see, reinforce the idea that animals are important to the child's sense of self.

Understanding how important animals are in the child's sense of self is the main purpose in this chapter. First, let us look at a range of episodes from my transcripts and field notes. Next, we will see in greater detail how they add up to a case for the child's self-in-relation to an ecology of subjective other beings. To anticipate, several patterns of activity relate directly to animals: interest in them, a desire to interact with them, increasing skill with them, and caring for their needs. Animals are also potently symbolic to children in a special sense—a sense that reveals the power of certain core properties of living beings. We will see how these all contribute to the self, which is a complex system of goals, and a special integration of experience. But a good place to begin is with the most simple kind of interaction of child and animal—times when virtually nothing appears to take place.

Children sometimes merely watch animals with rapt engagement, as when the children I was observing, themselves observed a dog in silence. Something about animals is able to truly hold young children's attention—a commodity of notoriously short span. Some children showed this inclination especially strongly; Solly was one such boy. Late in the school year, Mr. Lloyd brought two turtles to the class. During discussion, they were placed on a table in front of the class.

> Solly works his way close to the table and looks at eye level at the baby turtle, making a smiling, curious face. He reaches to touch the turtle, but is prevented by Mr. Lloyd—"We're answering questions now." Solly removes his hand but sits up closer, puts his hand on the table, and looks at the turtles again, still with a closed-lipped smile, eyebrows up. This close attention continues another minute. He is not oblivious to the discussion, about whether baby turtles survive in the wild (which most don't), as his lips become a frown. Fully two minutes after he started watching, Solly looks away briefly and then finally touches the little turtle with one finger. It moves toward his edge of the table, causing others to exclaim. Solly looks up at Mr. Lloyd,

smiling in open-mouthed wonder. Mr. Lloyd moves the little turtle back. It crawls again. Solly and others reach to touch it.

Solly's focus endured nearly two and a half minutes, despite an ongoing class conversation in the background and the fact that the turtles had been in the class an hour and forty minutes already. That young children have a great interest in animals is of course not an original discovery; the psychologist and educator Susan Isaacs showed it systematically in 1930.

Examples of pure attention to an animal were not uncommon in my observations, but even more frequent was direct interaction between a child and an animal. Interaction structures and sustains attention. It also presents many new dimensions, which we will explore in depth. The children had opportunities to interact with the larger turtle on the floor in groups of four, under the supervision of Mr. Lloyd. In one small group including the younger children Dimitri, Mindy, Toby, and Rosa, interaction was lively and continuous. Here is my contemporaneous record of less than a minute of it:

> Mindy gets the turtle in her hands and turns it around; the turtle faces her; she moves out of its way. Dimitri and Toby reach for it; so does Rosa. Toby talks to himself; otherwise the children are only intent on interacting. Toby looks closely, touching it several times, saying, "That feels so funny." The turtle faces Mindy and she moves back again suddenly: "Oooo!" Rosa moves back also, both girls in sitting positions. Toby: "Yikes. He looks mad, he looks mad." Mr. Lloyd: "Does he look mad?" Toby: "Yeah. Yikes. He's going to . . . he almost went over here"—Toby gestures to the floor between his legs. Dimitri now has his hands on the turtle; Mindy moves forward again, and actually picks it up, but then sets it down. Dimitri moves aside from the turtle as Toby and Mindy move closer. It crawls toward the bookshelf, all children around it. Toby: "Just let him go—just let him go where he wants." Dimitri: "Go this way . . ." Dimitri turns the turtle, looks at Mr. Lloyd, and smiles. Mindy and Rosa come around to be in front of turtle. Toby touches the turtle: "I just touched, I got to feel one of his claws." Dimitri touches it also: "Me too." Toby: "Hey, do ya wanta feel his shell?" Toby touches turtle and pulls his hand away quickly.

Even without describing the finer motions of the children, this is clearly intense interaction! Yet it was almost all nonverbal, save for some interpretation of what the turtle was doing or might do. The children were engaged in anticipating and responding to its actions. Animals are compelling as interactants. The children ignored the next group, each other, and much of what the adults said to them.

Another important theme emerged in the young children's time with the turtle. We just heard Toby ask the others to "let him go where he wants." This became the repeated and defining desire of the boys. But eventually, the turtle went too far away and they decided to bring it back, indicating a tension between wanting the turtle to be free but also wanting the interaction to continue. The evident concern over the turtle's autonomy is only one instance of a whole class of examples we will explore in this chapter. They involve the expression of concern for the animals' well-being, and they are central in understanding the significance of animals to children.

In a related case, the spider monkey that visited the class was very active. Although it was not dangerous, its owners held onto its tail, preventing it from moving freely or getting too close to the children. Drew, Solly, and others wanted them to stop this:

> Drew, interrupting, says to Ms. Dean: "Let go!" Solly: "When will you let go?" As Ms. Dean pulls the monkey back by its tail, Katra exclaims, "Aaaa!"

Later Drew directly challenged the monkey's keepers about the way they were holding its tail:

> The monkey strains briefly to get crumbs on the floor. Drew: "Why don't you let go of his tail?" Ms. Dean: "He's got my hand. I'd let go in a second if he'd let go of my hand." Actually, her hand is tight around the monkey's tail but its prehensile tip is visibly relaxed in her hand. Drew points to this, gesturing with one hand on the other: "He's let go'd of your hand . . . He let go of your hand." . . . Ms. Dean holds her hand behind her leg, out of Drew's sight.

These examples of children expressing concern for an animal's autonomy hint at one of the core features of animate beings that are most obvious and important in children's perception. The ability of an animal to move on its own, to have authorship of its actions—in short to show agency—is not only perceptually compelling. For children, it also conveys subjectivity—a sense of the animal as possessing its own interior life and goals. In response, children are inclined to respect these goals, in effect caring about the animal's own well-being. We will observe the same pattern in relation to other core animate properties.

There are more complexities to the child's concern for an animal's well-being. Ivy complained about the confinement of the baby snake:

> Ivy: "I don't think you should keep it in that cup, know why?" Ms. Nol, the snake keeper: "Well, I just brought it down in there, so it protects it from getting hurt." Ivy: "But know why? But know why?" Ms. Nol: "Why?" Ivy, indicating the size of the snake with her hands: "It could get bigger and it might squeeze"—she hugs her knees up tight to her chest, as if extremely cramped.

In passing, we may note Ivy's use of imitation, an important theme to come. But her complaint was not about restricted agency or about direct harm, as shown by her ignoring Ms. Nol's justification. Rather, it was that the baby snake could not grow. Ivy's concern extended to the snake's development. The animal can represent the child's own issues, paradigmatically in this case the inwardly experienced imperative of maturation shared by all young organisms. Animals—*just because they are living things*—may "symbolize" such issues. I put "symbolize" in quotes here to indicate a special and power-ful sense of the term, one not to be reduced to cultural construction.

I have just highlighted central aspects of children's experience of animals, using examples akin to those many parents may have observed. But such ex-amples—showing that animals command children's attention, that interac-tions with animals are compelling, that children readily care about animal's well-being, and that animals symbolize important issues for the child—al-though perhaps familiar, do not alone provide a theory or framework for understanding animals' importance to children. We must ask, is there an underlying thread of significance?

I suggest that the thread is the child's sense of self. The self is a uniting concept. It embraces activity, thought, and feeling. And as many psycholo-gists have argued, the self develops from patterns of interactions with others over time—that is, from relationships. Let us expand this to include animals among the "others" of the self. We feel a sense of relation to other species that seem to have "someone in there"; and we can explain something of who we are in reference to them. Animals provide clarifying points of comparison for the child and for our attempt to understand the self in general. Because animals interact differently with us from the way humans do, they can give us theoretical insight into the self in relation to other humans, too.

How does the idea of the "self" make sense of child's response to animals? First, we can view the self as a system of goals. These goals produce patterns of observable behavior. But the self is nothing if not also a subjective experi-ence. This we cannot observe directly. At the end of this chapter, I confront that problem and suggest a solution.

The Self as a Pattern of Goals

The self is a psychological "unit" with a high level of integration. For sim-plicity, we can think of it as an organized system of goals. This description agrees with the ordinary meaning of self, as in "self-interest." Continuity of the self is our primary goal. The bottom line is the survival of the organism, but the self is more than the organism, and its goals are not limited to bod-ily survival. Many different forces shape the self's various goals, among them genetic dispositions, social approval, and specific goals promoted by society. But since the "self" arises from relationships, continuity of the self also entails the maintenance of relationships. Thus, having a self predicts interest in significant others.

We can further infer that maintenance of relationships implies the exercise of the faculties that gave rise to them. Such exercise increases the person's skill, expanding his or her ability for furthering relationships. Thus, increase in interactive skills is evidence that a relationship (or kind of relationship) contributes to the self. From such an upward spiraling of ability and challenge, which the psychologist Mihalyi Csikszentmihalyi (1990) terms "complexification," more elaborate relationships become necessary to maintain the self. Indeed, the very process of increasing skill may itself become a derivative goal. In a final logical step, maintenance of relationships requires continuity of the others to whom the self is related; thus, their well-being may become a goal of the self as well.

An advantage of this approach is it allows inferences—from observed patterns of behavior—about aspects of the self that do not appear in conscious self-reports as well as those that do. The meaning of an event to the self is found in its consequences, as shown in behavior. We respond to events in ways that reveal their significance for our goals. Thus, a specific system of self can be inferred from behavior expressing the person's goals. Such behavior includes action toward the ends described previously, directed attention, preferences or values, and strong responses to certain events. What goals of the young child's sense of self do patterns of such behaviors involving animals reveal? We will now examine three central goals.

Interacting with Animals

Most of the young children I observed wanted to interact with animals. At the minimum, interacting meant sustained attention. Such "interest"—literally, "holding between"—means engagement. In a step still more engaged, actions by animals brought strong reactions or excited comments. The monkey grabbed the children's shoes. Being the recipient of its action was exciting! Solly said, "He bited my shoe!" and Drew exclaimed, "He was pulling on my shoe!" When the turtle scratched Mindy, she retorted, "Aaaaaa! You scratched me!"

The children had a strong preference for interacting with animals.[1] We have already seen one case. The young children with the turtle were not dissuaded from interacting even by the interference of adults—a clear instance of how the child actively shapes his or her own experience and socialization. More direct evidence comes from data I gathered one on one: I asked each child to choose one of several (randomly presented) activities. The choices were to draw with crayons; play with dolls; play with animal puppets; play with trucks; or feed the classroom guinea pig, Snowflake. Of the twenty-four children, nearly two-thirds chose feeding the guinea pig as their first choice of the five options—a striking result, since by midyear all of the children had had plenty of chances to feed the guinea pig.

But what about children's spontaneous choices? one might wonder. In the course of everyday activity, how important are animals? In the spring, I observed several children systematically and found that of thirty-eight animal episodes, twenty-three involved live animals, eight involved pretend, and in the remainder animals were the subject of talk or books. Of the children's total time, almost a tenth was spent in animal-oriented activity. Although this is not a huge figure, it is still substantial and comparable with time spent in other play activity settings that adults consider developmentally significant. Interacting with animals is a preferred activity and (among other things) expresses a goal of the self, that of maintaining the sense of self by engaging in relationships with important others. In these cases, the others are animals.

Expanding Relationship Skills

Over time, relationships with animals became more important to these young children. Interactions with the resident guinea pig show this increasing importance of the animal. I could tell this because Snowflake was familiar to returning students but not to those attending for the first time. During two months at the start of the school year, 39 percent of the instances I recorded of children involved with the guinea pig were of children new to the class, and 61 percent were of children returning for their second year. The individuals doing this accounted for 85 percent of the returning children but only 58 percent of the new ones. In other words, proportionally more of the children with the previous year's history of interacting with Snowflake chose to interact with it and accounted for more of the interactions. By May and early June, there was a more equal distribution: Fifty-eight percent involved "new" children, whereas 42 percent were ones who had been there the previous year also.[2] The children's interest in interacting with Snowflake appeared to increase with experience, at least in this age range.

Were the children getting better at interacting, too? Was a process of complexification at work? Most of the children's interactions with animals were not characterized by high degrees of "meshing," in the term used by the ethologist Robert Hinde (1976) for the precise coordination between the two participants' actions. The most intricate interactions were with the guinea pig; it was also the animal most accustomed to the children. The children could successfully feed it and hold it on their laps; they observed it in the classroom and helped with various needs like changing the newspaper in its cage. I did detect some improvement over the span of ages in the class. The younger children tended to have less knowledge and less skill at holding and feeding the guinea pig.

Regardless of age, however, differences between individuals showed that experience in interacting goes with increasing skills. Four children in the group who seemed especially adept at observing and interacting with animals spanned a one-and-one-half-year age range: Ivy (five years, eight months in the spring), Joe (5 years, 4 months), Solly (4 years, 11 months), and Toby (4 years, 3 months). In addition to their interactions with the guinea pig, they had multiple animal-related experiences outside school, which may help explain their abilities. Ivy had fish at home, had been to the zoo four times in the past year, and had kept Snowflake over spring break. Joe made frequent visits to the zoo. He had exposure to dogs in relatives' homes, his parents read to him about animals often, and he once had hermit crabs and a goldfish. Solly had fish and a toad and was very attached to the family dog, which had died in the fall. His mother reported he was always looking for insects and liked to watch birds; she herself had long had animals. Toby had spent time on his grandfather's farm, where there were cows; at home he had an ant farm. We have already seen examples of each of these children being involved with animals; these examples will multiply.

Similar examples are harder to come by for other children, such as Mindy. Her mother reported only three exposures to dogs or cats in the current school year and no pets in the home. Mindy said she preferred to talk about guinea pigs rather than pet or feed the one in the class. Actually, she did have frequent interactions (six) with Snowflake at the beginning of the year, the most of any of the new children. But these were often brief and awkward—enough so to evoke intervention from others:

> Mindy shakes the cracker box with the guinea pig in it. The other children tell her that'll hurt it or it'll die. . . . Later she lifts it up and down in the box, too quickly for my comfort. I try to get her to not do this. Then she fumbles the box and it hits the floor hard. Kevin helps her empty the guinea pig from the box onto her lap.

Most children were awkward with Snowflake occasionally, but Mindy seemed consistently so. During observation periods especially focused on, I saw few incidents where she was involved with live animals; the most involved interaction I observed her in was squashing bugs near the classroom door.

Another child toward Mindy's end of the spectrum was Dimitri. In the fall, five times he took action apparently just to make an animal react, more frequently than any other child. For instance, he chased pigeons and teased the guinea pig, once dropping a toy helicopter in the cage, then hitting the top of the cage, prompting Chris to admonish, "Don't do that." Dimitri's interactions with Snowflake were chaotic. He attentively fed the guinea pig, but like Mindy tried to control it physically:

> Dimitri wants to hold the guinea pig. Mrs. Ray helps him ask Rosa for it and puts it on his lap as he sits, legs extended, on the floor. He feeds it greens for a long time, sometimes straining to see its mouth. He tries to feed it a pellet of food. It doesn't take it. The guinea pig drops to floor between Dimitri's legs; he holds it there and says, "I got you."

Actions such as these were performed by most children at one time or another, but this pattern of control was typical of Dimitri. Data from Dimitri also do not entirely support the idea that experience and skill spiral up. He had extensive animal experience: year-long relationships with two cats, a neighbor's dog, and several visits per year to a pig farm and the zoo. During the year, one of his mother's cats was sick, but got well, thanks to a "doctor who fixes cats and dogs," whom Dimitri admired very much. But toward the end of the year, Dimitri was noticeably more adept at holding and feeding the guinea pig. Of course, not only individual differences in background but also instruction, development, and life events increase interactive skills and self-in-relationship.

The Animal's Needs

A child may incorporate the animal's well-being in his or her own sense of self, since this serves the child's goal of continuity in relationship. Altruism and caring are possibilities for humans on several theoretical grounds, and a sense of self-in-relationship is one of them. Examples of children's strong reactions to events and stories about animals, and actions they take as a consequence, reveal that meeting the animal's needs, is a goal in the self's underlying goal structure.[3]

Drew's desire to see the monkey move freely and Ivy's concern for the baby snake's growth exemplify a common concern. For example, the ferrets were put in harnesses, but they could wiggle out, and they chewed at their leashes. This attracted the children's attention:

> Billy looks and points: "Look what he's doing . . ." Solly turns to Drew: "They're trying to get out of that." Drew had been straining to look. At this point he starts chomping his teeth together.

Concern for free movement was expressed with less energetic animals, too. Toby asked that the snake be let go: "Why don't you let it just crawl around?" Ms. Nol did not reply but set the snake on the floor. Later, just before his small group time, Toby asked again, "Why don't you let him crawl around?" As we saw earlier, this was a strong theme for Toby. With the monkey in its cage to go home,

> Mindy and Rosa are on the floor looking in. Toby arrives: "Look [he's] trying to get out of his cage. He's trying to get out of his cage. Yikes." . . . Ms. Dean: "Do you think he's happy in his cage right now?" Toby: "No, see he's trying to get out." Mr. Dean: "You think he wants to get out?" Toby: "'Cause look-it, he's sticking his claws out."

When the monkey's movement was constrained, the previously implicit and unspoken meaning of the monkey's action—its expression of the monkey's agency—was revealed. Sometimes, children actually intervened with each other or with animals:

> Abeo pushes at the turtle's head again. Chen: "Don't push him, don't push [his head] inside"; he removes Abeo's hand.

In the introduction, we saw Toby "free" the caged birds—a fantasized intervention. These children clearly are concerned for animals' agency and autonomy—key aspects of their well-being.

Another concern for the animal's health was revealed in children's caring response when an animal was harmed—distressed, injured, or killed. Even mild injuries were troubling to the children. The dog owner, Mr. Grier, told the class a story about one time when Pogo, as a puppy, came to the grade school class he taught:

> Mr. Grier: "And the kids really enjoyed me bringing him in, and he got used to them and they got used to him, and you know, they could still even do their work and he would be walking around and he might sit with them and they would pet him. . . . Well, let me tell you what happened one day. One day, the class was all kind of seated down, and I was talking to them. And I'm talking and I started walking backward a little bit, and I guess I didn't look where I was going and I didn't know that Pogo was right behind me and as I was walking backward I stepped on him. And he let out a squeal, you know." The children's faces are quiet, attentive; Yasmin nods. Mr. Grier: "Like a yelp . . ." Someone makes a high faint squeal. Mr. Grier: "When you hurt, it wasn't just like a bark. It was really, he was in a lot of pain." One or two children are making squeals now. Reuben: "It was like this, go . . ." He makes closed-mouthed forceful and pained squeal. Mr. Grier: "Uh huh, something like that." Other pained squeals continue.

The children's sympathetic response to a violation of the animal's integrity and the pain it caused is familiar to anyone who knows young children. The incident was reported by two of the children to their parents. Joe told his mother about it:

> Joe: And the bad story when they were leaving our class, um was when . . . ah . . . ha . . . uh . . .
> Joe's Mother: Did something happen?
> Joe: Uh huh, um, um . . .
> Mother: Did something happen with the turtles?
> Joe: No, with um the dog.
> Mother: Oh, what happened with the dog?
> Joe: When he was a little puppy, his owner was a teacher, and he brang him to school, and he was dr—, and he was going to draw on the blackboard with a piece of chalk, and he didn't know that Pogo was right there, so he stepped on him by accident. But then everybody looked, but from then on all the kids were saying um "Don't walk around when Pogo's right there."

The incident was referred to later by Joe as the "bad story." Dawn brought up the story as soon as her father asked her about the dog's visit:

> Dawn's Father: And what about the dog?
> Dawn: A . . . ahm . . . when he was little um the . . . in the um . . . in thaaaa, ah, when he was little and he came to school with Mr. Grier when he was a teacher, and he laid on the kids' laps and it, it didn't even bother them. But and um as Mr. Grier was walking back, he stepped on it.
> Father: He accidentally stepped on the pup?
> Dawn: But he didn't get hurt.

It was fairly unusual for any event involving the animals that visited the class to be reported to parents, and these examples stand out.

The children's responses were more striking when the harm occurred to a living animal in the class. When an animal the children knew was harmed to the point of death, even greater emotions—and another aspect of the child's incorporation of the animal's needs—were revealed. Drew was very interested in the turtles' feeding behavior during their visit. He revealed why:

> Drew said to Mr. Lloyd: "My turtle died." Mrs. Ray to Drew: "Was your turtle that big?" Drew: "No. . . ." Mrs. Ray: "That was sad." Drew: "And it wasn't eating its food."

In fact, Drew's turtle had been a fifth-birthday gift, and after a brief life of six weeks it had died just ten days earlier. He had been careful in caring for it and was "very upset and sad to discover it had died one night," according to his mother. Drew discussed this further in his small group with Mr. Lloyd. He wanted to know what Mr. Lloyd was feeding his turtle and if it would "eat other stuff." The concern over the death of Drew's turtle was talked about among the other children, and Dawn reported it to her father.

The entire class suffered the loss of another animal, coincidentally on the same day that the turtles visited. The classroom's pair of doves had finally succeeded in hatching one of a series of eggs. The offspring was only a couple of weeks old when it was found motionless that morning on the floor of the cage. Ever since the egg had been laid, and especially after it hatched, the baby dove was an object of great attention. Mrs. Ray discussed its death extensively, including the cause—perhaps it caught cold or the mother did not have enough "crop milk." The children talked about this loss, and Dimitri brought it up with his mother. And in yet a further coincidence, another dead animal appeared on the same quite death-ridden day—a gray-cheeked thrush whose "sad eyes" impressed Mindy. All these dead animals were mentioned to Mr. Lloyd minutes after his arrival:

> Drew: "You know what?" Mr. Lloyd: "Hmm?" Drew: "I have a turtle except it died." Mr. Lloyd: "Why did it die?" Drew: "It wasn't eating its food, turtle food." . . . Abeo: "We found a dead bird outside." Mr. Lloyd: "You did, what did you do . . ." Drew (interrupting): "Brunged it inside . . ." Mr. Lloyd (interrupting): "Did you just leave it there?" Drew: "And our baby bird died inside here, today."

The death of an animal is recognized to be a traumatic event, as the study of people bereaved of their pets has shown (see the work of the human–companion animal researcher Lorann Stallones, 1994). It carries dual aspects. On the one hand, it constitutes a breach in a relationship within which the self had taken its bearings and thus threatens continuity of self. On the other hand, through relationship the goals of the other—goals like continuity and well-being—come to matter for the *other's* sake. Death can seem an ultimate violation of those goals.

American parents tend to feel responsible for their children's outcomes. Theory reinforces this with the idea that we construct every experience for the young. In some of the preceding examples, adults attempted to moderate the impact of harm or loss. But the impact had occurred; the adult's intervention was just a response. Even when the event was anticipated, its impact was felt despite adults' attempts to construct the problem in a more positive light. Of course, this is not to deny children's need for help in dealing with painful feelings! But it appears that events within children's own relationships with animals can determine children's responses. The effectiveness of adult construal is limited. Indeed, the meaning of such events is "overdetermined" by children's own forms of self and relating. Events with contents such as we have examined here—the animals' agency, affect, coherence, and continuity—are fundamentally important to children themselves. We are beginning to see how the separation of person and animal assumed by traditional theories presents a limited view of our potential.

Symbols of the Animate Self

In the previous chapter, we looked at animals as cultural symbols. Such symbols have come to be regarded by cultural psychologists such as Richard Shweder (1984) as "arbitrary code." Little but other cultural meanings determine what an animal symbolizes. But the meanings of animals to the children I observed related to specific psychological and developmental issues, such as Ivy's concern for the baby snake's need for room to grow. Indeed, for this particular concept, the developmental psychologists Karl Rosengren, Susan Gelman, Charles Kalish, and Michael McCormick (1991) showed an early developmental basis. By age three, most children understand that growth over time is a property of animates. In fact, so salient is this conception that they overgeneralize it to inanimate objects. By age five, children's performance does not differ significantly from adults'. Growth is a conceptually prepotent feature of living things. For us, however, what is at issue is not just children's conceptual grasp but the psychological significance of such meanings.

Children evince a fine appreciation of the meanings implicit in the features of living or animate things. These features resonate with the child's own self. Turtles, for example, had a particular symbolic meaning related to coherence. During the first session of the class as a whole with the turtle, the following exchange occurred:

Mr. Lloyd: "How do you think it feels, what does it feel like to be a turtle?" Solly: "Safe . . . *Safe*." Mr. Lloyd: "You think it feels safe, why?" Solly: "Because you have a shell."

Solly stated it first, but this theme was repeated many times. The children identified readily with the younger turtle, but they also expressed the desire to be invulnerable by identifying with the turtle's ability to "be safe" in its shell. Here is another example:

Billy: "When a shark comes . . . when a shark comes to get the turtle, it—he pulls . . ." Sam tries to join in. Mr. Lloyd: "Let's let Billy talk." Billy: "He just puts his whole body in his shell, and he just puts it right in." As he says this, Billy pulls his arms in tightly toward his sides. Billy: "And then he, and when it's all gone, when the shark is all gone, when the shark is all gone, he just puts his body back out." Billy extends his arms back out again.

For Billy, the turtle symbolizes not only safety and coherence but also the whole affective experience of surviving an imagined life-threatening situation. Notably, Billy's symbolization took the embodied form first of a tightly closed-off protective posture and then of an expansive, mobile, and agentic one—conveying affective qualities that would be hard to represent verbally. Imitation and incorporating the animal's well-being were united in this symbolic activity.

One time, I asked two boys if they would want to be the guinea pig. Their response showed both empathy and their interpretations of confinement:

> Mr. Myers: "Would you like to be like the guinea pig?" Drew: "No. In a cage? Would you?" Mr. Myers: "I don't know." Solly: "And crawl in things!"

Drew disliked the idea of a cage, but the agentic potentials of being a small animal appealed to Solly. Agency is a key value for children's own sense of self, and animals' autonomy symbolizes it.

The death of an animal is significant because it symbolizes issues of loss-in-relationship. A day after the baby dove's death, Dimitri explicitly brought up his own father's death in a talk with Mrs. Ray. For him, the bird symbolized the basic issue of continuity of self and other. The qualities animals potently symbolize for children are not just arbitrary. They include agency or autonomy, coherence or wholeness, feeling, and continuity. These qualities will become quite familiar to us and are central in the child's own experience of self. Animals represent them because they display them with immediate compelling vitality—a fact with broad implications for our understanding of symbolism.

To summarize, the functional sense of self posits the goal of self-maintenance; when translated into relationships this means interest and engagement in, and increasing abilities for, interaction. It also means caring about the others who help constitute the self and experiencing one's own vital issues through the other's experience. Following the German philosopher Martin Heidegger (1962), we can describe the human being by *Dasein* (German for "being-there"), which "itself is to be made visible as *care*" (pp. 83–84). The self emerges in the context of relationship and shows itself by links of caring. In this section, we have seen such links. They attest to our developmental potential for a sense of connection to other animals. The young child's self takes form in the available interspecies community, constituting itself among an ecology of subjects. But we have yet to understand in detail the exact interactive sources and full implications of these relationships.

The Self as a Pattern of Experiences

Before moving on, I want to take a step back to address the problem of the subjective self. The early American psychologist William James (1890) gave two meanings to the "self" as it is experienced by each of us. Experientially, he said, the self refers to the sense of a "me," or self-concept that one can describe in objective terms. On the other hand, it also refers to an ongoing sense of a *subjective* "I," meaning our feelings of continuity, agency, wholeness, and awareness. The "I" and the "me" have their origins in interaction with others and help elucidate the interactive sources of the goals of the self as a functional unity, as I described previously. But these two meanings also pose a dilemma for studying the self and its development.

James (1892/1961) said the "me" is "the sum total of all a person can call his" (p. 44). In other words, it was the person's material possessions; social positions; and distinct mental qualities, including consciousness, thoughts, and psychical mechanisms. These are all "objective" properties, and so James called this the "objective" self. This is what many psychologists mean by the "self-concept," and it can include *knowledge* of one's subjective self, or "I," but *not* the "I" itself. Many researchers have focused on what a person thinks of himself or herself, which is assumed to have a strong influence on the person's conscious choices, social relations, and so on. Such thoughts have traditionally been communicated and studied via language.

An example is a child's narrative about the self, which expresses self-attributed categories such as gender. The process of language socialization is crucial to this kind of development. In the school years, children make comparisons with others, leading to the perception of group and individual differences, including psychological traits. Such aspects of the self are clearly influential in a child's experience and are shaped by his or her particular speech community.

The American psychologist Jerome Kagan (1990) criticizes the nearly exclusive contemporary focus on the self-concept. It overvalues consciousness, he argues, reflecting our conviction that our conscious intentions are important. But this bias, translated into methods that ask the person to report on the contents of his or her mind, constrains the material available for theorizing. Many biological and psychological processes lie outside of awareness, inaccessible. For example, many adults cannot explain how they (successfully) solve certain problems. There is also the difficulty—especially acute for young children—of forming grammatically comprehensible linguistic responses to self-concept questionnaires or interviews. Particularly telling is the fact that self-reports rarely contain inconsistencies, although many situations could easily evoke contradictory responses. Likewise, objective measures of mood and feeling tone "usually have very little relation to self-reports" (p. 364). For all these reasons, Kagan predicts that the meaning of "self" in future studies "will emphasize a family of processes rather than a unitary one" (p. 365). Interaction with varying interactants, such as animals, is one place to look for such processes!

James's concept of the "I," or subjective self, is the personal experience of individuality and is underlain by processes such as those Kagan seeks. James discerned four features: (1) an awareness of one's agency over life events, (2) an awareness of the uniqueness of one's life experience, (3) an awareness of one's personal continuity, and (4) an awareness of one's own awareness. These four kinds of experience, which make us aware of the "I," all have profound consequences. Agency leads to the belief in the autonomy of the self and the sense one actively structures one's experience. Distinctness produces the sense of individuality—that "other [people's] experiences, no matter how much I may know about them, never bear this vivid, this peculiar brand" (James, quoted by the social psychologists William Damon & Daniel Hart, 1988, p. 6). The experience of continuity lends stability to the self; it and the sense of distinctness are especially important to identity and self-concept. Self-consciousness allows one to reflectively define what one's identity means. But the "I" *is* just that aspect of ourselves that can never be pinned down—the dynamic present sense of self. Whereas the "me" is the self-as-known, the "I" is the "self-as-knower"; it is ever changing and enters into the person's every action and interpretation as the backgrounded acting, knowing self. This is especially evident from the fluidity of agency and reflectiveness.

Wonderful and recognizably true as this description is to us, the fluidity and privateness of these experiences of self inclined many philosophers as well as James and his followers to despair of ever "capturing its essence in a scientifically objectifiable manner" (Damon & Hart, 1988, p. 4). Still, the self is not just a fiction; people do report experiences that endow the self with a compelling reality. Since it is not open to consensual validation, however, it can only be studied indirectly. But the alternate research focus on the self-concept collapses the "I" into the "me." Some researchers ameliorate this reduction by studying, as did George Herbert Mead, the "me"'s concepts *about* the "I"—that is, what the person believes about his or her agency, continuity, and so on. But this still is not equivalent to "self" in the full sense, and it has a further disadvantage in our case. Young children do have basic concepts of others' minds, and of their own, as entities possessing beliefs and desires. But more advanced concepts of psychological traits are some years away. Thus, measures of children's *knowledge* of the self's subjective qualities will underestimate the self's actual extent and detail. We *have* subjective selves long before we can tell much about them. If we want to understand how animals come to have such important places in the child's self as we have seen they have, we need another way of asking about it.

Fortunately, there is an alternative approach. It depends on a degree of inference, but within a theoretical structure this is customary in studying subjective experience. Recently, Daniel Stern (1985) has modified James's set of characteristics of the "core" subjective self to comprise agency, coherence, affect, and continuity. Basic experiences of self are attained in infancy through interacting with others—others whose actions allow the infant to make critical contrasts about who (self or other) is the source of agency, continuity, and so on at the moment. Crucially, Stern bases his ideas on early and probably innate talents of the infant. He explains James's idea of self-awareness as an acquisition based two further kinds of interactions: intersubjective and verbal. Together with the "core," Stern thus describes three distinct interactively defined domains of relatedness and self.[4]

Adopting the general strategy suggested by Stern's solution, we can make some inferences about the subjective "I" by studying the structure of interactions and relationships within which it arises. This is a similar strategy to that of Harry Stack Sullivan (1953), who wrote that the structure of a relationship is a clue to its significance to the participants. In studying children's interactions with animals, we can employ this strategy in a productive way since the characteristics of the interactants vary in interesting and regular ways.

We have already seen that children's incorporation of animals in their range of interests and concerns foreshadows the importance of the core subjective features of agency, coherence, affect, and continuity. A close study of their interactions will teach us exactly how animals attain such importance.

4 The Immediate Other: Animate Relating

ONE DAY, DAWN'S FATHER brought her baby brother to visit the preschool. Dawn begged her father to let her show Peter, who was barely able to walk, around the classroom. Finally, he acquiesced. First, they "walked" (Dawn lugging Peter along) to the guinea pig's cage and stood before it. Next, they stopped to watch the other children making Halloween "witches' brew." Then, Dawn awkwardly carried Peter to the glass doors and they looked out at the birds on the bird feeder as he rested his hands on the glass. The next stop was the pair of doves, to which they returned shortly after a visit to another activity table. Dawn was nearly five, and this was the beginning of her second year in the class. As she introduced Peter to her familiar setting, it was clear that the animals were important members of her classroom community. Perhaps, Dawn felt that her infant brother would be interested in animals, too.

Why do young children take such an interest in animals? Perhaps it is simply because animals are a novel stimulus—especially since urban children have little contact with animals. Yes, but can this be all? It is of course possible that animals are no different from other phenomena that are equally novel. The idea of novelty applies to occurrences in which a person loses interest once he or she is habituated to the stimulus. It might account for Peter's interest, but Dawn had the ability to be very absorbed even with familiar animals like Snowflake. What accounts for the spiraling engagement, as if "novelty" continued indefinitely, seen in people who spend their lives working with animals? "Novelty" fails as an explanation for it is too general: It tells us nothing about the particular structure and challenge provided by continued interaction with animals.

In fact, research now backs up what may have been Dawn's intuition that infants take a special interest in animals. As we will see, insights from infant studies provide important pieces in the complicated puzzle of why animals matter to us. In brief, from a very early age infants have the ability to construct a coherent experience of self and other from "invariant" properties of interactions. Because animals are much like humans—but not identical to them—in their properties as interactants, they provide a unique structure for the development of the self. I have introduced the basics already—agency, coherence, affect, and continuity; in this chapter we will explore these basics more fully as I show how the animal emerges for the infant and young child as a truly *subjective* other whose immediate presence is compelling.

An objection could be raised—indeed, we might expect several objections based on the traditional ways child-animal interaction has been interpreted. Is not the child being anthropomorphic when he or she experiences an animal as possessing an inner, subjective life? Is not the child's feeling toward the animal rather based on egocentric projection or culturally constituted linguistic meanings? Why should we think it is based on a genuine sense of self-in-relation, with all that implies about the dynamic adjustment to the other?

Today, it is rather easy to suppose that human mental and cultural constructions so override the natural world that the latter cannot have any inherent significance for us. The assessment of animals' importance to children is only one case in point. But the sense of subjective immediacy that arises in infancy and childhood is not secondary; we will see that it both precedes and continues after the child learns cultural frames. After analyzing the dimensions of this sense and learning its basis in early development, we find one fact stands out: Children's interactions with animals *vary* systematically depending on the animal. And these variations provide a response to some of the objections discussed previously. But we must start with a close examination of actual interactions. Indeed, until we have a clear account of human-animal relationships, we may be bound to look at them as distorted human-human relationships.

The Animate Other

One morning, the teacher instigated a game of "circus" with small slugs in the play yard. The children held sticks as the attached slugs dropped slowly along their strands of slime. My first impression was that the children treated the slugs as essentially objects, manipulating them mechanically. I do not mean they "objectified" the slugs in the sense of disrespecting their subjectivity—for it seemed there was no question of such an inner aspect of the slugs at all. In another case, which like the other examples in this chapter was transcribed from my videotapes or field notes, the children turned the turtle in its tracks to make it change direction:

> All kids seem to have their hands on the turtle; then Chen has hold of it. Drew: "Turn him around." Other kids sit back; Chen turns the turtle.

The animal seems essentially passive, inanimate and without its own agency. These examples involve slow, relatively nonmotile, "passive" animals. But the children also moved the guinea pig around physically, manipulated it, and ignored its own activity, such as the time Mindy shook it in the box or a time Drew and Solly played with it, trying to control its motions. Is it possible for children to see animals as if they were not alive?

Consider an alternative interpretation. We can reverse the "parsing" of such events, focusing not on the child but on the animal as shaper of the child's responses.[1] In this light, in interacting with even such a passive animal as a slug, the child *had to* adjust the height and position of her hands in ways that were responsive to the animal's movement and slime trail. When the children lifted the turtle, its ability to bite *caused* the children to avoid putting their hands near its head. This language may seem stretched, but in context it makes sense. And when the children did treat an animal as inanimate and unable to initiate or respond, they were often stopped in their tracks by some action of the animal or, in the case of Drew and Solly, by the guinea pig's squeal alerting an adult!

Is this kind of reinterpretation just conceptual sleight of hand, making much of the animal's supposed agency where at first glance it seems to play a minimal role? At the root of this problem is the child's concept of animates versus inanimates. Jean Piaget studied "childhood animism" by asking young children about inanimate objects such as the moon, clouds, and wind—"Why do they move?" The children told him it is because they intend to move (1929/1975, chap. 7, esp. 215ff.). This is "animism." They confused animate and inanimate causality. We now know that for a number of reasons, including linguistic cueing, this pioneering researcher underestimated children's abilities. Fortunately, recent work shows even infants have a clearer animate-inanimate distinction than Piaget concluded.

Infants and Animals

Some of the earliest evidence stemmed from James Watson's "conditioning" of a fear response in an infant. In 1920, Watson, a booster of behaviorism, and his graduate student Rosalie Rayner paired an unpleasant loud noise (the unconditioned stimulus) with the sight of a live rat and showed that eleven-month-old "Little Albert" quickly learned a fear reaction to the rat. In behaviorist theory, it should not matter at all what the conditioned stimulus is—instead of a rat, it could have been a rock. But in 1934, the psychologist Elsie Bregman tried replicating the infamous experiment, only she paired a loud noise not with a live rat but with wooden blocks and pieces of cloth. After numerous attempts with fifteen infants, she found no evidence of long-lasting conditioning. We can take this as a clue that an animal is not the same kind of stimulus as just any other thing.

Others have found more direct signs that infants are prepared to notice animates. Three-week-olds give different responses to the sight of inanimate versus animate objects according to the psychologists and infancy researchers T. Barry Brazelton, Edward Tronick, and Mary Main (1974). The psychologist Lonnie Sherrod (1981) showed that six-month-olds clearly distinguish animate from inanimate—although in these and other studies the only animates presented were people. Another psychologist, Gail Ross (1980), found a distinct category for animal stimuli by twelve months. In another study a few years later, the psychologists Roberta Golinkoff and Marcia Halperin (1983) found similar affective reactions to most animal as opposed to nonanimal stimuli in one eight-month-old boy. Although only one living animal was used (other animates were merely drawings), they also concluded he possessed a preverbal category for animal. The psychologists Kenneth Roberts and Martin Cuff (1989) placed at age nine months the ability to discriminate basic categories, including "bird"; and at fifteen months, the superordinate category "animal." Notably, animal words and sounds are among first in the infant's vocabulary (see also the work of the psychologist and researcher of language development Eve Clark, 1979).

But the strongest evidence comes from research employing living animals. The psychologists Aline Kidd and Robert Kidd (1987a) studied 250 infants at ages six, twelve, eighteen, twenty-four, and thirty months and found an increase across this range in proximity-seeking and contact-promoting behaviors directed to the family pet as compared with a novel battery-operated toy dog. From twelve months on, babies smiled, vocalized, and maintained interactions longer with the pet. And finally, the work of the Canadian psychologists Marcelle Ricard and Louise Allard (1993) stands out for presenting a living animal with which the infant was not already familiar. They found differentiated patterns of response to a rabbit versus a strange person or a mechanical toy between ages nine and ten months. The rabbit evoked an intermediate mixture of responses. The infants tried to get closer, as they did with the toy but not with the stranger; they made fewer communicative smiles than toward the stranger but more than to the toy; and they did an equal amount of looking as toward the stranger. With both the rabbit and the person, the infants looked back at their mothers less than when encountering the toy. The authors concluded, "The spontaneous familiarization behaviors they resort to when confronted with an unfamiliar yet not frightening animal suggest that they do not confound this class of objects with people or with inanimate toys" (p. 14).

These rather little-known infancy studies contain a big lesson: Children's concepts of nonhuman others may be based on and exhibited in *interactions* with them—and this has implications for the self. Instead of looking only at what the child can say about self and other (which would reveal James's notion of the objective self, or the "me," which is usually studied), we can come closer to the elusive sense of the "I" by looking at how actual interactions are structured, as we noted in Chapter 3. Young infants respond to basic features of other animates. As children mature, they become able to handle more complicated kinds of interactions; later we will explore the consequences of children's more complex abilities, for example, language. But the basic or core features of animates do not just vanish as the child gets older; they continue to structure the interaction, providing a basis for a sense of animate self and other that persists across development. Looking at children's interactions with animals, the features that stand out are the main constituents Daniel Stern (1985), following in the footsteps of William James, said are necessary for the first coherent sense of the "I."[2]

Agency

Agency is a cardinal feature of animals as young children encounter them. The animal can initiate action. For example, the animal's ability to bite was of concern to the children I observed and came up with every animal. Early on, fears that the snake was poisonous were raised and discussed among the children:

> Joe: "Is it a rattlesnake?" Chris: "No." Ivy: "What kind of snake is it?" Laura: "If it was a rattlesnake it would bite."

Even the snake owner's reassurances did not settle the matter, and the snake's potential to bite remained salient in the children's interactions. During one small group session, the snake's presenter suggested that my presence might be cueing the children to act out fearful responses, since they had been calm before I arrived. I reviewed the videotape and, sure enough, there were some fearful gestures when I was present. But this explanation ignored the snake's movements. While the children were calmly attentive, the snake's head was toward its keeper. When I was present, the snake happened to be positioned with its head outward, and each child pulled back precisely when its head was pointed at him or her. Indeed, *before* I arrived, the three exceptions to the calm attentiveness each occurred at the moments the snake's head was pointed at a child.

In other cases, the children verbally expressed concerns with biting. While feeding the ferrets, Dawn observed, "He's biting the bottle." The ferret presenter later cautioned the children repeatedly not to put their hands near its mouth, but this became relevant to Billy only once the animal was free on the floor. Then he asked, "Does it scrape and bite—bit people?" The monkey was very interactive and liked to bite at feet, which pleased Solly: "He bited my shoe." Katra, however, was not amused. I asked her, "Are you afraid of him, Katra?" She shook her head. Mr. Dean added, "A little bit?" Katra nodded twice. Further questioning revealed biting as her reason. Indeed, as Toby observed, "Everything we give him he bites."

Biting was not the only way the monkey initiated interactions. Its activity was regularly punctuated with attempts to grab the children's feet, which were extended toward it on the floor. It would first look away and then slide its body, arms extended, toward a child's foot. Mostly, this resulted in the children quickly withdrawing their feet, but sometimes they permitted the contact. Once, the monkey crouched down by Ms. Dean and then hopped first toward Yasmin and then across the semicircle to Chen and Drew. Chen retreated, exclaiming, "Hey!" The monkey touched Drew's shoe. Drew leaned back laughing, touched his shoe, and said, "He was pulling on my shoe."

Biting was not only something initiated by animals; it was also a response to action by the child. Anticipating bites, the children registered agency not only from overt action but also from the omission of possible action. When the dog visited, Billy asked if he bit cats; he was told the dog chased cats. Sitting next to the dog a little while later, Billy reached for its face and then sat up. He proclaimed: "I touched his tongue. . . . He *let* me touch his tongue." Mr. Grier responded, "Really?" Billy: "He didn't even bite me."[3]

Recent research supports the importance of agentic action to young children. It pervades their causal thinking about animates, as shown by many researchers since Piaget; see, for example, the work of the psychologists D. Dean Richards and Robert Siegler (1986). The developmental psychologists Susan Gelman, John Coley, and Gail Gottfried (1994) reported experiments in which young children were asked to judge whether videotaped unfamiliar objects and animals moving across a surface were moved by an external cause (a person moved it), an internal cause (something inside it moved it), or an immanent cause (it moved by itself). Some children saw all the target objects being carried by a human hand; others saw them all move without any apparent human help. Surprisingly, Gelman and colleagues found that four-year-olds "consistently deny any external cause to explain the biological events, even when a human bodily carries an animal. Rather, biological events are viewed as resulting from immanent cause. Children regularly appeal to intrinsic factors even without knowing the internal mechanism" (p. 349).

It could be objected that children attribute agency to animals because of cultural conditioning—for instance, the pervasive personification of animals. Some of the examples given do indeed occur within cultural scripts elaborated around petting/being petted, holding/being held, and feeding/being fed. Often, all three co-occurred with the guinea pig, and the children themselves transmitted this cultural practice within the nursery school. But although such interactions occurred in a cultural frame, the detailed moves are not deducible from it. Instead, such activities, as well as touching/being touched, biting/being bitten, pursuit/escape, seeking/hiding, and throwing/fetching are examples of "complementary" interactions (defined by the ethologist Robert Hinde, 1976, as when the action of one organism elicits a different but linked action by the other). Most interactions observed between children and animals were of this contingent form.[4] Partaking in extended bouts of linked moves is a social activity based on fine-grained responsiveness.

In a complementary interaction, either the child or the animal may be the initiating party. One example is "chase." Most often, the children pursued the animals, but the activity can occur the other way around:

> The turtle starts walking toward Billy. He gets up and goes behind Ivy, then moves to one side as the turtle approaches Ivy, who moves away backward. Ivy: "Oh oh, he's coming at me." . . . Billy continues avoiding it.

Being the recipient of the animal's own agency is a significant experience, as being touched by the monkey was for Solly and Drew. Mindy said she wanted to squeeze the snake. After having her hands on the snake for a while and evidently squeezing it, Mindy proclaimed five times, "I squeezed her." Then, the snake's reaction registered. Mindy interjected, "I feel the muscle, I felt the muscle." Children easily recognize and respond to the agentic qualities of animals, just as we would expect from the preparedness for such interaction that they have exhibited since infancy. The interactions this makes possible are the constituents, rather than the effects, of learned cultural scripts.

Coherence

The second key feature of animals is their coherence. Young children perceive animals as paragons of coherence. First, children receive a basic impression of wholeness from the animal's body. Young children are very concretely oriented in their approach to animals.[5] Petting an animal is culturally framed, but it also provides a tactile, concrete sense of the animal. It is a highly sought-after activity, and the children asked repeatedly for turns to touch the animals that were brought to class. When they were not allowed to do so, they tried on the sly. The children commented on surface textures they felt when petting the animal, such as its softness.

Some petting or observation focused on a part of the animal. The children remarked on animals' teeth, claws, paws, and so on. Benson touched the turtle's hind foot and remarked, "I touched his claws and he didn't scratch me." Pogo's bushy tail was another such part; it drew attention for its sweeping motion: Drew pointed to it, saying, "Look [what] it's doing; it's sweeping the floor." Solly suggested its name should be "Sweeper." Then, Mindy moved close to Toby and the dog's tail, Dimitri and Rosa also approached, and all put their hands under the dog's wagging tail.

The body parts the children remarked on in this way stand out from the whole animal, which possesses an unmarked primary unity revealed by the child's readiness to hold an animal. The small size of the animals in the classroom that the children petted enabled them to touch the entire animal—giving a very concrete sense of its coherence. This sense is reflected in the comment Dimitri made while feeding Snowflake. While holding the animal between his legs, he told it several times, "I got you." Dimitri had created a space for the small, calm, furry guinea pig that matched its coherence. The child's readiness to hold an animal often thus reflected its specific shape and character. On the other hand, one animal literally held the children:

> Yasmin: "I want to do, could you do that to me?" . . . Ms. Nol puts the big snake around Yasmin; she is calm and laughs. Ms. Nol: "It's got ya. It's just holding on tight." Yasmin, fairly calmly: "It's just squeezing me." Ms. Nol: "It's got its tail under your arm, just holding on—it probably thinks you're a tree." Yasmin: "Maybe." Ms. Nol: "A good solid branch to hold onto so he won't fall—she, she." Yasmin: "It touches. Please don't touch." She keeps her hands away from the snake: "Make it unravel by itself." Ms. Nol lifts it off.

The large, mobile snake embraced the children as it constantly extended and changed its position, tracing, as it were, not only its own, but also the child's basic experience of being a coherent unity.

Naming is a cultural practice that works within the reality of organismic coherence. One of the first questions children asked about a new animal was "What's its name?" Although they also wanted to know the kind of animal, species identification was not sufficient. It did not mark the animal's primary individuality. Sometimes, I invited the children to make up names for the animals. Here are some distinctive names they gave the ferrets:

> Laura: "What's his name?" Mr. Myers: "What do you think would be a good name for a ferret?" Laura: "Ferr-at." Dawn: "Ferrie." Solly: "Duster." Dimitri: "Duster." Angela: "Buster." Chris: "Nibbles." Sam: "Drinker." Ms. Collins: "Drinker?" Sam: "Yeah, because he drinks a lot [from the bottle]." Chen: "Drinker." He repeats this many times. Adrienne: "Furry." Ivy: "Furry, cause it's, it's furry." In the back, Adrienne and Dawn are saying "Ferrie" over and over.

Once they learned the ferrets' names were really Ben and Bojangles, they used those names frequently in talking about the animals. Naming is a cultural practice that merely underscores the animal's particularity—the sense of uniqueness between subjective self and other.

The animal does not talk to the child. Later, we will explore all the implications of this, but here we can gain insight into animate coherence by contrast with the verbal relatedness. Since it does not talk, the animal is unable to place the child in the "double bind" described by the family systems pioneers Gregory Bateson, Don Jackson, Jay Haley, and John Weakland (1956)—that is, the animal cannot persistently present contradictory messages through verbal versus nonverbal channels of communication, as do significant human others who essentially tell the child two things at once. For this reason, animals may not foster fragmented self-perception in the child but rather reinforce self-coherence.

Affectivity

Affect also consistently enters the child's experience of animals. How? One possible route, much studied in human emotion, is facial displays of discrete affects like "happy," "sad," "angry," and so on. These are powerful human emotion carriers and may be universally recognizable. Nonetheless, they are likely to be a weak route since animals' facial musculatures are relatively less intricate than humans', their facial structures are so different, and most of us lack the species-specific ethological knowledge needed to guess well. This is not to say that people do not frequently make wrong guesses—anthropomorphic attribution based on facial emotion display is not infrequent. But in fact, facial expression may not be the main way people get information about animals' emotional states.

Another dimension to emotion besides categorical affect is called vitality affect. Vitality affects are patterns of arousal over time and are displayed by both humans and animals through qualities of motion and prosodic qualities of voice. Words that describe some of these subjective affective patterns include "surging," "rushing," "drawn-out," and "fleeting." Such qualities are perceived across differing sense modes and situations and can be evoked by internal feelings or the actions of others. Stern (1985, p. 56) likens the expressiveness of vitality affects to that of music, of dance, or of the way puppeteers utilize a vocabulary of patterns that could be designated by such terms as "lethargic," "jaunty," "forceful," and so forth. All convey feeling despite a lack of facial information.

For humans, perception of vitality affect has roots in early infancy and is critical in human emotional communication. Within a certain range, these affects are also communicable across species. The writer Elizabeth Marshall Thomas (1993, pp. xvi–xvii) describes how her dogs rapidly and accurately read her moods from her behavior, even at a distance. Masson and McCarthy (1995) recently catalogued many examples of animal emotion, many of which hinge on vitality affect. Granted, the "vocabulary" may not be identical across species—excitement for a sloth must have a different rhythm, for example. Other species' affects may have no analogue in humans at all and, conversely, humans may be capable of feelings that no other animals have. Little research has been done on these clearly difficult questions. Nonetheless, we—children included—perceive that animal experience changes in arousal and affect quality.[6]

The children I watched responded to affect intensity and the qualities of arousal of the animals. The kinds of responses varied but usually included an unlabeled but enacted recognition of the animal's affectivity. In a simple example, when the children were invited to throw the ball for the dog, the animal's excited and expectant affect were conveyed to the children by its quick pacing and turning; the alertness of its face; and its nondirected, nonthreatening barking. The children's response showed recognition of the mood— they were very excited. For all, this mood waxed and waned with each episode of ball throwing and fetching. The children's excitement did not just come from wanting to throw the ball, which could be interpreted as the governing cultural frame of the interaction. That a deeper level of vitality affect was operating was shown in the variety of responses showing a similar affect. Two girls scrambled around and clung to each other, as if afraid. But they were smiling and verbally denied they were really scared. Their arousal contours followed the dog's excitement, illustrating how vitality affects can be expressed or experienced in a variety of concrete actions.

The ferrets provided a contrasting affect. They were initially too active to be let free and had to be kept in hand, where the children took turns feeding them with a bottle. From being held and fed a cloying oil-vitamin mixture, the ferrets became extremely passive, an affect reinforced by the way they relaxed when the presenter held them by their neck skin, a standard way to carry them. Reflecting this predominant vitality affect, the session ended up being the calmest of all the animal visits.

Vitality affects associated with activities the children experience in their own lives provide another avenue to the animal's affective side. Feeding the toad provided an analogy to familiar mealtimes. The children never tired of watching the toad eat. The teacher would place it on a sheet of paper along with whatever bugs the children had gathered from outside. The toad searched the paper, then stalked and finally snapped up the bugs it found. The vitality affects of these episodes were shared by the children: eager anticipation in avidly collecting bugs to feed it; building tension shown by the children's crowding around the paper to watch; and satisfaction upon completion.

Continuity

The three aspects of animals discussed here can give the child the feeling of being the *same* self in relation to the *same* other if there is continuity over time. Young children remember previous episodes of interaction with animals and generalize about them, transforming interactions into a relationship. The case is strongest when interactions with the animal are repeated many times and attain a degree of regularity in the actions of each participant, as in the children's relationships to Snowflake. A concrete history existed on both sides: The guinea pig had long been in this environment where it felt, saw, heard, and smelled the humans' activities; and since some children were in the class for a second year, a culture of guinea pig knowledge was passed on not only by the teacher but also by the children. This history included such things as the enacted knowledge for the children of having the guinea pig sit on a towel on their lap and holding food for it—and the enacted knowledge for the guinea pig of being placed on a child's lap and chewing the food and not the child's fingers. Where a relationship has a history like this, interactions can become predictable. For example, over repeated feeding episodes hesitant children who withdrew the food learned that the guinea pig was persistent; fidgety children learned the guinea pig would leave if they tossed it too much on their laps. In both cases, the children—often with encouragement—increased their success in feeding the guinea pig.

Earlier, I noted that the children returning to the class for a second year showed a greater sense of relatedness to the guinea pig, as indicated by the greater proportion of interactions with it and the percentages of children partaking in such interactions. Data on interaction with the diamond doves provides a comparison. The doves were brought to the class at the beginning of the year. Among the instances of children being involved with the doves, however, the attentions of the two groups of children were more equal: Fifty-three percent involved returning children, and 47 percent involved new children. Furthermore, these represented more equal proportions of the two groups: Sixty-two percent and 75 percent, respectively. Thus, the difference in the guinea pig data may not be due to the older age of the returning children but, indeed, to the role of continuity of self-with-other.

In a developed relationship, differences between children in interactive style become evident. Ivy frequently "babied" the guinea pig, cuddling it closely or rocking it proudly. Dimitri, by contrast, regularly attempted to scare the guinea pig, by banging on its cage or dropping in toys; he told me he did not like the animal. On the other hand, Mindy, one of the new children, accounted for a third of the guinea pig episodes from that group, and like Dimitri she sometimes provoked it. But she also told stories about a guinea pig she had known in a city in which she had previously lived and how someone who had been afraid of it learned not to be. Both a sense of grappling with the scary agency of the animal and growing continuity were reflected in her tales.

Out of these basic invariants of experience, a core animate domain of self and other takes on compelling reality. This is the reality of comings and goings; touching, observing, and responding to each other's overt actions and affects; and apprehending a basic sense of the other's inner experience.

The Infant's Social Self

We began by noting that even infants differentiate animals from other kinds of living and nonliving things on interactive bases such as the ones just discussed. At this point, a short theoretical digression will underscore the significance of these findings by showing the continuity between experiences of infant and young child.

According to the associationist tradition, very strong through much of the twentieth century, infants are born unable to perceive the world in a very coherent fashion. The stereotype was that the infant's world was, in William James's words, "blooming, buzzing confusion." Even Piaget believed that much learning had to precede the ability to represent external reality (1936/1963). Today, a revolution in infancy research is showing that infants are preprepared to notice many invariant features of experience. So far-reaching is the new work on infant perception that the infancy researcher Bennett Bertenthal (1993) has commented "No longer can we assume that basic concepts about number, people, causality and so forth must await the development of concrete operational thinking . . . or even preoperational thinking" (p. 175).

The invariants infants notice are patterns of "sensations, perceptions, actions, cognitions, internal states of motivation and states of consciousness" that are *analogous across sense modes* and so are experienced in terms of "intensities, shapes, temporal patterns, vitality affects, categorical affects and hedonic tones" (Stern, 1985, p. 67). It has long been known, for example, that *intensity* of stimulation is analogous across sensory systems; we now know this is true for infants and in all preverbal modes of perception. For infants as early as the age of one week, features experienced in one sensory channel—the bumpy texture of an unfamiliar pacifier in the mouth—can be represented and recognized in another—at first sight the infant can distinguish the bumpy from a smooth pacifier visually. According to the older perspective, such an act was not expected so early, since it would require development of different touching and seeing sensori-motor schemas *and* of coordinating schemas between them.

Stern (1985) suggests that "infants do not attend to what [sensory] domain their experience is occurring in" (p. 67) and that data from the different senses are fused in "highly flexible and omnidimensional" mental representations that have a global quality. This is perhaps clearer in contrast to language, which alone allows us to abstract visual, auditory, and tactile sensations from the amodal representations of concrete situations that the infant's body and brain automatically create. Language also lets us label objects in a way that makes them seem independent of experience. None of this is possible without the generalized reality created by language.

All of the foregoing has special relevance for the self, because certain invariants of interaction give the infant the data that reveal where self ends and other begins. Before the age of about three months, no organized, globally represented self has coalesced. During this time, Stern (1985) suggests, the infant may have experiences of "emergent self" when a new pattern of stimuli come together as a sense of "I." But after three months of age, the infant responds as a social being to others, as is so well recognizable in its "social smiles." We can identify the invariants in agency, coherence, affect, and continuity as critical ingredients in this core or animate self.

The infant experiences authorship of her or his own action through at least three routes: "(1) the sense of volition that precedes a motor act, (2) proprioceptive feedback that does or does not occur during the act, (3) predictability of consequences that follow the act" (Stern, 1985, p. 76). Evidence of these includes volitional motor plans such as hand-to-mouth, gazing, and sucking skills and, later, at four months, shaping the hand to fit an object being reached for. As is clear from studies already cited and from studies on animate versus inanimate motion, infants notice the agentic quality of others (see the work of the infancy researchers and developmental psychologists Elizabeth Spelke, Ann Phillips, & Amanda Woodward, 1995). Variation in the mother's role in helping the infant self-regulate "permits the infant to triangulate and identify what invariants belong to whom" (Stern, 1985, p. 106).

The infant also experiences self-coherence, or "unity of locus." The infant visually orients to the source of sounds and is thus in a position to see that others' behaviors are specific to them and different from the infant's own. Coherence of motion, temporal structure, intensity structure, and form add more information. Especially important is the demonstration that four-month-old infants detect cross-modal synchrony. For example, when viewing two films simultaneously, they watch the one with which a sound track corresponds (Spelke, 1979). This finding supports the contention that the infant can coordinate all sensory inputs emanating from another person into a coherent whole.

Affectivity and the emotions are higher-order self-invariants based on experience with a range of feelings. The discrete affects (joy, anger, surprise, disgust, and so on) give unique invariant organizations of feedback from stereotyped facial displays, patterns of internal arousal, and specific qualities of feeling. Patterns of arousal over time may be perceived with or without a co-occurring categorical affect and are experienced as vitality affects.

Continuity, or self-history, is based on memory of the other invariants. Infants are well known to register perceptual events in memory and have motor memories, or what the developmental psychologist Jerome Bruner (1969) called "memories without words." Episodic memory, or "memory for real-life experiences occurring in real time" (Stern, 1985, p. 94), enables integration of the other invariants, from specific to more general episode classes. The infant generalizes several similar memories of interactive episodes to create her or his first integrated sense of self and other. In the sense of self that these invariants make possible, "The emphasis is on the palpable experiential realities of substance, action, sensation, affect and time. Sense of self is not a cognitive construct. It is an experiential integration" (Stern, 1985, p. 71).

Let me hasten to clarify what early infancy realities mean for the young child's relation to animals. First, they provide a plausible explanation for how the infants we met earlier distinguish animals from objects and people. Animals are core others for the infant. This is to say, they are apprehended as first of all *subjective* others who display their own invariant patterns of agency, coherence, affect, and history. Because of this, they can also affirm the infant's self-invariants. The child receives roughly this experience from the animal: "I (the child) actively reach and touch; you affirm I did so by rubbing against me (or leaving, striking back, and so on). We fill a present together." I will have more to say about this shortly.

Second, and crucially, each form of self persists—once present, it continues to function even as later forms of self become operative. I have touched on emergent and animate (core) selves. As more abilities come "on-line," a preverbal intersubjective self gels from the awareness that subjective events can be shared. According to Stern (1985), this happens at around seven to nine months of age. This self is virtually unavoidable, because the caregiver matches the infant's vitality affect *in a different modality*, for example, cooing in response to the infant's calm hand motions. This communicates that the infant's *inner state* has been detected and shared. But note, with this achievement animate relating does not cease! As we all know, it is possible to non-verbally deceive others about our true feelings, and to an even greater extent, feelings can be at odds with what is spoken. The verbal self arises around twelve to eighteen months, when symbolic play and representation first occur. Like the earlier abilities, these new ones *create* a new domain of interaction. It vastly increases our potential for self-consciousness, but the other organizations of self persist with and after it.

The point here is that the specific aspects of concrete interaction characterizing each domain continue to be present throughout life. Senses of self, as used here, are not like Piaget's stages of logical operations, which overtake and transform the preceding one. Rather, domains of relatedness emerge and then coexist: "The subjective experience of social interactions seems to occur in all domains of relatedness simultaneously" (Stern, 1985, p. 31). This framework allows us to look at enduring senses of self and other in development beyond infancy.

Third, and most important, since experiences that are relevant to the self entail correlative actions by other persons, every sense of self necessarily emerges interdependently with the "other." The infant is social from the beginning, and the other becomes more complex as the infant's abilities blossom. Each new domain of relatedness depends on developing cognitive and other abilities, but each is realized through the use of these abilities in interactions. Since animals as interactants have different capacities for interaction from those of other humans, the child's interactively derived sense of self with the animal may differ from that derived with another person.

From these three theoretical reference points—the subjectivity of animate self and other, the endurance of senses of self, and the interactive interdependence of self and other—we can see (in later chapters) how the animate, intersubjective, and verbal domains together constitute the child's relations with animals. But first, we can answer the question of how the differences of different animals register in the domain of animate subjective relatedness.

Optimally Different Animals

At the start of this chapter, we considered the idea that animals are interesting because of their novelty. The problem with this idea was that it failed to account for situations in which a balance between environmental novelty and the person's capacities leads to development. Optimal arousal theorists and others, such as Csikszentmihalyi (1990), note that a challenge that just exceeds the person's present skills offers an optimally discrepant environment for development. And this is just what animals offer as interactants: new information—incongruities, interruptions of expectation, challenges—in the context of familiar otherness. Animate otherness underlies children's connection with animals; but within this otherness many challenges are available. Cognitive researchers suggest that the young child's explicit concept of "animal" is mammal-like. But on the animate or "core" level all animals offer gradient variations on the themes of agency, coherence, affect, and continuity—and thus opportunities for differentiated experience and thought.[7]

Qualities of animals' agency vary across taxonomic groups and across other factors such as domestication, training, and individual history.[8] Toward one extreme are highly responsive animals such as trained dogs. At the other are invertebrates—informatively, for example, insects. Arthropods' agency and affectivity are radically different and seem especially unpredictable to us mammals.[9] The children were shown how to let a tarantula walk on their hands and how to make it twitch slightly by puffing on it. But some children blew too hard, causing the spider to make a dramatic jump, which elicited even more exaggerated responses in the children! Occasionally, a fly would get into the classroom. In one exciting instance, Toby noticed a fly and stood up, exclaiming, "Fly! Fly." Chris, Ivy, Katra, Dawn, and others also saw it and joined in, calling, "Fly!" Katra pointed to it and Chris put his hands out to clap them over it, but in vain.

There is a huge variety of animals, each dictating a particular response to its whole form. The range of animals in this book clearly shows this. The very act of touching or holding another creature calls for sensori-motor accommodation to the size, shape, textures, temperature, and other qualities of the animal. Immediate contact conveys the unique, concrete coherences of animals to the child.

Interestingly, different species convey characteristic vitality affects. The monkey's unpredictable and stealthy way of approaching the children's feet created an atmosphere of suspense and liveliness. The characteristic vitality affect of an animal may be vivid enough that it overrides even strong societal biases about the species. For example, these four-year-olds knew enough stories to make them afraid of snakes. But in actual interaction with the living snake, many were remarkably calm. Had the snake's movement not been quite lethargic and smooth, even the reassuring presenter would have had difficulty keeping the children calm, as evidenced when the snake did make a sudden move or pointed its head toward the children. Contrary to stereotyped images, the children kept more distance from the monkey than the snake. Conspicuous differences in the vitality effects of the tarantulas, the ferrets, and the dog were also noted.

Variation in self-other continuity is implied by all these differences in animal interactants—compared to humans and compared across animals. An important dimension of interactions is the meshing or synchrony of moves by each partner. Meshing is never perfect, thus contributing to the distinctness of animate sense of self and other. To the extent higher degrees of meshing happen, for example, with the guinea pig, continuity would gain clarity and depth, increasing awareness of the animal's discrepancies from human patterns.

These observations can be generalized and are central to understanding how the children are not egocentric or anthropomorphic in their approach to animals. *As interactants,* animals present both important continuities and important discontinuities from the human pattern. Indeed, we saw that even young infants discriminate animals from humans. Carey (1985) found that four-year-olds put humans in a separate category from animals; they do not develop a domain of biological concepts that is independent of human social behavior until middle childhood (see also the work of the psychologists Frank Keil, 1990; and Graziella R. Rusca & Francesco T. Tonucci, 1992). But more recent work suggests that the domain of biological knowledge has origins independent of psychological knowledge (Coley, 1995; Hirschfeld & Gelman, 1994).

In either case, children draw on both kinds of knowledge in interacting. Children's interactions demonstrate they have implicit knowledge of the classificatory and behavioral differences of animals. No child interacted with Snowflake exactly as she or he would with another human—not even Ivy, whose tendency was to baby it. Children cannot be simply anthropomorphizing when they adjust interactive moves to fit the animal. Indeed, interaction is what produces new explicit concepts and distinctions.[10] For example, many names the children proposed for the animals—such as "Sweeper," "Drinker," "Duster," and "Nibbles"—bore close relationships to the actions of the animals.

Because animals, like other humans, are animate others to the child, relatedness grows in similar ways. But the animal is a discrepant other. Children by this age are adept at detecting and responding to these differences. The discrepancy is often optimal, triggering differentiation of basic abilities. The children I observed did not treat animals as humans; nor did they treat all animals identically.[11] When we look at interactions, we see a continuation of the infant's discrimination of animals as a distinct class, not just assimilation to a human pattern. This will become clearer as we add other interactive abilities to our analysis, and the window of pretend play will confirm it.

The Animal as a Subjective Other

The animal is a subjective other to the child; thus it can serve important psychological functions. Many interpretations of animals' significance agree in this regard but assume that these functions must be projective and egocentric. Before looking at some illuminating episodes, let us review some of those interpretations. In Chapter 2, we already encountered the psychoanalytic interpretation of animals, illustrated by Freud's case study of Little Hans. Following the child psychologist D. W. Winnicott (1971/1989), some have supposed the child projects his or her creative powers through the animal-as-transitional-object (see the work of Cecelia Soares, 1985, on pets in the family system). The psychiatrist Karl Menninger (1951) argued almost any action or attitude toward animals revealed unconscious motives—usually sexual or hostile repressed childhood urges. Animals may be security or authority figures. Because of these projective meanings, many clinicians believe animals are useful in the working through of intrapsychic conflict.[12] Recently, even psychotherapy techniques specifically calling for identification with "inner" animals have emerged.

The idea of a psychologically potent human-animal bond has been the focus of much research also, as reviewed by the human–companion animal researcher Beth Ellen Barba (1995). The idea is derived from the psychiatrist

John Bowlby's (1969) theory of mother-infant attachment.[13] It is a compelling idea, partly because it is easy to see pets in the framework of human-human relationships, especially those between parent and child.[14] The parallels include the need for continual care; the need for protection from dangerous ingestibles, things, and situations; the need for having problems explained to the doctor; and the performance of behaviors at the owner's will, such as petting and touching, as enumerated by the psychologists and pioneers of pet-person relations Alan Beck and Aaron Katcher (1983). Both pets' and children's range of movement is restricted, their sexuality controlled, their excrement tolerated, and their dependence accepted. Pet keeping occurs in many cultures, which the animal behaviorist James Serpell (1986) and many others hold is because an innate nurturant response to infantile features makes us react positively to animals with large eyes, round faces, and other "cute" looks.

The idea of a bond, projective and anthropomorphic though it may be, highlights how the subjective meanings of an animal may be positive, neutral, or negative. Positively, animals provide enduring interactions and good feelings. Contributions here have been copious from the use of pets in therapeutic settings of every kind. The psychotherapist Boris Levinson (1969) was a founder of the movement that now includes the use of dogs, cats, birds, horses, and dolphins, among others, in such settings as psychotherapy, residential programs, geriatric care, jails, rehabilitation, and treatment of autistic children. Pets also contribute to normal social development and family integration in a number of ways.[15]

The negative pole of the bond is shown in tragic cases of children, severely victimized by abuse or war, who torture animals and may later show sociopathology according to the psychologists Frank Ascione (1993) and Alan Felthous and Stephen Kellert (1987). Yi Fu Tuan (1984) suggested that a less extreme urge to dominate often co-occurs with making the other an "object" of one's affection. Unfortunately, history abounds with examples of human cruelty, including toward pets. Institutionalized gratuitous provocation and cruelty to animals is found today in rodeos and in every historical period and across cultures.[16]

We can take from this evidence the indispensable insight that animals are psychologically potent to us. But the challenge, as posed by two consistent contributors to the study of animals across the human life span, Aline Kidd and Robert Kidd (1987b), is to determine how the human-animal bond *diverges* from the human-human bond and from two other models: animal-animal and human-object. Interestingly, recent research on the mother-infant bond focuses on dynamic interactive and affective processes. We can use the same approach to understand how the animal is a *different kind of subject* for the child.

My focus on actual interactions with animals showed increasingly finely tuned actions. The child's basic abilities as a social being are not just set in one pattern but are capable of differentiation. The child is not merely projecting onto the animal. Such a view would miss the most concrete and basic relationship of the child to the animal. For example, a child cannot long mistake a living animal as a transitional object since the animal's independent agency conflicts with the child's projected sense of authorship of the object. Core connection to the animal suggests an alternative frame of interpretation of animals' psychological importance.

Specific Subjective Qualities

Then what subjective dimensions of the animate other are evident in children's actions? First is a nearly ineffable sense of "aliveness" that children can experience with others of any animate species. Vitality affects are continuously present in the other's action and in the self's inner experience; animals unavoidably convey them in the qualities of their movement. Stern (1985) argues that for the infant vitality affects are a more primary way of experiencing others than seeing each behavior as discrete. In a stream of interaction with the animal, its subjective presence is continuously available and (my second point) thus *confirms the child's own self.*[17]

For example, the animal's agency confirms the child's, as seen when children I observed provoked an animal to react. The children delighted in chasing common urban outdoor animals, such as squirrels and pigeons. After such episodes, some children reported, "I made it fly" or "I scared it." These children focused on their own agency, but agency means something achieved only with an animate other. In flying away, the action of the pigeon confirms the child's own agency in a way that an inanimate thing cannot. Even a child such as Solly who was usually very mild toward animals was capable of using an animal this way:

> As Ms. Collins retrieves the ferret, Solly moves his right arm up and down, roughly in karate-chop fashion, aimed just behind the ferret's tail. Solly: "Can't get away from the snapper, snap, snap," bringing his hand down on the "snap"s.

Mindy seemed unusually obsessed with pest animals, mentioning how there were mice and ants in her home, and at other times wanting to squash bugs. She also liked to tease the guinea pig—which is not a pest:

On another attempt to poke the guinea pig, Mindy pulls her hand out fast, making a noise on the cage, and it jumps. I point this out, which leads her to drag her hand on the cage to make loud noises, causing it to jump more. I ask if she likes to scare it. She nods and smiles.

In extreme cases of neglect or mistreatment, the desire to confirm his or her own sense of agency and self may impel a child to abuse an animal.[18] We can construe both the negative and the positive poles of the bond with animals as results of animate responsiveness. As the science fiction and fantasy writer Ursula K. Le Guin (1990) put it, both love and cruelty occur in the *otherness*, in "the space between us" that needs to be respected, not eliminated (p. 12). Animate connection, created through concrete bodily interaction, is the precondition, not the result, of "projective" processes.

A third subjective feature is that optimal discrepancy means *implicit self-other clarification*. The child encounters the animal's differences on a concrete level demanding immediate accommodation and interrupting the child's expectations. When multiple comparisons across animate interactants are possible, this enriches self-other clarity. These experiences may not be easily made explicit but inform the child's sense of self nonetheless. As we will see further in the next two chapters, a depth—but not a gulf—is thus added to the sense of being a human self.

Fourth, recall the baby snake's meaning of "growing" for Ivy: Special *symbolism* stems from shared animacy. Animals are not symbolic to the child in the flat sense of representing familiar cultural concepts such as laudable or despised human qualities. Rather, because they are living animates and thus display (sometimes more vividly than do other humans) agency, affectivity, and other life processes, they embody important qualities shared in common with the child. Symbols stemming from this core commonality constitute a special category of animal symbols, ones with great subjective relevance.

One striking example was provided by Yasmin, in interaction with the diamond doves, which she enjoyed watching. Early in the year, she would stand close to the cage and hold her hands close together, as if preparing to clap, or perhaps mimicking their positions, and then watch. In the spring, one remarkable video segment shows her silently facing the doves and their new hatchling and seeming to carry on a dialogue in motion with them, gesturing in imitation and anticipation of their movements, sometimes remaining still in turn as they moved. She held her hands together, index fingers oriented like their heads, as they landed together on the perch. She also did twirls before them and motioned as if to rouse or encourage them.

The dancelike quality of the whole episode is hard to capture in words. The episode ended with her dawning realization that the other children were already eating, at which point she herself "flew off," arms flapping, to get her lunch box. Notably, Yasmin also had a great interest in flying and the character Tinkerbell from *Peter Pan*. For her, the birds' capacity of flight inspired a sense of animated agency different from her own and endowed with rich subjective meanings. It is in this sense that animals are symbolic for young children.

Finally, the animal provides a vivid sense of *connection across essential difference*. This is not the same as accurate knowledge of the other, although it may initiate and motivate the search for that. Much of the sense of connection and meaning on the animate level is apprehended in an immediate manner without conscious inferences and realized through interaction and later in pretend or reflection. The fact that animate properties are shared is not incidental. It means that a common reality is felt to define both the child's and the animal's experience.

The children learned that agency has a shared meaning across species by feeding bugs, beetles, worms, slugs, and so forth, to the toad. The toad would eat these only if they were moving or made to move. This was well known by the children; animacy is meaningful for Toad, too! Likewise, the guinea pig was a continuous presence in the class in more than a physical sense. The children regarded Snowflake as a member of the class. They brought it food such as carrots, which they gave it at lunchtime. But there is more to it than just the children's actions. The guinea pig could smell the food when it was brought out at lunchtime and on at least one occasion it squealed. Ivy then fed it, and others who had heard it talked about it. Thus, the children constituted a common cross-species world, yet this world also embraced all the subtle and dramatic gradient differences animals present.

Conclusion

Animate qualities of animals—and of other humans—are continuously present in all face-to-face interactions. Thus, the sense of animate self and other is a constant dimension of experience, carried on with subtle variability, creating connection across degrees of difference. It is this, I argue, that primarily underlies the concern for animals voiced by children in the previous chapter and that explains how the child's sense of self is constituted among the available interspecies community. I have shown that cultural frames cannot produce the phenomena I observed; that the position that children are relentlessly anthropomorphic is challenged by their response to optimal discrepancy; and that egocentric and projective interpretations must depend on something deeper. The core animate level precedes any of these interpretations. Thus, it should be given greater emphasis in our ideas about the generation of the self from human-human interaction, too. Understanding the full implications of this idea requires also considering the child's capacities for intersubjectivity and language, to which we now turn.

5 The Creature
That Connects:
Sharing Feelings,
Words, and Minds

M any of the things children say about animals show they see them as feeling, thinking beings. Reuben had been watching squirrels outside the window when I joined him; one was turned toward us and he told me, "It's watching us." Reuben was attributing a subjective act—one that seems completely natural and undoubtable—to the squirrel. Of course, since children experience animals based on animate characteristics, the animal world is very "present" to them. The animate world is populated by subjectivities, aware of each other to some degree. But the opportunity to *express* the situation in this way stems from our intersubjective and linguistic abilities—which we acquire for the most part only in the company of other humans. Yet, once acquired, these forms of relating put their stamp on our experience of each other and of animals, although in differing ways. As on the animate level, children make distinctions based on such interactive abilities.

Children do more than see animals as subjective—they may see them as *sharing* the children's own subjective states. Dawn, for example, felt attracted to more animals than most children and was inclined to think they felt the same toward her:

> One ferret approaches Dawn, who is seated on the floor with her legs out in front of her. She draws her hands back to her sides and giggles: "He likes me."

What made Dawn think this? The ferret's keeper, more experienced with the animal's behavior, explained, "He likes *socks*." But Dawn's reaction was a feeling of mutual "liking." This example taken from my transcripts of videotape is like many others in the first part of this chapter. In them, interactants in some way mirror each other's behavior. Such episodes have special significance for how children judge three types of shared subjective states with animals: affects, attention, and intentions.

All of these kinds of sharing tap the child's understanding of others' minds—the beliefs, intentions, and feelings they guess fill the ongoing experience of the other. Consider Ivy's thought process here:

> Mr. Lloyd attempts to feed the turtle a small piece of meat held on the end of a stick. . . . Mr. Lloyd: "Maybe if we move it a little bit." Ivy smiling: "Think it's *alive!*"

From her wording, Ivy might have meant to encourage the turtle, or she could have been describing what she guessed it was thinking. Her meaning is not clear. What is clear is that to her turtles have the capacity for cognition. Ivy, one of the older children, has a five-year-old's theory of mind, which I will discuss later and relate to intersubjectivity and language. This example is especially revealing because she assumed the turtle understood animatelike motion in the same way she does—as indicating aliveness. In the mental states children attribute to animals, we find confirmation that animate qualities dominate their perception.

Shared attention and affect; the theory of mind; and, especially, shared intentions have close ties to language development, which makes possible many important advances in relatedness. The ins and outs of language compose a third major focus of the chapter. Sometimes, the children drew the animal in to the linguistic realm with striking or humorous disregard for difference:

> Dawn helps search for bugs in the dirt, together with Cassia, Yasmin, Angela, Reuben, and the teacher. She shows me the bugs in her hand and continues looking. . . . Cassia tells the others it's time to go. As she leaves, Dawn says to the bugs in her hand, "We're going," and runs off.

As in most cases, Dawn did not "communicate" anything of much sophistication to the bugs, but the implications of speech for our potential relations to animals are far-reaching. There are two main points. On the one hand, language is a *means of* interaction. How are children's interactions with animals affected by the fact they have this tool? How does it shape their conduct and experience of interactions with animals? On the other hand, children's ideas about animals may come from specific meanings *transmitted by* language, thus indirectly affecting their experience of them. In this chapter, I take up the first concern, leaving the second for later.

Young children are apt to be careless (as are many adults) in what they assume animals can understand. Indeed, to stay clear on how children make such inferences, I start with the developmental precursors to language—the nonverbal forms of intersubjectivity—and move on to examine how the structure of language depends on assumptions we must make about the cooperativeness and meaningfulness of communication. This chapter expands my analysis of children's interactions with animals to include the abilities that make us uniquely human. Language has usually been seen as setting us apart from animals or, rather, above them. But ironically, language is essential in making us the creature that connects.

Intersubjectivity

A special condition gives the child a sense of shared experience. Earlier, I discussed "complementary" moves in interaction, in which each participant responds with a different but linked action. "Reciprocal" interactions, on the other hand, are when a given action elicits a *similar* action from the second individual (Hinde, 1976). Fewer interactions between children and animals showed this quality, but ones that did deserve special attention because of the subjective experiences they afford. When another reflects our actions, we sometimes infer a shared experience or meaning.

Imitation is a case in point. In the class, the monkey scratched itself, and Ivy began scratching herself in imitation. She was not doing it to amuse the other children; she may have meant to establish a shared feeling. In more remarkable cases, twice the monkey appeared to imitate the children raising their hands. Chris noticed and imitated back, pointing at the monkey, raising his right foot approximately as the monkey had raised its, and exclaiming, "Wooo—! He raised his foot! He did this!" Although these reciprocal moves are remarkable and suggestive of subjectivity to the children, another ingredient is necessary for true shared subjectivity: confirmation from the other that the state of feeling or thought *is* shared.

Simple reciprocal affect, attention, and intention are evident in my data, but at most only very partial confirmation of sharing. In the last analysis, intersubjectivity mostly depends on normal human interactants to develop and occur. Nonetheless, in each case, the animal fits differently into the human framework. When the children respond to this situation, we find complex patterns, not a simple imposition of human schemas or socialized meanings. Each of these divergences deepens the sense in which the animal is a significant and discrepant other for the child.

Interaffectivity

Interaffectivity is an emotion that is shared and *understood* to be so. Is it possible between children and animals? Answering this question requires first determining if a child can grasp the emotions of an animal at all. In a broad sense, this is empathy. Many definitions of it exist, but most entail temporarily taking the other into ourselves and then imaginatively comparing the internalized other's feelings with our own (see the work of the psychologist Janet Strayer, 1987). Although unavoidably imperfect, there is no doubt that empathy is important in understanding animals,[1] and also that it can be greatly improved with knowledge of the other. Of crucial importance is how one interprets signs of the other's feeling.

Categorical emotions (happiness, anger, and so on) are less likely to enter into children's interpretation of animals' feeling than are vitality affects. We infer both partly from the series of events that lead up to an emotion, but direct cues are essential. Facial clues to animals' categorical emotions are absent or very ambiguous, but reading vitality affects (changes in intensity and quality of arousal) does not depend as much on knowledge of species-specific signals. Indeed, the children mirrored vitality affects displayed by animals, such as the excitement of the dog, the lethargy of the ferrets, and the calmness of the snake. Similarly, when the guinea pig was restless, some of the children became restless while feeding it. These kinds of cases resemble something simpler, like the mood contagion observed in infants and toddlers. In an exercise of truer empathy with the turtle, Dimitri and Toby read behavior and drew on concepts of others' minds:

> Mr. Lloyd: "What does he do when you touch his tail, what does he do?" All the kids are looking very closely. They pull back as Toby answers: "He puts it inside his shell." Mr. Lloyd: "He pulls it inside his shell. Why do you think he does that?" Toby: "Maybe um . . ." Dimitri (interrupting): "'Cause he's scared." Mr. Lloyd: "'Cause he's scared. He doesn't want . . ." Toby (interrupting): "Maybe he doesn't want us to do that."

From all these examples, we can say that children do—within limits—understand animals' emotions. But does this produce the confirmed sharing of affect? To answer this question, let us look at the origin of shared feelings in infancy.

A primary—perhaps original—means of establishing interaffectivity between parent and infant is attunement to vitality affects. This process occurs when the mother mirrors back the affect contours expressed by her child, the mirroring being performed in a *different modality* (Stern, 1985). For example, if the infant hits something playfully on the floor, the mother might make a sound like "kaaaa-*bam*," analogically reproducing in the verbal mode the arousal contours of the suspenseful preparatory swing and then the hit. This is called a *cross-modal* match, and unlike imitation it necessarily carries the information that the mother registers the infant's subjective feeling, not just its external motions. Thus, it confirms shared affect, in a process that occurs largely out of the awareness of either partner. This is one of the key kinds of interactions that make intersubjectivity a domain of self-other experience among humans.

Shared affect of this sort may occur between members of other species with multimodal social communication. In child-animal interaction, interaffectivity could conceivably be created by the animal attuning to the child; however, I did not observe it. Indeed, the early development of the ability to share affect probably depends on the active empathy of a mature human caretaker.[2] The cases of mood contagion noted previously could be child-to-animal attunement but did not involve cross-modal matching. So we cannot say for sure, but there is no evidence for true interaffectivity between children and animals.

But children (and adults) may be biased to read animal actions as conveying interaffectivity. Infants learn early that cross-modal matching signals shared feeling. This has an intriguing implication, since animals do not respond in language. Their responses to human speech (or action) are in a bodily modality or in a voice that primarily conveys vitality affect. Thus, when a child says something and the animal responds, it is likely to be doing so cross-modally. If the response is at all similar in vitality affect, this may bias the child to read into it a state of attunement to the self's. Animals "liking" children illustrates this pattern. Dawn, as noted, liked many animals and felt they liked her. She said the dog did; its behavior may have confirmed this. She said the ferret liked her when its behavior—approach—matched her own attraction. And this same affectively important behavior may explain yet a third case:

> The turtle crawls toward Dawn, who declares: "He likes me." Mr. Lloyd: "He likes you? He's going to crawl right under you there, huh?" Dawn backs up, spreads her knees on floor, and laughs.

Dawn probably felt a sense of mutual attraction between herself and these animals. These examples do not show true or confirmed intersubjectivity, but they do show that some kinds of affect reciprocity occur and blur into what could certainly be interpreted by participants as interaffectivity.

Important though the intersubjective domain may be, it has its limits even among humans. To compare the quasi-interaffectivity children may feel toward animals with a false conception that human intersubjectivity is complete would conceal important reasons why animals seem to share our feelings and why they are so effective as cotherapists. Because human affect attunement (that is, parent to child) occurs only occasionally and sometimes is wrong, children probably do not base judgments of shared affect on a perfect standard—there is always the sense that the self is somewhat opaque to others and vice versa (Stern, 1985, p. 218). So the animal's occasional response in apparent harmony with the child's own feeling may be apprehended as more than adequate evidence of a general capacity to share affect. And since the whole process goes largely unnoticed (even in adults), it is not often open to critical examination.

Furthermore, humans are not simply imperfect at sharing affect; we do it manipulatively as well. Parents, above all, enact multiple agendas through variations in attunement. "Misattunements" occur when another attunes, establishing, for example, a shared happy affect, and then alters the situation to serve a different purpose. This ultimately motivates children to learn evasions that "keep their own subjective experience intact" (Stern, 1985, p. 214). Attunements are also used to convey prohibitions. Animals as nonattuning others do not pose these threats and thus may provide "safer" zones of interaction.

Patterns of attunement communicate what is private versus sharable. Socializing agents systematically attune to accepted parts of the child's feelings and omit attuning to affects that are not part of the public realm. This in effect creates culturally agreed upon "private" experiences. Such "selective attunement" is especially salient in Western culture given the overlap between what is private and what is considered marginally human, or closer to the animal state. In particular, reproductive and other bodily functions and feelings associated with them are kept private and are considered "lower" in the ranks of human concerns. This convergence means children very likely feel more commonality with animals around these issues than they do with adults who have learned to keep such matters private.[3]

For example, children who are interested in feces face the difficulty that exploring their own is prohibited and even their interest in doing so is not attuned to by adults. But they can take advantage of animal feces and adult tolerance or inattention, as several children did during the year. The following episode captures one associated affect:

> The teacher points out a pigeon, up on a ledge as the children play in a neighboring courtyard. Dimitri, Chris, and others run at it, to no effect. Toby stays longer, watching it. He says "pigeon" twice, gets on his hands and knees, and rubs his hands in the dry piled-up pigeon droppings. He gets up, steps in them, and screams—his mood interested and delighted. Then he runs off to join the others.

Since animals were used to talk about body functions and sexual anatomy in this nursery school, they acquired a special status as avenues for such interests. There were numerous opportunities to observe and talk about the genitalia and other body parts of the dog, the monkey, the guinea pig, and even the snake. The children were often the initiators of these discussions, as in the following example:

> Dawn sits forward over the dog, evidently looking at what Drew was pointing to on its belly. Joe taps Drew on arm, saying quietly: "It's his penis." Mrs. Ray breaks in: "It's his penis, you're right." Drew turns and taps the teacher on her leg and asks: "What's the yellow stuff?" Mrs. Ray: "Maybe it's urine. Is it a drop of urine, left from last time he urinated? I bet it is . . . it's kind of wonderful that you recognized the parts of his body." Mrs. Ray to Joe: "How do you know if he's a boy, Joe? You made a discovery. How do you know if he is a boy?" Several children respond, saying "penis."

Such a demonstration with a human as the object (except perhaps for an infant) would not normally happen in the presence of adults. Although no reference was made to subjective feelings that go with having sexual anatomy, the avenue is more open for children to make this association with an animal, whose sexual anatomy (and occasionally behavior) is at least visible, than it is with other humans. Since such issues are not verbalized in the presence of children, it is unlikely that such a felt commonality with an animal would be on a level of verbal awareness either. If present, it exists outside the realm of the explicitly marked and shared, although advertisers have long exploited the connection.

Sharing Attention

Interattentionality is possible when the child can realize that self and other each have a focus of attention, that these can be similar or not, and that they can be brought into alignment. Children ascertain an animal's attention by observing what it responds to and what it watches, for example, third-person objects. Play objects included toys extended by hand to the monkey. Other aspects of animals' attention the children observed were food for the guinea pig; fish; or, especially, for the toad. Toad would dramatically creep straight at a moving bug before catching it with its tongue. In object-related play with an animal, the participants shared a focus of attention. For example, in playing fetch with a dog, its attention was generally directed at the ball. If the child was focused on the ball and simultaneously realized that the dog was, too, she or he could have had a sense of shared attention. But did the dog notice the child's focus on the ball? Never very clearly. Likewise, although the dog might have been focused on the ball, the child might have been too focused on the dog to throw well, as was often the case. Thus, this kind of episode may not fit the conditions for true interattentionality, but it can feel very much like it.

Gaze was the children's main clue to attention. Snowflake was turned toward Drew, and I asked if the guinea pig was watching him; he said, "Yes." Drew also noticed the turtle's gaze and, indeed, experimented with it:

> Drew reaches toward the turtle: "I saw his eye turn this way, when I was touching his nose." He gestures on himself, with right hand to right eye.

Children are especially stimulated by an animal looking at them: a situation in which the self is the object of the other's gaze and attention. Some children spontaneously reported aloud that the animal was looking at them, as did Reuben; he also noted, "He's looking at me," when the turtle had its head turned in his direction. In some cases, as we saw earlier with the snake, this reflected a concern that the animal might bite the child. But in others, it indicated an intense awareness that the animal was (or seemed to be) paying attention to the child himself or herself.

Being looked at by an animal is potent because eyes convey direction of attention, *plus*, on the animate level, they shout out the interior and agentic quality of the animal. Live animals were denoted by a special term in the nursery school: *real animal*. Ivy, in a conversation in which I used a realistic fox puppet to ask questions, explained:

> Fox asks Ivy: "Am I real?" Ivy: "No." Fox: "Is guinea pig real?" Ivy: "Yeah." Fox: "How can you tell?" Ivy: "Because he has eyes, and he can eat."

There was no question of confusing a puppet with a real animal. For Ivy, the key indicator of the animal's "realness" was its eyes. The absence of this cue could confuse the children. The point is vividly illustrated by what happened when a dead gray-cheeked thrush was brought to class. During discussion, Mindy asked, "Is that a real bird?" The teacher, as she had done before, explained that real birds can be dead or alive. But such a conceptual explanation failed to satisfy Mindy, who interjected, "Why his eyes are like that? [*sic*]" She repeated variants of this query eight times, ignoring the ongoing group effort to identify the species. The dead eyes disturbed Mindy and were at odds with the bird's "realness." To the children, eyes conveyed living otherness as well as attention, a powerful combination of domains.

Noticing the animal's attention does not alone amount to shared attention. Between humans, either party can make it fairly clear to the other what he or she is focused on, since language and gesture can serve indexical and referential functions. For example, to point to something establishes *that* the pointer's attention is on that thing; to respond to the pointing contains the understanding that one is sharing the focus of attention. In the case of infants, the requisite abilities depend on the adult's capacity to share the infant's focus and begin before nine months of age, when infants can follow the mother's line of vision. By nine months, they can follow the direction of another's pointing hand; they can point and alternate their gaze between the object and the mother to confirm that she is sharing the focus. Mothers focus on the objects their infants are focused on and make clear that they share this focus. By twelve months, infants can discriminate the adult's object of attention regardless of other objects at different perceptual depths. They even use a person's line of regard as a clue to infer his or her behavior (Spelke et al., 1995). Sharing attention is a landmark in the development of a concept of mind and a beginning of intentional communication.

Of course, this talent is routinized and advanced by preschool age. But applying it to animals is likely to be a one-way street. Animals may notice and then reveal they share a person's focus, but this is probably rare, dependent on extensive interaction or training, and not necessarily easy to detect. The child may notice what the animal is focused on and share that focus, but the animal is not likely to notice the child is doing so or to signal it if it does notice. Thus, much of the time children "fill in the blanks" to gain a sense of quasi-shared attention. In "fetch," the dog responded enthusiastically when Mr. Grier retrieved a ball that had landed beyond its grasp. The dog's focus was obvious, and the game itself provided shared attention. Children can observe and share animals' attention, defining an intermediate but still compelling position for animals as social others.

Sharing Intentions

More clearly than the two previous types of subjective sharing, the confirmed sharing of intentions requires a concept of mind and depends on language-related abilities. Sharing intentions requires (1) that one attribute an intention to the other, (2) that one also know *that* the other's intentions can be aligned with one's own, and (3) that one direct an act to get the referent person to align his or her intentions to one's own. To my knowledge, this form is only rarely achieved with animals;[4] almost certainly it depends on a fully human context to develop. In considering children's grasp of animals' intentions, there are two intertwined issues to address. One is how intention reading and sharing alter the flow of interaction; the other is the child's theory of mind. As before, although animals fall short with regard to intersubjectivity, the interactive possibilities they do offer are not lost on children.

It is now widely agreed that infants possess social competences that are prerequisite for interintentionality and a theory of mind. Indeed, they seem to have an implicit theory of mind by age nine months or younger, as shown by shared attention. They can tell what is intended by a communication by reading gesture, intonation, and simple utterances well before they can understand or use word meanings and combinations. Such achievements are always embedded in the here-and-now context.

The infant achieves interintentionality with acts aimed at another and intended to evoke an intention in the other. Before they can talk, infants use protolinguistic gestures to indicate their desires. These may not be initially intended to be communicative, but they become so when others treat them as if they were—for example, by delivering the cookie for which the infant is reaching. Reaching soon becomes pointing. Once used on purpose for such ends, these acts, "directed at a referent person, imply that the infant attributes an internal mental state to that person—namely, comprehension of the infant's intention and the capacity to satisfy that intention. Intentions have become sharable experiences" (Stern, 1985, p. 131). Such nonverbal interintentionality is very close to the signaling behavior of language use. Indeed, it is a prerequisite: Knowing that the other's intentions can be aligned with one's own and thus that the other can be got to serve one's own ends are pragmatic bases of language use.

Interintentionality is the third key interactive basis for the sense of intersubjective self and other. As such, even as a theory of mind and language develop, interintentionality persists as a distinctive dimension in children's interactions with animals. Again we find a quasi-shared phenomenon. Consider a child trying to catch a playful dog. The dog must read the child's potential body moves regarding obstacles and so forth in "keep away," and vice versa. In this way, the two share a space, reading each other's intended motions. Some episodes during "fetch" with the dog showed this simple reversibility of position and reciprocity of intentions—that is, a series of moves can proceed because each participant remains a coherent occupant of space.[5] Although it is fair to point out that much human interaction depends on just such intention reading, this is not confirmed intention sharing.

Some activities by some of the youngest children I observed come a bit closer to assuming linguistic interintentionality. The expectation that animals understand intentions was implicit in some of the ways they talked "at" animals:

Toby comes to the cage and shouts, "Ha! Ah Ha!" at the birds. He leaves after about
10 seconds.

It is not clear what Toby intended to communicate, but his shouting shows a
dawning awareness of, and frustration at, the inefficacy of language with the
animal. Here's another case:

Billy is making loud noises at the bugs which are in the pan for Toad soon to eat in
front of the group. Dimitri asks Billy, "Why are you yelling?" Billy replies, "So they
can hear."

Talking at all implicitly puts the animal in the role of language receiver expected to respond. Billy's comment, "So they can hear," reinforces this interpretation—as if talking itself should work, he tried increasing the volume when he perceived a problem!

Children only one year younger than these treat language not as a separate system but as part of a communication matrix equal with gesture, affect, paralinguistics, and other channels, as discussed by the developmental
psychologists Peggy Miller and Lisa Hoogstra (1989). As for infants, action
and word are not seen as separate systems. Similarly, the developmental
psychologist Janet Astington (1993) suggests that very young children have
only a crude grasp of the speech act as distinct from actions and mental
states. They often infer the intention from the action:

Moreover, if what someone has said does not accord with the interpretation a young
child has given to the action, the child disregards what was said. Children don't interpret the words in isolation, they interpret situations, sometimes without understanding the words. . . . Their awareness of other people's mental states is an awareness of
those states expressed in action, not in language. (p. 73)

The corollary—and the point—is that they also do not clearly distinguish
which forms of intentional action animals respond to. It may be that the
process of differentiating animals with respect to intentional communication is an ongoing task, changing as more interactive abilities develop.[6] For
very young children who do not make a firm distinction between these
modes, the animal may not be apprehended as outside the "human" intersubjective realm simply because it lacks language. The children's use of ex-
clamations in the previous examples suggests that they consider animals
part of an interintentional world but are becoming aware that language
does not work equally with all intersubjective interactants.

The emergence of distinctions between these kinds of relatedness is seen
in older children who accommodate themselves more to the animal's abilities. The children I observed occasionally demonstrated more refined and

accurate attempts to communicate with an animal on a nonverbal intentional level. Several children attempted to engage the monkey in a game of
give-and-take with plastic blocks or other objects. After initial presenta-
tions of a new object, the monkey usually ignored it. Benson, who repeatedly banged a block on the floor to get the monkey's attention, gave up
when the monkey's attention quickly shifted. But Ivy persisted in her goal
of handing it a toy monkey:

> Ivy leans forward, offering the toy to the monkey, but pulls her hand back when the
> monkey suddenly turns and moves in the direction of the camera. Ivy extends her
> hand further, but the monkey is away, by Ms. Dean's side. It scoots around, but con-
> tinues looking at Ivy and the plastic toy monkey she's waving in its direction. The
> monkey climbs up onto Ms. Dean's lap, still regarding Ivy. Ivy drops the toy and
> pushes a larger block toward the monkey. It climbs up onto Ms. Dean's shoulders. A
> minute later it climbs down quickly and faces Mrs. Ray. The monkey is close to Ivy
> now; she moves closer and peers at him, her head tilted sideways, as if trying to es-
> tablish eye contact. Ivy crawls closer and lowers herself, continuing to look at the
> monkey's face. Then Ivy claps as if to make the monkey come.

Here Ivy varied the ways she presented the toy to the monkey. In a further
gesture of reciprocity, she had even picked a toy monkey! When this failed
to elicit the "take" response she desired, she tried another object. Then, she
switched to simply trying to attain eye contact with the monkey, indicating
she changed her aim to a more modest form of intersubjectivity, a shared
gaze. Her sophisticated interaction shows a great deal of attunement and active accommodation to the animal's capacity.

Ivy's episode can be compared to criteria for true interintentionality. The
linguist Elizabeth Bates (1979) described the evidence for it as including
"(1) alternations in eye gaze contact between the goal and the intended lis-
teners, (2) augmentations, additions, and substitution of signals until the
goal has been obtained, and (3) changes in the form of the signal towards
abbreviated and/or exaggerated patterns that are appropriate only for
achieving a communicative goal" (p. 36). Needless to say, animals were not
observed fulfilling these criteria, but Ivy's attempts to engage the monkey
fit the bill. Had the monkey taken the object (as it did at times from other
children), Ivy might have experienced a sense of interintentionality: The
monkey would have grasped her intention and confirmed it by complying.
Suppose, however (as is plausible), that her intended game was *give-and-
take.* Then, only if the monkey clearly offered the block back in the same
manner would one have been warranted in concluding that the monkey understood the specific intention. But on the occasions it did take a block

from a child, the monkey dropped it. Feats of such nearly verbal human re-latedness are beyond most animals, but we aim to give full significance to the kinds of interaction that are possible.

The Theory of Mind

Recall the earlier example in which Toby and Dimitri concluded the turtle withdrew its head "'cause he's scared," and that "maybe he doesn't want us to do that." Their conversation moved beyond physical description to men-tal explanations of the turtle's behavior. We rely on the ability to think about others' minds to make sense of the world, and here Toby and Dimitri each demonstrated the ability to attribute desires or feelings to explain the turtle's actions.

Psychologists believe children develop a "theory of mind" to interpret and predict their own actions and those of others. In general, a theory of mind, or "folk psychology," holds that people have beliefs and desires, which can lead to intentions and actions and which interact with situations in the real world and with emotions in the self. Each of these mental states has certain properties and relates to the others in certain ways. For instance, beliefs may be true or false and may be held with varying degrees of cer-tainty. Desires, intentions, and emotions may vary in strength and are not true or false. Mental states are differentiated by their relations to the real world: Desires may only be fulfilled or not, whereas intentions combine a belief with a desire and thus call for a certain action; only if that is carried out is an intention fulfilled. Neither fulfillment nor its lack pertain to emo-tions themselves, although we experience the emotions in relation to be-liefs and desires. The attribution of intentions—or any mental state—to an animal depends on a theory of mind. How do children develop a theory of mind that relates such mental predicates?

Strong evidence of such a theory appears around eighteen months of age. Toddlers demonstrate they can think ahead and plan, and they register dis-satisfaction when plan and outcome fail to coincide, as reported by the cog-nitive developmentalist Alison Gopnik (1982). This shows the children can compare reality with hypothetical situations and have attained a degree of freedom from the here-and-now. They begin to pretend, can understand pretense in others, and can link their pretend play with that of others. Most researchers see this as demonstrating beliefs *about* beliefs.

By age three, according to another developmental psychologist, Henry Wellman (1990), children can distinguish real from mental entities, but they do not understand that mental things are constructed by the mind.

Dennett (1978) proposed that the test of whether an entity employs a theory of mind is whether or not it can recognize that a person holding false beliefs will act in accord with them even though the subject knows that the situation in reality differs. Three-year-olds cannot recognize false beliefs either in others (see the work of the developmental psychologists Joseph Perner, Sue Leekam, & Heinz Wimmer, 1987) or in themselves: They do not understand changed beliefs and are unable to remember their own earlier false beliefs (Gopnik & Astington, 1988). Also at this age, children have difficulty maintaining the appearance-reality distinction (as reported by John Flavell, Frances Green, & Eleanor Flavell, 1986), which may depend partly on the ability to encode and remember previous false beliefs.

Several further steps in children's theory of mind are evident around age four. Now, they do understand false belief, they use it to explain and predict others' actions, and they remember and admit their own previous false beliefs. They grasp how someone can believe something different from what he or she knows is actually the case. This implies they distinguish a state in the mind from a state in the world. As might be expected, at roughly the same time they understand the appearance/reality distinction, and the possibility that two people may have different views of the same object. At this age, they also start to tell deliberate lies, deceiving others by creating false beliefs. A range of other abilities also become more enhanced: empathy, helping, and so on—actions oriented toward others' understandings of the situation. Thus, one may argue, they have a representational theory of mind. Wellman (1990, p. 118) refers to it as an "entity" concept, as opposed to adults' "process" concept: Children believe the mind is a repository of ideas and beliefs such that people take their beliefs to be how the world is.

In the years from three to six, children move to a more active conception of the mind as an interpreting, representing, understanding faculty. They distinguish desire-based versus belief-based actions more clearly. Among the developments beyond the age of the oldest children in the nursery school are ideas about mental traits (shyness, generosity, and so on) in understanding another's behavior; these are not apparent in young children.[7] But certainly they should be capable of attributing simple beliefs and desires to animals and probably also communicative and other second-order intentions. Did they do so?

Many of the mental states children attributed to animals were wants or desires, often in close relationship to interactions. Toby's and Dimitri's attribution of fear and displeasure to the turtle reflected an awareness of its possible feelings toward them. Drew gave a simple desire as the reason for the snake's movement:

Drew holds the snake: "He's unraveling . . . he doesn't want to be in a ball anymore. He doesn't want to be in there anymore. . . . He opened!"

Questions such as why the bigger tarantula would chase the smaller one usually generated mentalistic explanations:

Ms. Tanner: "Ivy had a reason why they might be chasing." Mr. Dean: "Well, let's hear it." Ms. Tanner: "Do you want me to say it?" Ivy nods. Ms. Tanner: "Maybe the big one is trying to hug the little one."

Such direct attributions are common. Less common is a first-person narration of an animal's thoughts, which Drew made while the ferret rambled about:

Drew: "He's looking all over, woooo, 'I can't go that way, so where . . . let's see can't go that way' . . . " During this no one is obviously listening until Billy looks at him and laughs.

The thoughts Drew attributed here imply the ferret entertained a series of beliefs that were proven incorrect as it explored. Drew, at five years and two months, applied his understanding of false beliefs to its behavior.

Thus, the children over this age range become more adept at applying mental states to animals and at recognizing the limits of intention sharing. But the lack of child-animal interintentionality may seem at odds with the strong impression, held by many who know animals, that shared intentions do enter the process of interacting with them. To take a simple case, either a dog or its owner may be in a mood to play with the other, and either may successfully initiate play. But calling this "wanting to play" obscures the mutual second-order intentionality required by "getting the other to see I want to play," which is implied. Our bias to assume that the latter has occurred stems from the advance in our theories of mind made possible by language.

The theory of mind probably has innate origins (see the work of the psychologists Jeremy Avis & Paul Harris, 1991; Alan Leslie, 1991), but its full development almost certainly depends on language use. "Speech acts" are uses of language to affect others. Astington (1993) explains their relation to states of mind: "Like mental states, speech acts consist of attitudes to propositions. However, the attitude is usually referred to as the force of the speech act. The force is how we want the proposition to be taken by the hearer, that is, as a statement, or a request, or a promise" (p. 70). Force may be conveyed explicitly, by nonverbal aspects of language, or by types of utterance (declarative, interrogative, imperative). Thus, the "force" of a speech act corresponds with a mental attitude. Examples include the mental state of desiring and the speech act of requesting; intention and promising; belief and assertion; regret and apology; gratitude and thanks. Because these correspond most of the time, language can work as a means of sharing mental states, and so the use of language goes hand in hand with an understanding of minds—one's own and others'.

Thus, language is part of what underlies the ability we saw previously to ascribe wants and beliefs to animals, as well as to attribute second-order intentional states. Indeed, how language affects interaction is an intriguing question in itself, and one that animals—as interactants for which this feature is absent—can help us answer.

Language and Verbal Relatedness

The themes of the animal that speaks a human language or the human who can understand animal language have long lineages in world mythologies and contemporary culture. The German ethologist Konrad Lorenz (1952/1962) noted the wide appeal of a misreading of 1 Kings 4:33—that King Solomon talked *to* (rather than *of*) animals. Plato, early in the *Statesman* (272c), has the stranger recount to the young Socrates how people in the past could converse with animals and could "learn from each several tribe [*sic*] of creatures whether its special faculties enable it to apprehend some distinctive truth not available to the rest." Ursula K. Le Guin (1990), putting a feminist twist on the issue, remarked that it is the myth that "civilized man" alone has a soul "which all talking-animal stories mock, or simply subvert. So long as 'man' 'rules,' animals will make rude remarks about him" (p. 10). Or perhaps, such animosity is explained by events told by the Argentine fantasist Jorge Luis Borges in *The Book of Imaginary Beings*: "Ages ago, a certain South African bushman, Hochigan, hated animals, which at that time were endowed with speech. One day he disappeared, stealing their special gift. From then on, animals have never spoken again" (Borges & Guerrero, 1974, pp. 80–81).

If animals do not speak, at least to domineering adults, some writers have imagined they might speak to children. Lewis Carroll (1871/1946) astutely imagined the outcome when the Fawn and Alice entered the meadow where things have names: "The Fawn gave a sudden bound into the air, and shook itself free of Alice's arm. 'I'm a Fawn!' it cried out in a voice of delight. 'And dear me! You're a human child!' A sudden look of alarm came into his beautiful brown eyes, and in another moment it had darted away at full speed" (p. 227). It seems that language introduced distinctions for the Fawn that were not operative before. This tale shares the spirit of our quest to understand how the nature of language disposes its youthful users to regard and interact with animals; what the animals say in return, I will not attempt to guess!

Many people believe children talk to animals a lot, although only sparse data are available. Although several writers have suggested that children confide in animals more than adults do (Serpell, 1986, p. 97), there is little evidence apart from clinical case studies. One group of children in middle childhood reported to the psychologist Brenda Bryant (1986) that they talk to pets, about feelings of sadness, anger, fear, happiness, and "secret" experiences. Among ten-year-old children, 66 percent reported liking to talk to their pets, and 69 percent said they share secrets with them (Rost & Hartmann, 1994). Nielson and Delude (1989) found day care and kindergarten children directed more talk to an unfamiliar cockatiel (69 percent of the children) than to a dog (36 percent) or to a rabbit (16 percent). I did not hear my young friends talking abundantly to animals, however. More typical was silent, tactile interacting or watching.

We might expect significant amounts of talk to animals to be due to adult modeling. Adults use a special form of talking to their dogs, which the psychologists of language development Kathryn Hirsh-Pasek and Rebecca Treiman (1982) called "doggerel." It is similar to "motherese" used with infants. Utterances in both are short, simple, in the present tense, repetitious, and well formed. One difference is that doggerel uses fewer words to point to objects; mothers use such talk to tutor children on words and names. The authors suggest the similarities and differences in these two kinds of talk may be stimulated by the social responsiveness of the different recipients. This may be, but adults' talk to animals can be very complex. For example, one assistant teacher said to the monkey when it crossed the line on the floor separating it from the children, "I'm sorry, but there's a boundary here." Both her words and the abstract boundary she mentioned were completely foreign to the preverbal realm of the monkey.

In contrast, the content of the children's talk to animals was simple and kept a close tie to immediate animate action. The children verbally stated aspects of concrete physical interaction, such as movements in space, as Dawn did in telling the bug in her hand, "We're going." The children marked comings and goings of animals with hellos and good-byes—often using the animal's name, a marker of individuality and coherence. Or consider again Dimitri's talk to the guinea pig:

> [Dimitri gets help from the teacher in holding Snowflake and feeding her. He then holds her a long time, carefully watching her eat. . . .] He holds her between his legs and says, "I got you." Later the guinea pig gets away and Dimitri excitedly goes to intercept it. Trying to get it to come back, he puts leaves in its cage and says, "Over here, guinea pig" over and over.

This talk simply verbalizes immediate preverbal relatedness. "I got you" expresses the present situation of contact and the boy's subjective sense of power. "Over here" indexes the pair's relative concrete positions and intentions. These children's utterances refer closely to a core level of interaction and pertain to subjective feelings generated by present events. Adults can be quite casual about the high degree of sophistication their talk assumes in the recipient animal. The point is not what the animal actually understands but how far removed are adults' thoughts from the preverbal domains of re-latedness. Children seem to be in the midst of figuring out how to accommodate themselves to the differences animals present.

Indeed, the fundamental issue is not quantity of talk or even the content. Rather, how do children's assumptions as language learners and users affect their interactions with animals? Without an analysis of the nature of language, how can we judge the significance of children's talk—and animals' silence? The interactive implications of language derive from how the structure of language allows us to use it to *intentionally* communicate. And this means attributing to the hearer a special kind of higher-order intentional state. Understanding the child's assumptions as a language user will reveal yet again how the child's interactive abilities become differentiated—and how a sense of connection develops.

Pragmatics and the Structure of Language

At this point, a somewhat technical digression is needed to lay the ground-work for the rest of this chapter and the following chapters. Our subject is how language use (pragmatics) relates to the structure of language as a system. We can pick up from where we left off in our earlier discussion of in-terintentionality. The main point for us—which the following aims to explain—is this: Using language imposes the demand to link preverbal meanings to the requirements of interpersonal communication. Preverbal meanings include all of the animate and intersubjective aspects of interper-sonal events, plus other practical knowledge about the world. Interpersonal communication, on the other hand, entails certain assumptions about *com-municative intentions* and word meanings. The gist is that there must be a meaning meant by the language user, and language must provide a system of designation independent of that meaning.

Let us take up that last point. As noted by the Swiss linguist Ferdinand de Saussure (1959), the central requirement of linguistic communication is that signs (such as words) and rules (such as syntax) must be independent of the meanings they are used to convey. In terms of the pragmatics of the language event, this is because of the crucial role of intention in linguistic communica-tion. Consider the prototypical language event. It involves a message sender who (1) has a goal, (2) wishes or desires to enlist another in attaining it, and

(3) trusts or believes that the other party will help (Bates, 1976). What will ensure that the other party will understand that its help is desired?

This desire will be understood if the *intention* of the first party to get that help is communicated. Suppose the goal—a nonverbal meaning—is self-preservation from a threat. An animal in trouble certainly might wish to enlist others in this goal. Could that be accomplished by an alarm call? Presumably, such a nonlanguage sign is emitted as an expression of the distressed inner state of the animal and may arouse programmed helping behavior in another. But such a call contains "natural" meaning—it communicates without anyone intending it, according to the philosopher H. P. Grice (1957). It does not necessarily *communicate the sender's wish* to arouse the other and thus does not ensure that the other will respond to that intent, which could entail doing things other than the programmed response.

A word, on the other hand, does not "naturally" express the feeling of the moment. To utter the set of sounds designated by the letters *h,e,l,p* evokes not a native altruistic response but rather a learned or learnable one. It bears an arbitrary relation to its meaning. To use a word instead of an alarm call *does* require that the listener attend to the intention of the speaker, for the word must be interpreted. This is what Grice (1957) meant by "nonnatural" meanings: They depend on the other person grasping *that* a meaning is intended. Language entails communicative intent.

How does the listener know what was intended? Partly by knowledge of word meanings. The meanings of words are negotiated between speakers, who use the words in various contexts. They are thus "conventional signs" (Mead, 1934/1962). When roughly shared meanings arise from this process, either party can use such conventions to evoke an understanding of what is intended. This is "reversibility," as described by de Gramont (1990):

> When my cat Rover meows to go out, she clearly intends to have an effect upon me. But the effect of Rover's meow is not reversible. That is, meowing does not call out a comparable response in her. If I meow to Rover, she gives me a puzzled look, but she does not appear to think to ask what my meow means; and she never attempts to open the door for me. Rover does not use signs with the understanding that they intend a meaning, so as to call out a response in the other. She cannot use signs this way because she does not have a system of conventional signs that are distinct from what they stand for. (pp. 74–75)

We can understand this relative independence of conventional *signs* from the *meanings* they stand for with the metaphor of "files" containing information, and "file labels" that tell what is in the files. The files are the preverbal (innate and learned) meanings; the labels are the words—the generalized signs referring to the meanings. When I say a word, I refer to a meaning. But this referential process is not—in fact, must not be!—exact. Since the contents of a file are complex, a given word, when heard, might refer to several meanings, although the speaker intended only a particular one. Thus, the conventionality of word signs alone is not enough for the system to work! Both participants have to engage in recalling shared meanings, assessing the context, and guessing the other's point of view and intention in order to use the language system effectively. Linguistic communication requires interpretation to anticipate the hearer's frame of mind and to discern the sender's intended meaning. De Gramont (1990) summarized how language use thus fulfills the productive and receptive demands of interpersonal communication:

> The genius of language is precisely in the fact that it does not fix a reference or a propositional content. Rather, it leaves those slots open so that they may be filled by those who are communicating, based upon the setting their communication pertains to, and the assumptions they make about what they say. . . . A speaker must be capable of investing his or her words with meaning in a way that anticipates what the listener will hear. (p. 76)

So language use rests on a general ability to apprehend one's actions in a social context and guess how one's words will be heard. It is an *interpretive* act.

Two key things are assumed in interpreting conventional signs. To infer the other's intended meaning, the listener normally *may* take for granted that what is said is relevant, orderly, unambiguous, and appropriate for some communicative purpose. This tacit assumption is the "principle of cooperation" (Grice, 1975). But since an utterance can be indirect, biased, or deceptive, assuming cooperation is not always safe. Still, the listener *must at least* assume that the words do communicate meaning if there is to be any hope of deciphering them. The upshot of this "principle of communication" is that "language makes cryptographers of us all" (de Gramont, 1990, pp. 77–78). Words succeed in communicating by employing generalized signs that we assume we must "fill in" with particular contents or meanings. It would not work if we did not routinely make these assumptions.

Let us briefly look at three consequences of how language works. First, language works as a structure independent from meanings. Thus, "The generalized reality we convey with language, exists *because of language*" (de Gramont, 1990 p. 72, emphasis in original). And, "Language is responsible for our ability to perceive reality as independent of our experience" (p. 19). In particular, language helps us abstract out and label our own and others' mental states from the flow of consciousness and interaction with the world.

Second, language as a system independent of preverbal meaning frees us to respond in novel ways. Because words are *about* meanings, words, or labels, can be detached from nonverbal meanings and compared across file contents. Metaphors do just this. The metaphorical function of language enables us to deliteralize word meanings and to realize more what meaning is *about*—to integrate the "novel implicit meanings which had been (till then) excluded from verbal meaning" (de Gramont, 1990, p. 151).

Third, because language demands coordination of preverbal meanings with the requirements of interpersonal communication (the independent structure of files and their interpretation), language creates discontinuity with the animate and intersubjective realms. Consider these contrasts:

Preverbal Domain Meanings	*Linguistic Domain Meanings*
concrete and embedded	abstract
analogical, gradient expression	discrete/categorical expression
pertain to particulars	pertain to generalities
immediately meaningful	require interpretation
amodal and globally represented	separated out from sensory fusion and streams of action

Language use requires breaking the preverbal context and then productively combining word labels according to the grammatical and linear structure of spoken language. This presents young users with a formidable challenge: conveying a specific meaning using words that express generalities. For example, a toddler might repeat "eat" many times before the adult understands the specific instance (bread) from the general class (foods) the infant intends (Stern, 1985, p. 177).

This very abbreviated summary of language should make it possible now to appreciate how language—and its absence!—define the interactive opportunities offered by animals. We will look first at children's talk to animals and their interpretation of animal behavior according to linguistic assumptions.

Talking to Animals and Understanding Them

The animal that was talked to the most was the dog, but the words directed at it were mostly typical trained commands—especially "Come!" and the dog's name. Commands do make it seem as if language is effective in altering the recipient's behavior. But a command evokes only a trained and not an interpreted response. Animals do not use conventional gestures. The closest the animals in the nursery school came was the dog playing fetch or the monkey accepting objects, but these do not qualify since the animals did not use the gestures reversibly. Nonetheless, children (and adults) do not always appreciate this limitation.[8]

The children I observed expected that interintentionality and conventional signs would work with animals.[9] One older girl felt her pointing gesture communicated her intent to Snowflake:

> Cassia comes to the cage and drops in celery pieces for the guinea pig to eat. Then she holds the foil they were in over the pieces. Snowflake comes and gets one. I ask if she was pointing with the foil, and she says, "Yes." Mr. Myers: "Did the guinea pig see you do that?" Cassia: "Yes."

Children's use of language also showed they thought the animal capable of interpreting intent:

> Pogo is lying on the floor. Billy asks Mr. Grier, "Can I shake his paw?" Then he gets down, looks the dog in the face, holds out his hand, and says: "Give me your paw. Give me your paw."

That Billy did not use the command "Shake!" suggests that he assumed any appropriate set of conventional signs would work. In other words, he assumed that the dog understood words as a person does, by interpreting them. Earlier, we saw Billy yelling at bugs so they could hear him. These examples might reveal different expectations about dogs versus bugs as interactants. But Billy was also seven months older when he asked Pogo to shake and maybe better at accommodating himself to animals' different qualities. When the dog failed to respond to his words, Billy did eventually touch its paw, thus reverting to a more effective, animate level of interaction to accomplish his aim.

The children also expected that animal behavior requires decoding similar to speech. Language and theory of mind together make this possible, but it brings a subtle bias to animate experience. For example, some children "gave" animals appropriate words to "say." This tendency was most pronounced in a few of the more verbally inclined older children, one of whom was Drew. We already saw him give words to an exploring ferret; two weeks later he read meaning into the monkey's motion:

> The monkey tries to get something from its owner's hand. . . . Drew interjects, "He's like, 'What's in here?'"

These adroit words Drew put in animals' mouths clearly relate to the concrete, animate-level activities of the animal in its environment—the most immediate aspect of the animal for children. It is not surprising he would find such meanings, but a rift has been introduced by verbalizing them. Only language as a set of markers independent of preverbal experience can denote specific intentions and aspects of the world in an objective manner. To communicate his impression of the monkey's experience, Drew had to change it.

Children attributed language-like thoughts to animals, but no example yet has shown the attribution of a specifically communicative intent to an animal's motions, sounds, or other expressive actions. It would be surprising if children did not do this, for the adult-created media surrounding children portray fully linguistic animals as cartoon and literary characters. Furthermore, the adults themselves often spoke for toy and real animals for playful or didactic purposes. Consider the snake owner presenting a baby ball python, a species that wraps itself into a tight mass for self-defense:

> Ms. Nol takes out the little snake, and explains that it's very afraid: "See, it says, 'Oh please don't hurt me, don't hurt me, I'm just a little baby snake.'"

Strictly speaking, an animal that does not use language can intend a set of affairs including that it not be hurt, but not by affecting the mental state of another—it cannot intend that you not aim to hurt it.[10]

The following transcript does show a child—again Drew—attributing linguistic intent. It also shows more children attributing core-related mental states to the animal:

> Mr. Lloyd attempts to feed the turtle a small piece of meat held on the end of a stick. The turtle turns toward the meat. Mr. Lloyd: "He's thinking about it. . . . No, now he's going to scratch his head." Drew, gesturing with his hand in imitation of the turtle, as if to wave something away, and turning slightly to one side: "'Aw, no, I don't want it.'"

Drew repeated the motion and words several times. Rather than simply giving the animal thoughts as in the examples before, the words, "Aw, no, I don't want it," in the social context of feeding, carry a communicative intent directed at the intentions of the feeder. The imputed pragmatics are clear: "I want you to know I don't want this food so you won't offer it." In this type of case, then, fully linguistic abilities are implicitly attributed to the animal.

Animal Language

Children thus assimilate animals to the language model they are learning—but do they also distinguish them within it? Once, two girls denied the monkey could understand them:

Ms. Dean, rhetorically: "Why? Does he speak English?" Adrienne, Laura: "No." Adrienne: "He speaks, he speaks . . ." Laura: "He speaks . . ." Laura and Adrienne together: "Monkey talk."

But a dawning explicit awareness that animal communication differs from human language was evident in one of the most linguistically sophisticated children, Joe (five years, four months). When the dog visited, this exchange occurred:

> Mr. Grier: "If I'm up in my apartment and he's out in this park by himself, I've got to know when to go get him, right, when he's ready to come in. So you know what he does?" A child barks. Mr. Grier: "Exactly, who said that?" Ms. Tanner and Drew indicate it was Joe. Mr. Grier: "Exactly, I'll be up in my apartment, maybe reading or something, and I'll hear from outside 'Woof woof woof' just a couple of times, and that means he's waiting right by the door outside and he's ready to come in."

Note that Joe did not answer the question in words. Rather, he demonstrated the answer, implying that barking contained the meaning about which he was asked. Mr. Grier's reply confirmed that barking had a language-like meaning. That evening, Joe's mother taped a conversation with him in which he gave his account of how the dog barked to be let in. Then, Joe told his mother how dogs talk:

> Mother: Is Pogo happy [in the city]?
> Joe: Uh huh.
> Mother: Hm. That's good.
> Joe: Well, we don't know if he's happy.
> Mother: How come?
> Joe: 'Cause we're not him. We don't know. We're not other dogs, so we can't ask him.
> Mother: Oh, do you think dogs talk to each other?
> Joe: Yeah.
> Mother: So other dogs would know because they'd talk to him? What did—how do they talk to each other?
> Joe: Just a minute. (pause)
> Mother: So when, ahh, I'd really—I'm interested in what you said about dogs talking to each other. How do they talk to each other? I've never heard a dog say anything . . .
> Joe (interrupting): They bar . . . they bark, they have their own way of talking—they bark to each other.
> Mother: Ah!

Joe went on to explain that wizards (which he admitted he had never encountered) can talk to animals—instances being one in a book and another in a movie called *The Man Who Talked Animal*. Joe stated the opposite of what especially younger children's behavior implies, and which they seem to have assumed: that intentional human language is effective with an animal. This represents a further development into reflective awareness of the differences animals present in interaction. But Joe has not realized that different communication systems may be fundamentally different. Joe's version of dog language incorporates ordinary assumptions about human language: that it is both the privileged route of inner access to another's mental state and a shared code. This reveals an interesting fact about his concept of communication. Notions of human language form his implicit model. In this, however, he is not different from most people. Indeed, perhaps the biggest limitation in our understanding other species is our lack of awareness of our own communicative biases.

Key Assumptions

Some other aspects of language also determine the interactive significance of animals. Language is the communicative channel that usually carries the demand for accountability (Stern, 1985)—that is, it is much easier to deny information conveyed in a gradient channel such as prosody, gesture, or positioning than in a categorical channel such as words. If a nonverbal act is challenged (for example, because it caused offense), one can often deny the meaning ascribed to it. But one is held accountable for what one says. The reverse is true when interacting with an animal. The animal misses the discrete content of all but a few learned words and does not hold the speaker accountable. The effective channels are direct action, body language, tone of voice, volume, and other gradient features—features that have their analogues in the animal's own repertoire, to which a child can respond. This again leaves interaction with an animal free of a very severe social demand that is imposed almost as soon as the child can speak.

Gradient, or analogical, channels carry information that is of vital importance to social mammals—information about relationships (Watzlawick et al., 1967). As Bateson (1972) put it, mammals "are concerned with patterns of relationship, with where they stand in love, hate, respect, dependency, trust and similar abstractions, vis-à-vis somebody else" (p. 470). Perhaps, oversimply put, interacting with an animal has special salience since children know to "read" contact and gradient information for messages about the basic status of the relationship. The animal does not present or provoke a divided or "double bind" situation (Bateson et al., 1956) since it does not present verbal messages that clash with nonverbal ones. The animal offers one message—that conveyed by behavior, which is the channel to which children (and adults) look to see what is "really" meant by what others are saying.

Although it is ambiguous and opaque, animal behavior (albeit nonverbal) would seldom directly contradict the principle of cooperation by being patently deceptive.[11] In human communication, we learn by the experience of being deceived to suspect the cooperative assumption. Although people can interpret animal behavior as deceptive, the interpretation is usually very difficult to confirm one way or the other. If, as we saw, children tend to regard animals' behavior as meaningful and decodable, they may also unconsciously assume it conforms to Grice's (1975) principle of cooperation. Because animals' behavior is in the channel children trust for important information, because they do not contradict themselves or create double binds, and because confirmed deception is a rare event, animals' activity is apprehended by children as especially "authentic," if also hard to decipher precisely.

One key conclusion about the role of language in children's interactions with animals is that it inclines them to assume that animal behavior is interpretable and therefore meaningful. Children bring the communicative principle to bear on animals' action. This may result in misinterpretations, such as wrongly attributing shared intentions, comprehension of words, intentional communication, the possession of an animal "language" with features like human language systems, or a simplicity and honesty of action. Certainly, the history of human misunderstanding of animals (for example, as evil agents or as having extraordinary abilities) shows the power, universality, and defects of our biases. But our interpretive habit also may lead out of these and into the realms of science, reflective practice, and concern. Ironically, rather than setting us apart from other species, our nature as language users is what makes it possible for us to wonder about the meanings of other species' activities and ultimately to care about their subjective worlds and welfare. Society has barely begun the task of bringing our full interpretive faculties to bear on understanding other living creatures, but many young children are very engaged by the first steps of this project.

The Animal Outside Language

We have found some ways children assimilate animals to the assumptions of language but also other ways in which they distinguish animals as in a separate interactive realm because animals lack language. They talk less to animals and gradually adjust their biases to fit what animals do and do not do in response to words. There are some indications children may treat animal behavior as less problematic than that of their conspecifics. But the fact that animals are outside the worlds of language has other far-reaching and nonobvious consequences.

Animals do not place demands for proper language use on children and thus afford interactions with novel qualities. With animals, children are free from the demand to negotiate meanings. Words can be used to express exactly what the child wishes to mean without the demand to clarify; the problematic general quality of words does not interfere. The child can express her or his preverbal meanings without the constraints imposed by the phonetic, grammatical, narrative, turn-taking, and other structures of language that serve its interpersonal functions. One need not worry that the animal will tell anyone what was said, either.[12] But in contrast to monologue, in which, according to Katherine A. Nelson (1989), an expert on language acquistion, the speaker does not attend and respond to another, language with an animal is connected to the flow of the interactions and may help the child interpret the animal's behavior.

That the animal does not require the child to fit his or her meanings into the forms and structures of language and yet is responsive on a core level places the animal within the preverbal, personal world of early childhood and outside the social order. These two worlds often exist in tension. The sociologists Peter L. Berger and Thomas Luckmann (1966) described the experience of this tension: "I encounter language as a facticity external to myself and it is coercive in its effect on me. Language forces me into its patterns" (p. 38). The developmental psychologist John Dore described the transition when language becomes an effective mediating force between mother and infant:

> At this critical period of the child's life . . . his mother . . . reorients him away from the personal order with her, and towards a social order. In other words, whereas their previous interactions were primarily spontaneous, playful, and relatively unorganized for the sake of being together, the mother now begins to require him to organize his action for practical, social purposes: to act on his own . . . to fulfill role functions . . . to behave well by social standards . . . and so on. (quoted in Stern, 1985, p. 171)

This passage emphasizes the difficulties of a transition that is not entirely past by the age of four or five—or perhaps ever! Children are very much in the midst of being socialized at this age and still also very much in touch with the intimate, analogical, concrete, and direct preverbal world. The social order is constituted by speech acts: Others create action categories and enforce behaviors that could not exist without the language that denotes and elaborates them. Animals (although some are themselves intentional social products of domestication) do not compel actions through situation definitions, linguistically defined goals, adherence to conventions, or selective affect attunements. To this extent, children may enjoy a voluntary quality in interactions with an animal—it is not out to socialize them.

Roles are one social force and product of language. Adults may impose such a scheme on animals;[13] and, indeed, they use animals extensively in the role socialization of young children. But animals do not impose roles on children, and their interactions do not operate according to ascribed (or achieved) expectations or responsibilities. Role performances are subject to impartial evaluations that do not take into account the personal qualities of the actor. An animal does not judge in this way. Interaction with animals thus constitutes a domain without the conflicts typical of the socialization process. On the other hand, the child is free to imagine or impose whatever roles he or she wishes the animal to have. But there are limits to what an animal can perform or will tolerate, so such role frames may be broken before they get very far. In one example, an animal was given a culturally specific animal role: The guinea pig was placed in a vast building block maze and watched as it tried to escape. Paradigmatically for the present point, it ignored the passageways after a short time and climbed out over the walls, much to the children's excitement!

Conclusion

In summary, children gradually accommodate themselves to the fact that animals do not use language. There are ways that animals' lack of language may make children more apt to feel close to them. Animals do not demand sophisticated conformity to the structures of verbal communication, leaving children free to experience meanings and relatedness on nonverbal levels. Nor do they require accountability or draw children into the complex worlds of linguistically constituted objects, roles, morally laden evaluations, deceptions, and paradoxes. But also, the assumptions that children make as language users affect the expectations they bring to interacting with animals. In particular, children expect that animals' actions are meaningful or decodable and even especially "authentic." Thus, the child's curiosity about the meaning of an animal's behavior and experience is a key contribution of language.

In discussing how animals do not impose social roles or linguistic rules on children, I do not want to give the impression that language is only a negative thing for children. To the contrary, it also enables many uniquely human and positive experiences. My point is simply that interactive differences matter and that children respond to them. Let us consider the positive side of language. The animal does not make metaphors, which give language deliteralizing and liberating powers. The intentional worlds constituted by language offer some of humanity's greatest solaces and creative adventures. Language creates community between people. This community is basic to who we are and who we become. Speaking and being listened to are fundamental forms of affirmation and recognition; silencing and refusing to hear are paradigmatic of inhumanity. Furthermore, since language can mark and "hold" a meaning, with it we vastly transcend the here-and-now. We can plan and project a future. And we can reflect back, reconstructing our experience with a new grasp of its significance. We can also isolate intentions from the stream of consciousness for reflection, thus opening a new realm of autonomy and conscious choice that can guide action. With these come new forms of interaction, negotiation, and commentary that define obligation, right, and common understanding—and new forms of accountability and the regulation of social conduct.

When we share such worlds with others and when we confirm them for another by listening and discussing, we realize our humanity in a way only other humans can help us attain. Although we may grapple with the roles of animals in our intentional worlds by such deliberate reflection and dialogue—or merely by assimilating them symbolically—animals themselves do not create these worlds with us. As Serpell (1986) notes, a pet does not offer human cooperativeness, altruism, advice, or moral support; understand worries, fears, or frustrations; compare experiences, opinions, attitudes, beliefs, or goals; or comprehend the depth, scope, and complexity of human relationships. But animals also pose less potential for deceit, competition, manipulation, betrayal, and rejection. Through words, we possess and change shared meanings, opening entire new domains of connection and relatedness—and of misunderstanding and separation.

A speech-spun world implies a self. The self that I consciously think or imagine myself to be is the "self-aware" or "reflective" self. Without considering it, our account of the role of animals in the child's sense of self is incomplete. We know who we are in relation to others partly because of how we verbally characterize ourselves—and each other—in the terms of all the kinds of talk I have mentioned here. Because of this origin, must there not be a radical discontinuity between the child's nonverbal sense of relatedness to animals and the self-reflective sense of being a human, with roles and so on? Is the animal superfluous to human selfhood, except as we linguistically "construct" it? This is the implication of the traditional view. In the next chapter, we will explore children's pretend play both to learn the meanings children detect in animals' varied qualities and behaviors and to explain how animals do in fact enter into the child's self-reflective sense of self.

6 Pretend Play: Self as Human, Self as Animal

THE U.S. CHILDREN'S ENTERTAINMENT INDUSTRY regularly dishes up new cartoon creatures for the current crop of movie- and television-viewing kids. Whether animal or human, these figures have magnetic and dynamic personalities that hold young children's attention. Children recount and act out memorable scenes they have thus learned in pretend play. While I was engaged in research for this book, prehistoric personages adapted from the film *The Land Before Time* were popular with the children I was observing, as shown in this excerpt from my field notes:

> Dawn attacks Joe—they butt, on hands and knees. She backs off. Kevin: "I'm Sharp-tooth. . . . " Dawn: "Are you Sharptooth?" Kevin: "Yes." Dawn: "Then I'll fight you"; she stands, then pursues him, saying, "I'm taller than you." She runs away. . . . Dawn approaches Kevin again, who is on the floor by me. She paws the ground. Kevin turns the tables and chases Dawn and the other children, pursuing slowly with big steps, hands clawlike and elbows bent *T. rex* style.

High drama also came from the *Teenage Mutant Ninja Turtles*, another cultural animal rage. These four anthropomorphic cartoon reptiles struggling together for the good and to discover themselves were irresistible identities, especially for little boys. In one instance, somehow incited by the presence of a real turtle, Billy and Benson pretended to be Ninja turtles in combat with it:

> The turtle, itself remarkably inert, is on the floor with the group of four younger children. Billy moves his fists in a tight circular motion, leaning toward the turtle. Billy: "Let's cut it up. I *got* your turtle, I got the turtle on his back." He reaches around to show where on his own back. Benson: "*Pucchhh!*"—he thrusts his fist toward the turtle twice. Billy: "Bang!"—making a hitting motion.

117

Pretend play episodes provide fascinating windows into children's minds. Several issues that pertain strictly to the human world are evident. Most obvious, children are completely swept up in their fantasies. In these examples, the children I observed even subsumed the turtle in a cultural script; no response from it was necessary. Second, animal roles are an avenue for working out tough relationship issues. Dinosaurs and Ninja turtles can be helpful outlets for urges toward aggression, power, and control. Not only do children use animal pretend play developmentally, but adults exploit it this way, too—usually with a milder tone:

> Mrs. Ray talked with Yasmin while pretending to offer her worms and calling her "little bird." Mrs. Ray told her how when she grew up she would fly away and leave the nest. Yasmin was silent. Then Mrs. Ray asked if that made her sad to think of that. She nodded. Mrs. Ray said, "That's what's so nice about being a person is that you never have to leave your family, you can keep seeing them as long as you want." This did seem to help Yasmin, but she continued as a bird.

In this example, issues of autonomy and dependence were clearly central. The "little bird" identity assumed by Yasmin (recall her special interest in birds and flight) provided a distance that made it possible to metaphorically discuss the primary issue. While being dinosaurs and baby birds, these children are developing in the familiar psychosocial sense.

But these examples—and this way of looking at them—confirm the traditional views of animals: that they are important to children only secondarily and human factors are primary. What is mainly happening is projection, or rehearsal of a linguistically created cultural script. The animal is just conveniently appropriated, or reappropriated, in the case of cartoon creatures. Or perhaps, as some researchers hold, the function of pretend play simply is to give practice in human roles; it serves socialization goals. Corsaro (1985), in an important study of young children's creation of their own culture, discusses two pretend episodes in which children play animals. These involve the roles of pets—kitties—with other children playing husbands, wives, and children. Corsaro's analysis touches on power and control and the fact that lack of language limits the possibilities of the kitty role. But his key foci are children's concepts of human social roles and the ways status is conceived of and negotiated through the language children use. In fact, Corsaro excluded roles that children "cannot reasonably be expected to enact or encounter in later life" (p. 78). Thus, despite the ubiquity of animal pretend play in nursery schools, the only episodes considered important are those that illustrate family roles.

Let us consider another example, much like those just discussed but with an element that helps distinguish a more unique developmental role of animal pretend play:

Yasmin, "meowing," is a kitty. Solly is "a dog, a space dog" on all fours and making "arfing" noises. Both are crawling about in the doll/play house area, and near the block play area. I help Solly with his suspenders, which are coming loose. His role as a dog is not greatly interrupted by asking me for help: He spoke, but continued his posture and noises. He pulls away, goes to the play house door, and looks in. His pose evokes a dog's alert "sitting" posture. Mindy, evidently "mother," is in the house. She tells him to get out; he butts at her. Yasmin comes over and sides with Mindy, telling Solly to get out. Solly gets in a play scratching fight with Yasmin—she is still a cat. Mindy intervenes, chasing him out with a saltshaker. He retreats a bit and meets up with Joe. They agree to "go after that kitty" and crawl to the doll corner. Mindy shakes the saltshaker at them again; they scratch at Yasmin, who is seated in the high chair. Then Solly and Joe play with the telephone cord, holding it in their teeth and stretching it. Yasmin likes that and does it too. At about this time, the teacher announces that it's snack time, but Solly continues a mild attack on Yasmin. Solly tells the others, "I'm playing ruff ruff superdog and underdog." . . . Later, I ask Yasmin what she was—no response, so I add, "A kitty?" She meows affirmatively.

Again, we see the assimilation of animal roles to the human "household." But it is the role of the body that stands out. Consider the scratching, pulling of phone cords with teeth, and Solly's sitting pose. Solly was leaning on extended arms, his "tail end" on the floor, knees down and pointing ahead, lower legs turned out on the floor to either side, back straight, head up. Solly's body is not a dog's, but it offered possibilities for translation to a dog's. As with other examples here, the fidelity of his posture to a dog's suggests attention not just to the appearance of the pose but to its inner "feel." In the dinosaur scene, Kevin's *T. rex* pose and motion were unmistakable. As Yasmin received worms, her neck reached up in imitation of real baby birds she must have seen on television or in real life. And as Corsaro (1985) astutely observed, use of language is also unusual. Yasmin faithfully avoided verbally responding even when questioned directly. In animal roles, children do sometimes talk, but the talk is truncated and fits closely with the actions: Yasmin told Solly to leave and followed up the words with scratching. Solly formed an alliance with Joe, wherein, as dogs, they verbally agreed to attack "that kitty."

This interpretation centers on the meanings of the interactive features of animal roles. If pretend play reveals (among other things) what animals mean to children, it confirms what we found before: The preverbal domains of animate and intersubjective relatedness are primary in children's connection to animals. In this chapter, I develop this theme, using pretend play as a window on meanings. But I claim it is more than that. It is also an important contributor to the development of the self-reflective sense of self.

Intentional pretending and imitation enhance the sense of self in relation to the nonhuman animal in two respects: The child sees himself or herself as being like the animal and thus feels *more connected* to it; at the same time, accommodation and differentiation are required, and so the sense of what it means to be human and not the other species is *clarified*. This itself is an important—even unorthodox—conclusion. But the implications go much further. The aware sense of being a human self that pretend animal play produces is not a sense of being *categorically* human. Pretend play creates and preserves *continuity* between animal and person *and* between the preverbal and the self-conscious realms of selfhood. Thus, it provides insight into larger problems of psychology, including certain discontinuities of experience and the mind-body dichotomy. Leading the way to a view of the full contribution of child-animal relations to social development theory, pretend play and the self—as developed in this chapter—will provide us with a model for looking at continuity of concern, interest, and community in the next chapter.

Language, Imagination, and Self-Reflection

The attentive reader may have noted that my assertions here raise an issue alluded to at the conclusion of the previous chapter. It is unusual to propose that self-reflectivity arises from nonlinguistic sources, such as pretend play. But here, the most fundamental issues about the role of the animal body—ours or another species'—are ripe for rethinking. To tie things together, an excursion into the idea of self-reflectiveness will be helpful.

In the predominant theory that self-awareness depends on language, the audible character of the word and the organization of social roles play special roles and the body is dismissed. All of these are questionable, and for our particular purposes this basis of human self-awareness is inadequate since it leaves animals entirely out of the picture. On the face of it, this exclusion is implausible. Do we not have a self-aware feeling of being *human* exactly because of the cross-species comparisons available? Granted, with language we can construe those differences flexibly. But we know now that children make distinctions between themselves and animals on other-than-cultural and linguistic bases. Indeed, they do so on interactive bases. Let us try to look beyond the constraints the earlier view set on our understanding of the self and see how children's cross-species interactions extend into self-awareness.

Our thoughts on the self have been greatly influenced by the work of the pioneer social psychologist George Herbert Mead. We need to examine his thinking here because he specifically denied that pretend play and imitation contribute to the self-reflective self. Why did he think so, and was he right? Mead (1934/1962) proposed an exclusive mechanism for how William James's objective "me" came into being: "I know of no other form of behavior than the linguistic in which the individual is an object to himself, and so far as I can see, the individual is not a self in the reflexive sense unless he is an object to himself" (p. 142). Two points are made in this passage: First, only language can objectify the self. When I speak or use a sign-language sign, my meaning is symbolized simultaneously to both the other and to myself. I have an inner response to my own gesture and *can confirm it by seeing the other's response*. In this way, a verbalized meaning *about me* lets me stand outside myself. The result is the "me," an object, the self that is perceived, known, and described with attributes much as another would use.

The second point is that such an objectified version of myself is required material for self-awareness. Self-awareness is a capacity of the "I," the subjective self, the actor, the knower. But the "I" slips from grasp in the very act of grasping: The "I" is not *what* I can be self-conscious of but *the faculty I use to be* self-conscious. I can have self-awareness only indirectly, when the "I" creates (based on words) an objectified image of itself in the "me." The whole self develops from the back-and-forth of the "I" and the "me": A new self-concept (me) can shape the next choice and action (of the I), and so on, dialectically. In general, this portrait seems plausible.

But Mead (1934/1962) gave language a role it cannot fulfill. He said it is the simple audibility of the spoken word that provides the person a way to identify with or have access to the perceptions of others.[1] There are problems here, for actually we do not hear our own words exactly as others do—due to anatomy, physics, and differing perspectives on what is meant. Words have to be interpreted; they do not work automatically, as we saw. With words, we can express ourselves or something characteristic of the self can be summed up—but if this is how the self becomes available then it is in a different respect than mere audition that language makes the self reflexively available.

The more important factor that Mead (1934/1962) left out is imagination, as the philosopher Karen Hanson (1986) has argued. We need imagination—the Cambridge philosopher Ludwig Wittgenstein called it "*seeing (something) as (something else)*"—to take the other's viewpoint on ourselves. This accounts for how words can express something characteristic of the self but not simply due to the broadcast nature of speech. In terms of its perceptual basis, analogy making is dependent on the general preverbal ability to apprehend one's own actions in a social context, which is a sense carried through the life span. But Mead assumed an incoherent body and an asocial starting point from which this should not be possible.

Mead (1934/1962) said the self must be distinguished from the organism. The eye can see the foot and thus objectify it; but only the self unifies the body. Hanson (1986) says Mead came close to denying the body's basic integrity. Consider his denial of self-coherence: "The individual organism, without the socially generated self, responds only to parts or separate aspects of itself, and regards them, not as parts or aspects of itself at all, but simply as parts or aspects of its environment in general" (Mead, 1934/1962, p. 172). Today, we have strong counterevidence. Daniel Stern (1985) examined two four-month-old girls who were Siamese twins born facing each other. Before separation surgery, they were observed to occasionally suck each other's thumbs. Stern tried pulling thumbs from mouths. As he did so, he found that when twin A was sucking on B's thumb, A's head would strain forward to maintain sucking, but B's arm offered no resistance. But when A was sucking her own thumb, the arm resisted. Stern concluded: "The results indicated that each twin 'knew' that one's own mouth sucking a finger and one's own finger being sucked do not make a coherent self" (p. 79). Indeed, Mead had it exactly backward: Only with language can anything be conceived of as truly independent of the self. Bodily coherence is first.

Of course, imagination and the self-reflection it supports take more than bodily coherence. Comparing, *seeing* (x) *as* (y), is founded on the innate ability of infants to detect invariants and patterns of experience. It is further developed in metaphorical, deliteralizing language play. And imaginative reflection on the self is rooted in the social world. As Hanson (1986) puts it:

> The self may not be given in a response which is immediately shared by others . . . but there must be a foundation of shared responses to support the vault of imagination. The whining complainer, for example, must share the winces of others. He need not, of course, now or ever react with a wince to his own tone. *Pace* Mead, we need not duplicate the behavior of others at the moment of sighting ourselves in reflection. (p. 102)

Granted these prerequisites—basic self-coherence, comparison making, and shared social responses—imagination enables the kind of perspective taking for which Mead (1934/1962) was looking. Such perspective taking occurs in pretend play, which thus *would seem* to contribute to the child's growing sense of self.

But no. Only organized social roles, for example, in games, are alleged to be sufficient. Mead (1934/1962) claimed that only the internalization of the "generalized other" enables the individual to objectify "the whole self" to him- or herself in reflection, and only the organized perspectives of other players in a game creates this paradigmatic social self. Hanson (1986) concedes imagination enables the apprehension of only *a* self, such as a role (a complainer; a leader); it does not seem to produce one single definitive self. Why did Mead argue so strenuously for the experience of "the" whole self? Hanson suggests his concern was autonomy and self-control (pp. 86ff.). For Mead, the "generalized other" enables the individual to *not* be ruled by the particular other people present at a given moment.

But Hanson (1986) points out the contrary implication of truly internalizing the "generalized other": "An individual who comes to be the incarnation of all the common attitudes might well be thought to have abdicated individual integrity" (p. 88). Thus, the "me" is too rigidly given by Mead's (1934/1962) concept of how language objectifies the self. Indeed, Mead was mindful of this danger of the overly conventional person. In effect, he conceptualized the "I" so as to supply spontaneity, and he stressed the unpredictability of its actions by excluding habits from the "I." But, Hanson writes, habits are very much the sort of thing that becomes incorporated into the person in the dialectic of the "I" and "me" that forms the self. Habits are also among the things we become aware of in reflection and which seem essential to a description of actual selves. This last point about habits emphasizes the fact that self-reflection is not as automatic as Mead would make it seem. It may happen, but it may not—much as would be the case if it depended on occasional imaginative reflection! So it may be that Mead's requirement of reflection on "the" whole self is unrealistic, at once too mechanical and too ideal. Reflection on "a" whole role of the self-in-context is more like life.

There are other reasons to doubt a too linguistically oriented view of the objective self. Development of the objective self is signaled by several roughly simultaneous events at about eighteen months (Stern, 1985, pp. 165–166). At this age, the use of pronouns ("I," "me," "mine") to refer to the self occurs. So, too, does touching the face when the infant sees a surreptitiously placed spot of rouge on his or her face in a mirror. We also observe early acts of other-directed empathy, and this is the first age of pretending and of planning. Given the diverse inputs implied by all these achievements, it would be presumptuous to give any one of them causal primacy in the emergence of self-awareness.

The need to explain "the" whole self led Mead (1934/1962) to focus on the organized qualities of games and to dismiss pretend play as a developmental means of achieving a reflective sense of self. Now that we have rejected his argument that the vocal gesture uniquely underlies taking others' roles, pretend play "is easily assimilated to an account of the self which places imagination at the core of reflexivity" (Hanson, 1986, p. 78). Precisely how is it a route to understanding how the child's self-awareness as a person is expressed and clarified by the enactment of animal roles?

Mead (1934/1962) admitted that the child pretending must, to guide his or her performance, "take the role of the other." But, he said, "the latter phrase is unfortunate [here] because it suggests an actor's attitude which is actually more sophisticated than that which is involved" (p. 161). The child in pretending is not so advanced as to be deliberate but is "simply exhibiting responses characteristic of the other because the other's attitude is also in the child, 'ready for expression'" (Hanson, 1986, p. 80). But could the child really *inadvertently* enact the part of the other? To the contrary, pretend is an intention-dependent concept.

To knowingly play the role of the other requires a delineation of self and other. Hanson (1986) illustrates this point with an example that is coincidentally harmonious with our focus:

> The child playing bears, pretending to be a bear, knows he or she is not a bear. That is just why pretense and imagination are necessary. If the child simply had growling among his usual repertoire of reactions, if growling were just among the responses "ready for expression"; if he were as likely as not to drop to the floor and pad about on all fours; then this growling, padding behavior would not be thought—by him or anyone else—to constitute a specific role-play. But the (normal) child who growls and pads and swipes with a hand held stiff from the shoulder, the child pretending to be a bear, does not normally exhibit this behavior, and that is just why it is appropriate to this pretending play, why the child has, so to speak, chosen it. (p. 83)

This concept of pretend play, unlike Mead's (1934/1962), involves conscious contrast between self and other. Although Mead intended to find in pretend play some contribution to self-other differentiation, his formulation of it as *un*intentional had the consequence of ruling out that possibility, and he let the important work fall on games. Hanson (1986) elaborates the achievement necessary in pretend:

> The child can be discovering which bits of behavior are most appropriate to the other and which are most characteristic of himself, for he must evidence or emphasize the former and suppress or disguise the latter. A more coherent sense of both himself and the other is thus obtained. Hence, as engaging in this sort of play does further demar-

cation of the self, it is reasonably cited in an explanation of the development of the self. (p. 83)

Language is still a part of the picture here—to see animal behavior as meaning laden may depend on the child assuming the communicative principle. And the formation of the very intention to pretend may also depend on a language-related theory of mind. But what we now can say is that the development of self-reflexivity is not the product of language exclusively; nor is it an achievement possible only in relation to other language users.

Pretend Play and Imitation of Animals

What can we tell about children's concepts of self and other from pretend play? Pretend play shows the differences children consciously perceive between themselves and animals. This might be revealed in the content of the pretend episode (what the child does) or in the deployment of different media (how language is used, for example) in enacting the episode. So long as the child must be deliberate in his or her action, either pretending or simpler imitation meets the criteria discussed previously. Accordingly, the imitative acts we will consider are all performances addressed to a (*usually* human!) audience. The most important thing that is revealed by pretend animal play and imitation is that the alterity, or "otherness," of the animal is preserved and represented. We find this in three areas: orientation to social forms, language, and the body.

Orientation to the Social World

Especially in pretending to be an animal, the child's orientation to the everyday human social world is changed. First, the roles enacted typify animals rather than humans. This was not always the case, as when an "animal" occupied a human role such as "baby," but more often pretended animals were predators, prey, combatants, pets, or working animals. These different roles are enacted by movement, the occupation of space, forms of activity and passivity, and so on that are uncommon in children's other roles.

Children's orientation to space and time while being animals is altered from normal patterns. In everyday life, space is patterned by social convention and cultural objects. For example, tables are not just physical objects; certain rules surround their use, as children know. But in pretend play, space is correlated to the "animal's" own shape.

Mr. Lloyd, the turtle owner, asks Katra, "Would you like to be a turtle?" At first she seems not to have heard him, but then begins pretending. Katra: "I'm going in my shell." She hunkers down into a turtle position, arms and legs tucked in. Both she and Angela tuck down, turtle style. Mr. Lloyd tries to address Katra: "Miss, dear. . . . " Katra: "I'm going to my shell." Mr. Lloyd: "Oh, you're going, okay, you're playing the part of the turtle." Katra moves toward the corner and climbs into the blanket shelf, a tight spot a bit bigger than herself. Then she rejoins Angela, and they both go off to the corner, Katra still intent on the blanket shelf.

I had never seen any child crawl into the blanket shelf before, but for a "turtle" it became an obvious option. Time also may be altered, as when Yasmin became so absorbed in nonverbal "dialogue" with the doves that she failed to realize lunch had begun.

Certainly, children's sense of time and space are not fully socialized to begin with, and many activities besides animal role play find their unique tempos. But the children's comments make it clear that identifying with animals frees them from social pressures. Sam and other children responded very positively when asked whether they would like to be monkeys and why:

Sam: "I would stay in trees and never climb down." Mr. Myers: "Really, how come?" Sam: "Because I don't want to come down," slapping his leg for emphasis.

Children perceive animals as not being subject to socialization pressures. Billy said he would like to be a monkey:

Billy: "I wish I wouldn't have a mommy so I could just do whatever I want to." Mr. Dean: "You wish you didn't have a mommy?—Do you think monkeys have mommies?" Ivy and Billy reply, "Yes." Ms. Dean: "Yeah, do you think their mommies tell them what to do?" Billy, Ivy, and Benson all answer, "No!"

Nor are animals burdened by school demands. I asked Solly if he would want to be a monkey:

Solly: "Yeah." Mr. Myers: "Yeah." Ms. Dean: "How come?" Solly: "Because they can swing by their tail, and they wouldn't have to go to school." . . . Ms. Dean: "You think their moms make 'em go to school?" Smiling, Dimitri and Solly answer, "No."

This perception is an added plus of pretending to be an animal: The child acts in a space that feels free of, or in opposition to, social structures. Rules that apply to children may be relaxed for "animals":

Mrs. Ray notes that the slugs which the children and she are holding have no legs but can move. She asks, "Do you know other animals like that? How about a snake? How does it do it? Watch and see if you can figure out." Mrs. Ray calls Ivy over; she looks a moment at the pill bug, and then leaves, seeming not too interested. . . . But not long after watching the slugs, Ivy, Cassia, Yasmin, Katra, Dimitri, and others get on their bellies in the sand area and squirm across it. Dimitri calls out, "Look! Tracks!" Ivy adds, "We're making tracks behind us!"

The children delighted in this activity, which had the special appeal of being normally discouraged, since it made them dirty.

Socialization teaches children to evaluate behavior. "Good" or "bad" can also be applied to animals, but they, like other pretend identities, offer freedom for exploring this evaluative dimension:

> Yasmin and Laura want me to watch while they are kitty and witch. Yasmin is the wicked witch's bad kitty, and scratches (gently) at me. I wonder out loud if she might not really be a good kitty, and she switches to be one. But preferring the bad kitty, she switches back. They both growl. Yasmin: "But they eat persons. But bad witches eat persons." . . . Laura: "Why would anyone want to be bad?"

Yasmin found it more acceptable to be a bad kitty than a bad person; she used the animal role to explore and express "badness" without threat of censure.

These examples indicate children perceive pretend animal identities as affording an orientation distinct from the ordinary human world with its structured time and space and its roles and rules of conduct. This confirms my earlier conclusion that because the animals differ as interactants on the verbal level, children perceive them as independent from role pressures. Children represent this contrast through pretend play. Correspondingly, the child's human self must be experienced as engaged in such roles and social patterns.

Use of Language

Pretend animal roles may or may not involve talking. Corsaro (1985) observed that as an animal a child cannot talk. Is this true in the following play?

> Rosa and Yasmin were playing in a cozy corner behind the "space capsule." The play was primarily pretend, and Yasmin alternated between being a guinea pig, making squeaking noises, and a kitty, meowing. In either case, the animal could make ice cream. . . . Rosa asked, "Do you want to go in a big cage?" When Yasmin didn't reply Rosa said, "Little kitties can't talk." Yasmin: "How can kitties talk?" Rosa: "Can big kitties talk?" Yasmin explained: "They can go 'meow, meow.'" The play continued, focused on objects and less on roles. . . . Later I asked Yasmin if kitties talk. She said, "No." "Can they talk to each other?" I asked. Yasmin said, "Yes," but offered no more explanation.

Here Yasmin broke the pretend play frame in which she, as a cat, could not talk, in order to explain the fact. While in a role, the children generally observed this interactional constraint of pretending to be an animal (notably, cartoon animal models do not suffer this constraint). Yasmin's responses to my questions make it clear that this is her conception of being a cat. But her responses also indicate that she considers the meowing she does as a cat to be far from meaningless: It signifies effective communication between cats. This is as we would expect based on my earlier discussion of children's assumptions about animal action and vocalizations.

As with other pretend role play, some talk in and around animal roles marks the pretend frame and confirms the play is a performance: It is meta-commentary. Talk is used to negotiate roles and plot. With human roles that involve speech, some in-role talk adds indirect definition of the role—for example, saying the things a mother would say indicates that one "is" a mother. So do animal roles require more out-of-role frame-establishing talk? As "animals," children are aware that their behavior needs a frame to be interpretable:

> Today at lunch, Abeo sits next to Angela and Ms. Tanner. She announces to Ms. Tanner, "I'm a beaver," and takes a bite from her apple, which is sitting on the table—without holding it with her hand!

Normally such behavior at lunch would be corrected. Abeo's play here illustrates exactly the intention essential to pretense. At lunch, pretending even for a moment to be an animal requires deliberate distinction from her normal behavior.

But when the context can serve to mark such advertence, children may dispense with verbal framing. Recall how Joe barked in answer to the question of what the dog does to get in. In contrast, Reuben then gave a mixed verbal-barking reply: "He goes, [three barking sounds]." But neither boy simply said, "He barks." Where humans talk, animals simply act—or bark; this contrast obviates the need for frame-establishing talk.

Talk within animal pretend roles revealed a variety of ways children exploit the freedom the animal role gives from the constraints of language. Talk may merely call attention to the nonverbal role-play:

> After looking at a beetle with other children, two or three boys, who before had been chasing and tackling, play at being the beetle. They repeat, "Beetle, beetle, beetle" and crawl over each other in the sand and on the grass.

Words spoken in most pretend play may stand in a flexible, open, and non-literal relation to action. One of the attractions of animal roles is that children are even freer from the demands of reciprocity and accountability that come with use of language. Occasionally this can cause problems:

> Out on the lawn, virtually everyone is a shark, or at least is chasing around. Ms. Tanner asks the sharks, "What do you want?" The reply: "Bones." Mindy dashes about, hands raised, fingers gripping, and growling continuously. Toby grabs her; she screams and lashes out in protest. The teacher admonishes her, "It's not fair for you to grab others but they not you." Mindy smiles. Mrs. Ray: "That's silly."

Mindy was enjoying the shark role as a chance for aggressive play but did not see it as a reciprocal and accountable kind of action. But the teacher imported different standards into the pretend frame. Reciprocity is more inherent in language use, and fairness is more typical of the formal and impersonal nature of social roles than of the animal activities Mindy pretended to perform.

"Animals" need not endure the demand to match meaning with word; action can mean just what one wants. Baby role play offers a similar safety, allowing the "baby" to fuss and intend the most indecipherable meanings toward its "mother." The following episode shows how baby and animal roles can blend around this common trait:

> Two pairs of "pet owners" and their "animals" leave the rug for the doll area: Reuben with Mindy as dog, and Angela with Abeo as cat. Each animal has a necktie around her waist and crawls on all fours behind the owner who tells her what to do. . . . At the doll house, Abeo gets in the crib but won't talk to me—she only meows somewhat threateningly.

Far was it from me to tell precisely what the cat-baby meant by this!

In sum, the role of talk in animal pretend play does not vastly differ from its role in human-role pretend. Talk is still necessary to negotiate the play episode, and can be used in role. But children sometimes avoid language and use animals' nonverbal nature to jump into a pretend animal role, and some children strongly avoid talking in an animal role. The lack of talk in an animal role affords a freedom from demands and constraints of language, confirming the interpretation that interactively defined differences are salient to children—a way they clarify the difference between human self and animal other. Arguably, this is realized in awareness through imitation and pretend play.

Embodied Meaning

To imitate or pretend to be an animal, children embody it, as when Solly translated a dog's qualities of motion into his own body. Words may help label the role, but the intelligibility of the play depends on fidelity to the constraints of the particular creature. In this play, the child must clearly *see* her or his action *as* that of the animal. It is possible to thus reflectively grasp the otherness portrayed, because the child has not only her or his own sensations and perceptions but also the responses of others. Children in complementary play roles hone each other's enacted agency, affect, and coherence, such as the aggressiveness of "cats" fighting, or the friendliness of a panting and attentive "dog." Or feedback can be more direct:

> Dawn crawls forward facing the turtle, crouches down on the rug, and tucks her head down. . . . She raises up suddenly, saying, "I know how to be a turtle in my shell." Mr. Lloyd: "Is that how it would be, like that?" Dawn: "Yeah." Mr. Lloyd: "But you couldn't see anything then." Dawn brings her head up to disagree: "Huh huh." Mr. Lloyd: "But the turtle stays in his shell and he sees things." Chris disagrees: "Yeah, and ah, I can." He is in "turtle" position, crouched down over his legs, but holding his hands by his face, and pointing his head forward rather awkwardly.

In response to Mr. Lloyd's challenge, Chris modified his pose to meet the objection. This gives us confidence that the play is a conscious self-other differentiation.

But these children are also telling us that the externals of the performance are not the essence of pretending. Chris and Dawn first denied their action was incorrect, suggesting that an important dimension of pretending to be an animal is not just how it looks but how it feels to the child—they *felt* they could see just like a turtle. The dimensions of embodied action together with subjective experience constitute the animate otherness of the animal as described in Chapter 4. Reflective portrayal of these properties, complete with their variations, are at the heart of children's pretend play as animals.

Animate Properties.

Core agency of pretend animals is revealed in movements, implicit intentions, inhabiting of space, and uses of objects. Children translate the animal's body movement into their own in creative, analogical ways. A child may use just a part of his or her body to show how an animal acts:

> Yasmin is asked what she liked about the dog. Yasmin: "He blows the wind on my hand with his tail." She gestures, waving her right hand over her left palm. (Earlier she held her hand on the floor below the dog's wagging tail.)

Careful observation led Ivy to notice how the dog chewed on its ball:

> Ivy bends down, looks into Pogo's mouth, sits up, and says to Mr. Grier, pointing at her mouth, "He moves his, he moves his tongue over here [she points to her right cheek] so the ball can fit over here." Ivy points to her left cheek.

Ivy interpreted the dog's implicit intention, but this required referring to her own face to show what the dog did. Just a little earlier, Ivy had shown why a dog could not pick up the ball, again making gestures that captured the bodily limits of the dog's agency rather than explaining it with words—which would have been quite difficult to do precisely.

Such translation of the animal's actions to one's own body goes beyond using its parts to the possibilities of the whole body:

> Ms. Nol asked, "Can you see why it's a 'ball' python?" Benson: "Ball." Ms. Nol: "It wants to roll up in a ball." Benson says immediately, "Like this," and quickly curls over, head to knees. Ms. Nol: "That's right. When it's afraid it rolls up into a ball to try and hide itself."

We have seen many other such examples in episodes already described.

The animals' divergent animate coherences were shown by portrayal of the animal's body as *a different kind of whole* from the child's own body. An animal's appendages—or lack of them!—can be a hurdle in pretend play, but the lengths to which children go reveal their faithfulness to the animal's different self-coherence. Several interesting techniques were used to illustrate the snake's body, as in this taped session at home between Abeo and her mother:

> Mother: The snake came today?
> Abeo: Yeah, there was a baby snake and a momma snake.
> Mother: Oh, there were two of them.
> Abeo: Um hum.
> Mother: How did they interact, how did they react?
> Abeo: I'll show you, I'll show you.
> Mother: Oohh, they were creeping like that, oohh, did you try to do that while they were there?
> Abeo: No.
> Mother: Oh I bet you like creeping like a snake. Abeo is creeping up and down. You like to creep?
> Abeo: Yes!

In class, Dawn took a similar approach:

> Mr. Myers to Ms. Nol: "How fast can a snake like this move?" Ms. Nol: "Not very." Just after my question, Dawn inconspicuously backs away from group, then extends on her stomach on the floor. She comes around behind Chris and Joe, pulling herself slowly along on floor by her hands.

Sam offered a different possibility, using part of his body:

> Sam taps Chen on shoulder and shows him a snake motion with his arm in the air. Sam: "Chen . . . makes a 's'—Sssssssss." Chen puts his hand on Sam's to make him stop, then makes a snake motion on the floor with his own hand. Sam takes this up also.

The turtles elicited much imitation, but of course entirely different embodiments than did the snake. Sometimes, children portrayed the animal's shell with their backs and head movements. Solly and Joe explored a different approach to being a turtle:

> During a whole class discussion of the turtles, Joe walks on his knees to the back of the group and falls forward on all fours facing Solly. Immediately, Solly places both his hands on the back of Joe's head and pushes it down in an exaggerated nodding motion three times. Each time, Joe brings his head back up by himself, to look toward Solly. Then, Solly grabs Joe's shirt, prompting Joe to try pulling it up over his head. Solly helps, but Joe's shirt only comes to his nose, and he pauses to look at Solly. Benson sees this activity and immediately begins pulling his shirt up also. Solly reaches for Joe's head, encircles it with his arms, holding him. Ms. Wick interferes at this point, first by calling, "Solly," and then by reaching out to touch him. He crawls away behind Joe. Joe desists and listens for half a minute to the discussion of the depths at which fish versus turtles swim. During this interval Solly leaves him and comes around behind on all fours, putting hands and knees down deliberately and emphatically. This stroll lasts a full 27 seconds.

This example also shows how animals' vitality affects are conveyed by qualities of motion in pretend play. Toward the end, Solly's turtle walk perfectly captures the characteristic slow, plodding "feel" of the turtle's gait.

The dog's vitality affect was effectively embodied when Mr. Grier elicited pretend behavior in the presence of the dog:

> Joe crawls around by the camera, "woofing." Dawn moves her legs as if to get up, but then crawls over by Joe. . . . Mr. Grier asks the group, "If you had your choice, do think you'd like to be like a dog, like Pogo?" Chris: "Yes." Mr. Grier: "Yeah, you'd like to be?" Joe and Dawn both come toward Mr. Grier, "panting," and assume sitting positions facing him with animated expressions. Cassia gets down from her chair and joins the others, dog-mode. Mr. Grier looks at them, smiles, and watches several seconds. Pogo lies on his side, wagging his tail slightly. Mr. Grier: "Pogo's going to think you're a dog." They move closer. Cassia barks, then Dawn also. Then they sit back up.

Here, the calm but eager and friendly demeanor of this dog—or of the dog the children want to be—is reflected in the children's dog imitations. Apart from their actual inner states, different species' simple qualities of motion can strongly suggest affects to children. Vitality affect is a discernible aspect of the core other that children embody in pretend play or imitation. The vibrancy and lively quality of the children's performance in these examples is hard to convey verbally—indeed, that is one main point of this theoretical discussion! It seems that among the most salient things embodied in animal pretend play is a sense of vivid animate aliveness itself.

A sense of core self-other continuity, or history, might be expressed in pretend play by a child's presentation of the same particular animal identity over time. Parents were asked, "Does your child like to pretend to be any animals?" and, "What animal identities does he or she take on, and when?" Parents of roughly half the class listed between one and seven animals their child liked to pretend being. Two-thirds of these included a cat or a dog, probably the animals best known to the children.

Interestingly, favored animal roles were unrelated to the animals children had at home. In fact, the four children who most avidly practiced pretend animal identities at home had no pets in the house: Yasmin's parent listed her being a "cat almost every day. If not a cat, she pretends different animals"; as we have seen, at school Yasmin had two of the most enduring animal identities of any child: cat and bird. Chen's home list included lion, crab, wolf, and dinosaur. Billy was lion, dog, cat, ape, frog, snake, and dinosaur at home; and Rosa was reported to pretend to be dogs, lions, and alligators. Taking the whole class, I found this relationship statistically significant: Children with no pets were more likely to have two or more pretend animal identities than were children with a pet.[2] A factor that might explain this relationship is siblings: Single children are known to fabricate more imaginary social interactions. But there was no relation between pretend animal identities and lack of siblings. Pretend animal identities substitute for real animals rather than being stand-ins for human relationships.[3]

Animals taken collectively were prominent among the roles the children took on in pretend play. A very wide variety were enacted: The children were beetles, slugs, sharks, dogs, cats, snakes, turtles, birds, beavers, ferrets, rabbits, spiders, crabs, alligators, dinosaurs, frogs, and more. These constitute a full and ever-available cast of divergent identities into which the children readily stepped.[4] Although there surely are cultural influences on animal pretend play, the animate qualities of actions like comings and goings, holdings and chasings, mutual presences and the range of vitality affects and so on are the material out of which more complicated cultural scripts can be enacted. Animal pretend play offers the special advantage that the child's meanings can be consciously felt and experienced as being of a piece with their actions, without the difficulty of aligning preverbal, global meanings with conventionally appropriate verbal symbols and syntax.

Consequences for the Self.

Every time a child intentionally imitates an animal's divergent space-time reality or variations on core agency, coherence, affectivity, and historicity, she or he must objectify the self. Language is not necessary. In the process, the child imagines what it is like to be the animal and thus feels closer to it. The process also enhances the differentiation of the self. And the differences children depict in pretending to be animals are the same ones we found to be salient in their interactions with animals. This supports our overall interpretation that direct interaction is more primary in children's concepts of animals than other factors such as culture, psychodynamics, or anthropomorphism. It is evidence that children see and represent animals in a manner consistent with our view of core relatedness.

Pretending to be animals clarifies children's sense of what it means to be human. The key point is that it is not a rigid kind of human-animal distinction that is experienced but one underlain by deep animate commonality. This is different from the emergence of a categorically human self. And here is a larger implication of the commonplace episodes we have witnessed. The behaviors children act out in pretending to be animals carry meanings; some they express verbally, others by animal-like vocalizations. But most they convey implicitly in action—in complementary interactions and in the ways the child bodily translates the animal's core agency, coherence, affect, and continuity.

In pretend play, these meanings are made self-conscious, but note an important difference between this and the old view that self-awareness is only possible through language. Language requires the separation and encoding— and by the recipient, the interpretation—of preverbal meanings into discrete, general, abstracted "labels," or words. By contrast, pretend play *preserves continuity* between the preverbal realm and the self-conscious. Using language, it would be nearly impossible, or at best very difficult, to present to self and to others a comparable sense of the otherness of the animal. Pretend play and imitation do not entail as much opposition or tension with preverbal modes as does language. Imitating lets the awareness of being a human self develop in more continuity with animals as core and intersubjective others—that is, as embodied beings like ourselves. Thus, children's relations with animals point to a resolution of the old and general problem introduced in Chapter 2—the relationship between the animal body and the self-aware human mind.

Continuity Between Preverbal
and Verbal Experience

What does the insight reached in the previous section mean for development? Answering this question requires some further steps of theory, but the upshot is that it is *discontinuity* that needs explaining. Again, our habits of thought—the high evaluation given to the linguistic mind and the low status of the animal body—have led us to overlook normal continuities.

Many thinkers have stressed the dichotomy between the nonverbal and the verbal, and we saw that language makes possible a generalized reality that would not otherwise exist. We compared how language works to a system of verbal "labels" on "files" containing nonverbal meanings. The ability of a label to act as a placeholder for a meaning makes self-conscious thought possible. This underlies, for example, the linguist John Searle's (1983) deliberate "prior intentions" versus nonreflective "intentions in action"[5] Certainly, this is an important distinction. But to the extent the difference is conceived of as a *discontinuity*, the linguistic pole is usually granted greater importance in our higher mental functioning. It is more closely related to abilities we regard as uniquely (and thus essentially) human. It is also simply more accessible for study and as a result is more demonstrably important in the meanings, plans, and memories by which people lead their lives.

But much of human life is also led by "intentions in action"—that is, without prior reflection. Fully conscious self-awareness may be the exception, as the English philosopher Alfred North Whitehead observed, "From the moment of birth, we are immersed in action, and can only fitfully guide it by taking thought" (quoted in Ingold, 1988b). But how much are our abilities really divided against each other? Interplay between conscious and preverbal forms of thought occurs in artistic and scientific creativity, in psychotherapy,[6] and in problem solving. Recently, the psycholinguist David McNeill (1992) has shown a unitary process of meaning creation underlying words and gestural communication, and the language acquisition researchers Martha Alibali and Susan Goldin-Meadow (1993) have shown children's hands tell more than they can say in solving math problems. Indeed, children must be able to bring world knowledge into conjunction with language. This should make us wary of assuming too great a discontinuity.

Despite social theorists' heavy emphasis on the constitutive power of language today, if we trace the emphasis back to its origins, we find earlier writers who stressed continuity centered on the immediate face-to-face social situation. Even P. L. Berger and Luckmann (1966), so impressed with the "coercive" power of language, nonetheless also noted that "the other . . . becomes real to me in the fullest sense of the word only when I meet him face to face" (p. 29). Their predecessors, sociologist Alfred Schutz and Maurice Merleau-Ponty also granted the nonverbal a foundational role in communication. Both drew on a tradition in European philosophical biology that was more friendly to the idea that the animal body is preprepared to find meaning in the world, and especially in interaction, than was the American behaviorism followed by Mead. An alternative to either behavioristic or physiological explanations of behavior was provided by the animal behaviorist F. J. J. Buytendijk:

> On the level of behavior there is an original identity of perceptibility and intelligibility. . . . For although there are realities which are perceptible without being intelligible, such as colors and figures, and realities which are intelligible without being perceptible, such as mathematical and logical relations, we believe that we have here singled out a level, behavior, on which, strictly speaking, perceptibility and intelligibility are given inseparably from one another, so that behavior cannot be perceived without at the same time being (although possibly wrongly) interpreted. (quoted in Grene, 1968, pp. 124–125)

As an analogy, we might ask, how do we understand music and dance? Their intelligibility is given immediately with how they sound or appear to us. These theorists are saying behavior, on the most basic level, is like these arts. Music and dance share with interaction the additional trait of entailing a duration of time. The founder of ethology, Jakob von Uexküll (1940/1982), spoke of the "melody of movement" (p. 62ff.). Schutz (1951) used the "mutual tuning-in relation" between performing musicians to illuminate interaction. This relation is "established by the reciprocal sharing of the other's flux of experiences in inner time, by living through a vivid present together" (p. 96).

More simply put, in our ordinary attitude we immediately "interpret" qualities of behavior. For example, we cannot precisely say all that it is about someone's greeting that tells us it is friendly or not, but we normally receive and respond to others' behavior with such information already "included." This is simply a phenomenological description of our findings on children's sense connection to animals: The animal is a subjective presence because of its agency, coherence, and affectivity in interaction. We do not experience action in its mere "behavioristic" minimum of physical motion in time and three-dimensional space—a minimum to which we must then establish connection through the use of word signs. Rather, the preverbal sense of meaning and the verbalizable meanings blend into each other. The two functions are not really separate.

This should not surprise us, because of what we already know about infants' abilities. Of special importance for the development of a reflective sense of self through pretend play is the ability to "*see* (x) *as* (y)"—to make comparisons. This ability precedes language; we saw it in the infant's ability to detect invariants across sensory modes. Even very early imitation might employ this ability in generating a sense of self. The psychologists Andrew Meltzoff and Alison Gopnik (1993) suggest, "Infants are launched on their career of interpersonal relations with the primary perceptual judgment: '*Here is something like me*'"[7] (p. 336, emphasis in original). This perceptual judgment is rooted in an innate ability to find correspondences between self and other, as revealed in imitation. According to Meltzoff and Gopnik, "The work on early imitation shows that even newborn infants recognize some equivalences between externally perceived behaviour—that is, perceived body movements—and literally internal proprioceptive states" (p. 339).

Such comparison making is later given a huge boost by the metaphoric mode of language. The ability to "detach" the "labels," or words, from the "files" and compare them across different files deliteralizes word meanings and enhances our sense of what meaning is *about*. It is about our complex and sometimes inchoate preverbal knowledge of the world, ourselves, and words. In this mode, language is not discontinuous with world experience but enriches it. The child engaged in seeing herself or himself as a cat is doing something similar to both invariance finding and metaphor. She or he enacts comparisons that are perceived as at once intelligible—and interpretable through more sophisticated metaphoric processes—by both herself or himself and others.

Understanding Discontinuity

If continuity is the primary relation between verbal and nonverbal, why should pretend play, which especially provides continuity, be so important? Perhaps, learning language is simply challenging and pretending is easier—and more fun, particularly with animals. But still, if the sense of self and other can develop with continuity, how are we to understand discontinuity? One hint comes from studies of autism: Discontinuity may be explained as the result of some *obstacle* to the normal process. Interestingly, children with autism have fairly intact language, but they lack a normally developed theory of mind. They also are unaware of their own mental states, do not distinguish between appearance and reality, and do not pretend. The Swedish child psychiatrists Christopher Gillberg and Peder Rasmussen (1994) reported a case of an autistic girl with symptoms of Williams syndrome who

> would be a dog from time to time. Her mother says she did not "pretend" to be a dog like another child might do: she would be a dog. If the family entered a shop, she would do so on all fours . . . barking and nosing, completely oblivious of other people (and of 'other' dogs). If anyone tried to stop her in this ritual she would tear down the shelves. In spite of her excellent performance as a dog she cannot participate in mutual imitation games. (p. 387)

One explanation, offered by the psychologist Alan Leslie (1991), is that these children lack the ability to represent their own representations. Normally, metarepresentation underlies the theory of mind and certainly is vital to metaphor. More broadly, the psychologist Uta Frith (1989) sees a pervasive cognitive inability to integrate information into larger meaningful wholes, a lack of cohesion-making (reviewed in Astington, 1993, chap. 9). The key point is that autism demonstrates a deficit in the abilities needed not just for metaphor but for even more basic forms of continuity between parts of experience. The consequence is impairment of social abilities and compromised self-awareness.

Normal children have no such basic deficit as an obstacle to development. But language can pose an ordinary—or severe!—obstacle when its generalized reality is confused with concrete reality. Patrick de Gramont (1990) analyzed such moderate, specific, and indeed common forms of the breakdown of metaphorical ability. Language, because of the independence of sign and signified, carries the risk that the person will not realize that a word is about a meaning and will treat the word meaning as thinglike. He or she may thus "reify" a meaning, losing the ability to "detach" the "label" from the "file" contents and perform a metaphorical comparison.

This poses a developmental challenge. Children can be trapped by confusing the sign for the signified—that is, they can reify meanings in their learning of language. Such distortion occurs in language learning because words start off as induced labels and are thus taken to be the things they name (de Gramont, 1990, p. 93).[8] The metaphorical function develops with the realization that words stand for things without being them.

Two broader classes of reification that afflict adults, too, are "capture" of meaning by affect or by ideology.[9] Both forces—emotion and unmovable dogmatism—are known for their ability to make us lose touch with the concrete and treat an abstraction as reality. "Distortion occurs not as a result of regressing to a preverbal mode, but of collapsing the metaphorical mode that emerges with language into a literal meaning that operates like a preverbal meaning" (de Gramont, 1990, p. 138). A vivid clinical example is "glove anesthesia," a symptom in which numbness or pain occurs according to the location as designated in verbal thought, not according to the body's nervous structure.

Just as metaphor making broke down for the girl afflicted with autism, affective capture can create confusions of the self with others—including with an animal. The influential American psychologist Erik Erikson (1958) noted that people with schizophrenia may become "dehumanized, and eventually even de-mammalized. These patients can feel like a crab or a shellfish or a mollusk, or even abandon what life and movement there is on the lowest animal level and become a lonely twisted tree on the ledge of a stormy rock, or the rock, or just the ledge out in nowhere" (pp. 103–104). The psychologist Harold Searles (1960) pointed out the occurrence of animal imagery and self-perception in schizophrenic symptoms. There are psychiatric syndromes involving the delusion of being an animal; a specific type with an old history in Europe is *lycanthropy*, the belief one is a wolf, usually a dangerous one.[10] Arguably demonstrating a related social pathology, a number of the German Nazi elite had powerful identifications with fearsome animals. Hitler had especially close attachments to dogs. They were constant companions, including one named Wolf that belonged to his landlady in the 1920s. Indeed, when he was young, he used the name Wolf. In the 1920s, with a woman who played the role of foster mother, "Hitler would often sit at her feet and lay his head against her bosom while she stroked his hair tenderly and murmured, 'Mein Woelfchen'" (O. Strasser, quoted by the sociologist Arnold Arluke and Boris Sax, a writer on animals and society, 1992, p. 16). Given the Nazis' ability to completely distance themselves from the feelings of other humans, it seems likely this evidence points to both affective and ideological capture of identity meanings.[11] In all these examples (and similarly to the autistic child), the self is taken not just to be *like* an animal in a metaphorical sense but to categorically *be* the animal.

Continuity Between Self and Animal

Although the cases discussed here of the human self being reified as animal are clearly pathological (albeit perhaps common in certain historical situations), it is possible that reification of the human self as *human* is a normative ideological capture of meaning in some cultures. That is, whereas early experience revolves around continuity, the culture may dictate human-animal discontinuity. In Western culture, this may have roots in the classical opposition of the simple animal body versus the human mind, defined by a high standard of self-reflective thought. Ironically, language itself is reified as a discontinuity between the body and the mind and between the animal and the human. One important implication is that in this culture there may be a complex set of affective and linguistic meanings (explored in the next chapter) that encourage individuals to draw the human-animal boundary *categorically* and that weaken metaphorical human-animal continuities.

We are now in a position to counter this particular reification in our psychological theories. First, animate commonality is primary. Second, it is ironic that language is reified as difference because *it* is what lets us wonder about the meaning of behavior—actually enhancing our sense of continuity. In light of this chapter, self-reflection and language can be employed *within* their matrix of bodily interaction, imagination, and metaphor. We have seen that for the young child, at least, the gap between the human self and the animal interactant, although real and intriguing, is far from absolute. And we have seen that this is based on self-consciousness in continuity with the interactive human animal body. This kind of difference-within-continuity *can develop further* rather than suffering reification.

What would development that fostered continuity look like? We can consider several aspects. Most simply, it could involve developmental trends in pretend play among young children. A bit more broadly, what kind of longer-term potential for understanding animals generally can we hypothesize? Finally, generalizing much further, how does the perspective here inform our thinking about ourselves generally and the relations between psyche and culture? I address these questions in what follows.

I can only speculate about developmental trends in pretend play. Children in the older half of the group I observed (over 4 years, 4 months) accounted for the majority of incidents of animal pretend play. But focal-child observations in the spring, in which I more intensively observed a subset of children, showed no age-related difference in tendency to pretend, and the four children reported by parents to have the most pretend animal identities at home were among the younger ones, including Yasmin, who accounted for thirteen of the twenty-four instances of pretend animal play by the younger half of the children in the fall. These three contrary indications support at most a conclusion that individual differences are important in preference for pretend animal play.

Differences in the quality of pretend animal performances are evident between children who do it frequently versus others, regardless of age. Frequent pretenders included Drew, Dawn, and Yasmin. In just one example, Drew imitated the turtle wiping its paw across its face, an action he repeated several times, giving it the words, "I don't want it." Dawn was the only child observed to imitate all the animals brought to class, showing how avidly a child can engage in embodying different animals. We saw Yasmin's long imitation/"dialogue" sequence with the doves. As noted already, being a cat was her other most constant role; in the following, she adorned herself for it:

Katra helps Yasmin make a 6-inch masking tape cat tail. Katra asks, "Do you need a bigger tail?" Yasmin answers, "No." Yasmin tells Katra that "cats have 'em, you know, those things that scratch with claws." Attaching her tape "claws" by the bathroom, Yasmin tells Reuben, "I'm a dog. No, a cat." She has lines of tape spanning from her nose to her cheeks for whiskers, and is busy mounting little pieces on her toes and fingers.

Katra helps by supplying pieces of tape, which Yasmin cuts with scissors. Yasmin: "Once, my grandma, she has a kitty, and I'm going to visit her, and . . . she has—[we] went to visit her and she has a cat, and ah it scratched me and that's its claws doing it. Sometimes it puts out its claws when it's playing 'n it accidentally scratches you."

Her observation and experience with a "real" cat informed the ways Yasmin modified her own body for the role of a cat. On the other hand, some children very seldom imitated or pretended to be animals. Chris, Adrienne, Dimitri, Irvin, Toby, and Reuben were among those showing low levels of animal imitation or animal pretend play in class, but they did not show less interest in animals than other children.

More broadly, what evidence is there that imitation of animals—and thus continuity—is *favored* in other cultures? Translating the shape of the animal's body into one's own—the key continuity—may be a broadly shared characteristic of childhood. Children's animal pretend play has not been studied cross-culturally, although Fernandez (1986) reported it in the Fang of Africa and among children in the Asturian region of northern Spain. Other cultures have specialized in animal imitation. Consider such examples as the old Kwakiutl ceremonies (recorded by the ethnographic photographer Edward Curtis in the 1916 film *In the Land of the War Canoes*), in which animals are vividly enacted by masked dancers, or the unusual imitative talents of one member of the Bushman group in the ethnographic film, *The Hunters*. Notably, these are cultures in closer contact to the animal world than is our modern urban one, but they hold clues to our own potential.

What efforts in our own culture to understand animals in their own terms deserve attention? Clinton Sanders and Arnold Arluke (1993) suggest sociologists and others should explore this area, taking their cues from those who work and live closely with animals. They go on to say people can go much further to "learn to speak in the animal idiom" with animals by exploring the "least human role," reproducing as much as possible the animals' own repertoire of movements and sounds in context (Sanders & Arluke, 1993, p. 383). For example, Kenneth Shapiro (1985, 1989) used a pioneering method to understand the subjectivity of his dog, Sabaka. It is worth examining for its advanced use of the kind of activities we have seen children do. He first considered how social constructions of dogs—popular and scientific—affected his preconceptions, and he became "a historian of the individual animal . . . under study." The principal method, however, was to recover meanings implicit in the dog's activity through "kinesthetic empathy" in which the investigator "attempts directly to sense or empathize with the motor intention or attitude or project of the animal" (1989, p. 185). Combined, these three methods provided interesting insights. Sabaka "is embedded in a lived rather than an objective space. It is a space shaped and oriented by his own position, interests, and projects." Shapiro concluded that space is fundamental to Sabaka in the way that time may be for humans: "He can just lie there for hours because he is not primarily waiting, he is not primarily anticipating, he is not thinking in our sense; he is already arrived, he is at home" (p. 189). A third central concern of Sabaka's is his relationship to Shapiro. After Shapiro reprimanded the dog, he reflected, "I directly sense his searching for my bodily attitude to him. He is, as it were, studying my kinesthetics." (p. 190).

Shapiro's bodily empathic attitude has much in common with animate relatedness and its elaboration through imitation and pretend play. Bodily empathy involves "the meaningful actual or virtual imitation or enactment of bodily moves" (Shapiro, 1989, p. 191). Its potentials with nonhuman animals demand sensitivity to a shared "prelinguistic region where meaning is and remains implicit, embedded, and more consistently enacted directly" (p. 192). Self and other are not assumed to be originally isolated, a conception that could only arise with linguistic distinctions. And this process does not necessarily mean a more limited access to the other's subjectivity than that available though explicit means, since "the comportment through which an animal's intention . . . is embodied is less deceitful, more visible, and therefore more directly inhabitable by us" (p. 192).

What might we achieve by stretching our human powers of understanding, including not just the cognitive and historical but also the bodily empathic? Children do something quite like Shapiro's (1985, 1989) practice spontaneously, and the knowledge it provides is brought into consciousness via pretend play and imitation. Noske (1989) noted with regret that authentic feral children were not studied for what they might have known about their animal "foster parents." "Principle investigators" in ethology might begin their research in infancy, with parents who nurture their relations to animals in addition to their normal human attachments. Having spent the period of greatest behavioral plasticity in a mixed species community, such individuals might, much later and upon further disciplined study, come to unanticipated insights into animal behavior.

Conclusion

On the most general level, continuity between preverbal and verbal experience has very broad relevance. It reinforces a deep understanding of the creative process and reframes the problem of knowing and understanding other subjectivities—human and otherwise. The dynamic whereby continuity can be blocked sheds new light on development and socialization, which we will explore in the next chapter. My findings have implications for our collective self-understanding, including as it is formalized in psychological theories. Perhaps, we should not be too proud of the things we achieve uniquely as humans, for our creative abilities depend on the foundation we share with many other species. Although we can never become other than human, what makes us essentially human is what we have *in common* with other creatures. Important values are at stake in our relations to nonhuman species as well as to our own human animal bodies. How these values are played out in the culture of the American preschool is the subject that occupies us next.

7 The Animal in the Cultural Context of Development

THIS IS THE AGE OF CULTURE—many now appreciate how each culture's beliefs and institutions shape its members' views of the world. And animals are clearly part of those cultural worlds; the variability in how animals are used, regarded, and symbolized across cultures is vast. In this chapter, I suggest that the variability (at least for young children) is not arbitrary. Instead, its patterns reflect the early developmental potency of animate relatedness. Just as we discovered that animal role pretend play fosters *continuity* between human self and animal other and between body and self-reflective awareness, so, too, do animals reveal important dynamics in the developmental realms of morality, cognition, and identity. Our interest here will be in continuity of three aspects of the self: *continuity of concern* for other living animals; *continuity of interest* in understanding them; and *continuity of community* between self and animal other. The cultural context of childhood has everything to do with the realization of these potentials, but such achievement happens only to the extent the culture *works with* the patterns of connection already operating on the animate level.

So strong is the consensus about the force of culture, however, that this proposal may appear quite radical. Admittedly, people appropriate animals in symbol and flesh in so many ways and to so many ends as to give reason to believe that the meanings of animals *are* wholly social constructions. Consider the social historian Keith Tester's (1991) look at the history of the animal rights movement. It has roots, he shows, in the "invention" of animal rights in the nineteenth century through the animal rights activist Henry Salt's juxtaposition of humans' similarity to animals with humans' perfectibility. These principles made it possible to believe in a natural source of obligations to animals. But Tester believes the invented nature of these concepts was systematically obscured. Their proponents ignored the sea of evidence of human cruelty, and they fetishized "rights." In truth, he writes, "animals are only made the site of moral worries to the extent that they are useful in establishing social definitions of the properly human" (p. 195), and the task of reading meaning into the "blank page" of animals' pain, "takes skill, know-how and subjectivity . . . abilities which only fully social human individuals are said to possess" (p. 197). Adult humans seamlessly construct all meanings of animals, we are to believe.

In developmental studies, a culture-centered approach akin to Tester's (1991) is familiar. It assumes culture makes the child; the mechanism, socialization, is the reproduction of occupants of social roles and statuses, of believers and speakers of the native discourses. Certainly, all the adults in the children's lives—and the children themselves—are immersed in cultural networks of belief and practice. But it is not just that morality, cognition, and identity cannot be complete without the cultural context; the claim is that culture mainly determines them.

But to accept such a one-way model of socialization ignores children's influence on socializers and on each other, together with any deeply entrenched or inherent dynamics to psychological development. More immediate doubts are raised by real interaction with animals, which proceeds with intricate accommodation to the animals. Far from not "possessing subjectivity," even infants form a social sense of self. Young children retain and flexibly employ these same core abilities with other species; pretend play confirms this. Animals' living subjective presence makes them powerful symbols for parallel matters in the child's own life—symbolic in a sense both richer and more determinate than cultural constructionist studies typically reveal. These patterns hardly paint a picture of one-way socialization in which childhood is a blank slate or primitive animal body to be shaped and formed. Indeed, other-than-human creatures themselves turn out to be important in our becoming who we are.

The relations of language, cultural messages, feelings in the body, and individual subjectivity in development are complex. We can take as a clue the *continuity* of connection-within-difference the child experiences by pretending. Rather than assuming that the preverbal and self-reflective selves are necessarily at odds, we found evidence for a particular dynamics of continuity and discontinuity. In this chapter, I apply these insights and locate similar patterns in different domains—patterns, that is, whereby cultural practices promote or harmonize with an aspect of the individual's unfolding subjective experience and others that thwart or distort it. In this search for wider implications, we will look in three domains—moral development, cognition, and socialization—for conditions of continuity in experience.

The Animal in Moral Development

We have seen many examples of young children's concern for animals' well-being. It would be odd to claim that this concern arises from cultural messages, for in fact nursery schools are pervaded by *conflicting* moral messages about animals. We will look at several facets of this and then come back to the events that children themselves react to in ways that are nascently moral. The importance of the patterns we find can be seen in light of several perspectives on moral development. These patterns indicate the conditions that allow *continuity of concern* for animals.

Perhaps, children simply absorb messages in adult-designed cultural media aimed at them. Children's literature and cartoons are full of animals participating in morally loaded narratives. The writer Margaret Blount (1974) noted several varieties of morality in children's animal tales, including didactic animals whose natural behavior is used to make a moral point; instructively amoral characters like Brer Rabbit; "people-with-animal-heads" enacting typical social situations; and animals used satirically to show the human race to itself, as in *Gulliver's Travels*.

Besides the various moral animal messages in books, the nursery school I observed was not isolated from the wider culture's conflicts over the moral status of animals, as data from my videotaped conversations and other observations showed.

> Joe: "Can you make him talk?" Ms. Dean: "Do you think I can make him do anything he doesn't want to do?" Several kids answer: "No." Ms. Dean: "How come? Joe: "Because he has his own rights."

Animals' rights came up again with a species at the opposite end of the anthropomorphism continuum:

> Ms. Dean: "[Would you] squish a spider in your house?" The children respond, "No." Ms. Dean: "No, how come?" Solly: "Because it has to have its freedom."

In both these examples, the questions posed by Ms. Dean had a rhetorical and highly suggestive tone, making it clear what answer was expected. In turn, their answers had a rote quality—the very picture of inculcation.

Indeed, Mrs. Ray brought her strong advocacy of human rights to the classroom, indirectly providing the opportunity for children to extend "rights" to animals. But her same principle worked in an opposite direction as well: In another instance, she related how people in other cultures eat snake, monkey, and turtle meats. That time tolerance and the interests of people took precedence over extension of "rights" to all species.

Another countervailing tradition is the motif of ecosystem as impersonal economy. Pests like bugs fit well in this frame, and the teachers sometimes tolerated ill-treatment of them:

> Mindy goes out the side doors with Reuben. . . . On the floor, Dawn says: "Oh-oh, a bug's coming." They look at it together. Reuben tells it, "Get out, little bug," and he pushes it under the door. As they look for more bugs they inch their way outside. Mindy says, "Here's one," and she reaches out. Ms. Tanner brings them back inside. Mindy continues to stand and look out, sights more bugs, steps on them, and says, "That one's dead."

Intruding flies or collected bugs—food for the toad—were treated dismissively. When the fate of a beetle was put up for a vote, eight children wanted it to be toad food, five wanted it left outside, and nine wanted it kept in a jar in the classroom. In the end, it stayed in a jar until it was dead.

Although some bugs did not matter, others were worthy because of their beauty or usefulness to people. Mindy was about to squish an ant, but Sam intervened, insisting, "*No*, don't kill it, he's a *good,* he's a good insect." Thus had lessons about good-citizen bugs been internalized.

Of course, human meat-eating can also be assimilated to the nature-as-smorgasbord image. Once, a hunter talked to the class about his sport:

> A man comes in with an elk antler. He says his guide found it while they were out hunting deer and elk in Wyoming. He shows a magazine cover with a picture of an elk on it. Mrs. Ray asks him why they shoot elk. He replies, perhaps too fast, "Food." He tells what they do with an animal: They use the hide for a blanket and cut up the rest for meat. He asks the kids, "Do you eat meat? Do you eat hamburgers?" Reuben nods, smiles open-mouthed and starts screaming quietly and crawls excitedly off the rug. The man adds that meat comes from cows and chickens. Mrs. Ray says that a long time ago everybody got their meat from animals by hunting, and some people still do, but many prefer to get it at the supermarket.

Killing animals and meat eating is officially okay, even though a deer is a much more immediate other than a bug.

But the children also learned the other side of the issue:

> Mrs. Ray says that when she grew up, her mother didn't let her eat pig meat, illustrating that "Some people are not allowed to eat certain foods. . . . And some people eat no meat at all." Kevin: "They're vegetarian."

Some children knew such people, such as Laura's uncle. But two-thirds of the parents said meat eating had not been raised as an issue or that it had but there was no disagreement. They conveyed acceptance of meat and justified the choice with nutritional and ecological reasons. None of the parents actively advocated vegetarianism to their children, though several did say they would allow the children to make their own choice when older. Shortly, we will look at the children who *did* have reservations about meat, but what is clear from all these mixed inputs is that simple internalization could not explain the concern children felt for animals' welfare. The culture speaks in many conflicting voices about the issue, and the children are exposed to all of them.

To the contrary of the cultural absorbtion hypothesis, the children expressed moral sensitivity to harm, often regardless of adults' attempts to directly construct the children's reactions. One series of such events began to unfold as the turtle presenter told about turtle reproduction:

Mr. Lloyd: "They lay [their eggs] in the sand and then they forget about them." Billy: "Why?" Mr. Lloyd: "They never—they never see their babies. That's the way reptiles are. Turtles are reptiles and they do not take care of their babies." Billy: "Do the babies die?" Mr. Lloyd: "Some—a lot of the babies die. Because so many things eat them and they've nobody to take care of them. See when you're born, your mommy and your daddy take care of you. A little turtle doesn't have anybody. So the turtle gets eaten by other animals and that's important too because if all the baby turtles that hatched out of eggs lived, we'd have far too many baby turtles, so some of them have to die to feed other animals and that's part of what we call the food chain. Everybody in the wild kind of eats everybody else. But a few of them survive. This [adult] one survived, and this [baby] one will survive."

This was clearly a challenging concept for the children. Being eaten violates core self in every aspect; in addition, here it was reported happening to vulnerable young creatures. This convergence of factors made the baby turtle's fate a vivid symbol for the children's core concerns. The teacher stepped in to try to soften the blow:

Mrs. Ray: "I had a question that I wanted to know. If they had many many many eggs that means that they don't expect all of them to live." Mr. Lloyd: "That's right." Mrs. Ray: "You know what? Some big animals have only one baby, and they're the kind of animal that take care of their young, but when an animal has many many many many babies like a mosquito or like an ant or like a bee, they don't take care of them, and some of them are *meant* to be food for other animals. Wow, that's wonderful to know."

Nonetheless, the sight of *this* individual baby turtle was impressive to the children, and *it* had received much attention from a caregiver. Despite the teacher's help, the baby turtles still carried a large symbolic load for the children, as reflected in later behavior. Several children, including Mindy, Katra, and Billy, told their parents. Only issues such as this were so common in these conversations:

Abeo: And you know what, um . . . um, the turtle has a baby and the mom was still at home, was still at home and the raccoon came into the yard, into the owner's yard, and ate up ten babies.

Mother: *Really?* Who told you this story?

Abeo: The owner.

Joe also discussed the issue with his mother. He had been attentive during the class discussion, and the teacher's rationalization evidently stuck with him, although his intonation in this passage was a blend of curiosity and dismay:

Mother: So then you were going tell me about the turtle and the ma . . . baby, the baby turtle and the mother turtle.

Joe: There's no mother. There's—the turtle's name was Flattop, because he had a flat shell. And Flattop's baby . . . survived, but some of the other babies had to be eaten by other animals.

Mrs. Ray's explanation of the babies' deaths seemed to calm Joe, but the supposed necessity of the deaths was prominent. In a later discussion:

Mother: You told me that some of the babies, that there were some other babies but they died?

Joe: Don't—I don't want to talk about that.

Mother: You don't want to talk about it? . . . How come?

Joe: 'Cause it makes me sad.

Mother: *Oh*, the other day I asked you if it makes you sad, and you said "No." Do you remember what you said? I said, "Why wasn't it sad?"—Remember what you said?

Joe: Yeah, but now it *is* sad.

Mother: Now it is sad. Yeah, I can understand why it's sad.

Joe: Don't—don't talk about it.

Mother: Well, I just wanted to ask you not about it being sad, but when you *weren't* sad about it, you told me why you weren't sad. You said it wasn't sad because, why? Do you remember that? You taught me something . . . I remember you said, "It isn't sad because it's part of life." I thought that was interesting . . . that you said that.

Joe: Well, now it is, it *is* sad.

Mother: I see. Okay, well, let's not talk about it then.

The teacher's reconstrual of the animals' deaths had at first been repeated by Joe, but it appears now that it only superficially buffered the sense of loss symbolized by the baby turtles' deaths. In this second talk, Joe was overwhelmed and clearly could not mitigate his feelings with the teacher's words.

This set of examples includes a definite contribution from the child, which bears the familiar mark of core-relatedness: concern about self-other continuity and the symbolization of issues that are personally meaningful to the child. This was even clearer when the animal involved was known personally. Indeed, although nothing threatened Snowflake directly, threats to the guinea pig were discussed. One day, Drew wanted to know why the animals were called "guinea pigs." I looked through a book with him and we found an explanation, but the passage also mentioned that people in Peru eat guinea pigs. He said little but seemed visibly disturbed. Later in the year, when the ferrets visited, several children guessed that they were carnivores. But this took on a concrete meaning:

> Mr. Myers: "Today I did something and I didn't think what I was doing, but Ms. Collins pointed it out afterwards. I took that ferret carrier with the ferret in it and I set it next to Snowflake's cage, to put it out of the way for a while. . . . " Ms. Collins: "I said 'I bet that guinea pig's going crazy.'" Mr. Myers: "And Snowflake was hiding under newspapers." Ms. Collins: "He smelled the ferret." Mr. Myers: "And in the wild . . . In the wild the ferret might be something that would eat a guinea pig . . ." Mrs. Ray broke in immediately: "So guess what, in this room we would not let that ferret get next to our guinea pig. We would protect Snowflake, right?"

This incident was reported by Drew:

> Drew, whispering: 'Cept those kind of animals do eat guineas.
> Mother: They eat *guineas*? Uh, so did you, what'd ya do, keep the guinea covered up?
> Drew: No, we didn't put it near the guinea.

Given Drew's response to this event, one might guess that people eating guinea pigs was an *entirely* foreign idea. Drew's sense of self existed in a connection with guinea pigs that would never conceive such an act.

Nascent moral feelings are strongest when several factors emphasize the animate needs of the animal. Pets' moral status is overdetermined for children, but not only because of cultural meanings. Granted, pets are assimilated to the family, treated as training ground for responsibility taking and being gentle. And caring for them is gender-role consistent for girls and not gender-role discordant for boys (Melson & Fogel, 1988). But deeper relational factors are more important.

Pets fit into two universal features of young children's experience that the psychologists Carol Gilligan and Grant Wiggins (1987) say constitute the seeds of moral development. One universal is that the child is relatively powerless compared to his or her caretakers. This experience is the root for later concerns about independence, equality, and the injunction not to treat others unfairly—in other words, for an orientation toward justice. Simultaneously, the child is also dependent on and attached emotionally to his or

her parents. This can generalize to a care orientation centered on responding to need, preventing harm, and the injunction not to turn away or abandon another. Gilligan and Wiggins's framework applies to pets in a particularly salient way. With a pet animal, the child is in the parental position in
both respects. The child is more powerful than the animal, and it is dependent on her or him. In this circumstance, the child's own emerging sense of
both moralities may readily generalize to the animal.

Consider the time Mrs. Ray trimmed Snowflake's claws. The day before,
she prepared the class by telling them that the guinea pig would not like being held tightly but the operation was really just like cutting our fingernails,
which does not hurt. The children were very interested. Ivy was clearly
worried and received reassurance. The next day:

> Mrs. Ray begins by saying that guinea pig will not like it. She holds its front paw and
> it struggles and whines. "Hey, wait," she says to it. The children smile. She tells it to
> be quiet, and notes it didn't understand her words. She compares the whole thing to
> taking a baby to the doctor. . . . "It's important to let the guinea pig know that we
> aren't going to hurt it," so she'll just clip one today so it won't get upset. . . . One
> claw is clipped; and then three more. . . . Mrs. Ray: "Nobody really likes getting
> hurt." . . . As she clips more the children crowd in to see. Ivy is very concerned and
> says out loud: "It won't hurt; it'll only take a second."

The teacher's response to the children's concern was adept. She helped
them assume the caretaker's morally active position in a relationship like
one in which they were usually the patient. Ivy especially responded.

In the examples of the baby turtles, the guinea pig–ferret issue, and the
guinea pig claw-trimming, adults responded very carefully to soften the
emotional impact on the children. But they are not just shaping the children's morality in these cases; they are responding as they feel they must to
respect and support the morality implicit in the sense of connection the
children feel to the animals involved. Mrs. Ray's analogies helped the children contain their concerns—and sometimes failed to help, as in Joe's case
discussed previously. The children are working though these early moral issues in their own terms, but they are not doing so from an arbitrary base,
nor one constituted only by culture.

It is not surprising that children have the early moral responsiveness to
animals we have observed. Several independent sources point to the universal importance of harm and to links between early empathic feelings and
morality. The cultural psychologists Richard Shweder, Monamohan Mahapatra, and Joan Miller (1987) declared that "the abstract principle of harm"
(p. 19) is one of a few mandatory features of any rationally appealing code

of morality and found that "kicking a harmless animal" was one of only a few items that Oriya (Indian) and American five- to seven-year-olds agree is wrong (p. 61). Core relatedness may underlie this apparently universal constraint. The American psychologist Jerome Kagan (1984, 1986) has pointed to the emergence of morality around age two, and notes, "The capacity for empathy is inherent in children. . . . Since W.W.I, American psychologists have declared you've got to teach children morality. We use the term psychopath, referring to a person who never learned a moral sense. *But one can only lose a moral sense*"(1986, pp. 87–88; emphasis added). A sense of morality itself is an expectable outcome of a normal early childhood.

I suggest that discontinuities in concern must be the result of some interfering factor. Intriguing evidence comes from the children's attitudes about eating meat. According to the parent surveys, two children did not like meat because of how it tastes. Four children had asked for information and three of these were hesitant to eat meat once they had learned where it came from: Mindy, Yasmin, and Joe. Mindy said, "Yuck, I don't want to eat cow meat anymore." Joe once told his mother he did not like to eat dead animals. Thus, despite the parental acceptance of meat eating there was some resistance to it, especially when the origin of the meat was clear. One reason may be disgust, but another is probably the children's recognition that killing animals violates the valued animate properties of the other:

Cassia, Ivy, Adrienne discuss meat eating at the game table. Cassia: "Do you know people eat animals?" Ivy: "And animals eat people." Cassia: "And animals eat animals." Adrienne: "*You* eat animals!"

The children felt conflicts over eating meat; although this may be unavoidable, it may also signal the loss of continuity of concern. The abstract quality of these three girls' talk should not be missed; the issue feels somewhat vague. Indeed, they have no contact with the reality discussed. The nursery school culture helps keep it out of the way; for example, children's books idealize farm life.

But so does the larger society. It uses distancing mechanisms to reduce the conflict between emotions linked to a sense of connection and harm linked with meat eating. These misrepresent exploitation, thus relieving the discomfort we might otherwise feel. What the children have not acquired—and are in the course of acquiring—are these distancing mechanisms that adults use to reduce the dissonance of harm to animals. Serpell (1986) wrote that humans' empathic responses to animals require that people distance themselves psychologically when they exploit animals. This is accomplished via mechanisms such as detachment, concealing the harm, misrepresentation, and shifting the blame. The psychologist S. Plous (1993) hypothesized other similar factors: conflict reduction; animals as an out-group; and, more positively, the "similarity principle" that accounts for differential extensions of caring, depending on how alike the recipient is judged to be. Hank Davis, an animal experimentalist, and Dianne Balfour (1992) proposed that a bond develops between animal experimentalists and their subjects, requiring some kind of psychic defense. Some have argued Western culture is built on a myth of human supremacy, buttressed by such psychodynamics.

This particular kind of cultural acquisition is not arbitrary but plays a particular function in development. Children's concern about animals reveals an inherent and self-organizing dynamic of morality. It does so more vividly than does their moral development toward other humans, because in the case of animals the culture encourages a discontinuity—or, at best, a complexity that is hard to navigate with moral sensibilities intact. If moral dilemmas are to be optimally resolved, then the fundamental role of core relatedness must be acknowledged and means of continuity fostered.

The entire mixture of cultural messages places animals at the center of a complicated set of moral sentiments. We are tied to animals by bonds of emotions and by the ways (whether truly necessary or not) they serve our needs. For the young child, the bonds are strong. Add to that how the animal can symbolize the self's vulnerabilities, as well as the self's needs for self-perpetuation, defense, and even aggression. With such various pulls, maintaining a continuity of concern is challenging. Where possible, the real conflicts should be removed; otherwise—and we shall probably never escape this—what can be done is to acknowledge and embrace our own vulnerable connectedness. This means helping children in their appreciation of animals' needs, whether through interaction, nurturing, or observation.

The Animal in Cognitive Development

Animals are relevant for many concerns of cognitive development, including topics I have touched on such as the child's understanding of causality, mind, biological categories, and social roles. But what about the unique intersection of thought and animate relatedness? In particular, how do we understand *continuity of interest* in the subjective worlds of other species?

The answer necessarily blends cognitive, affective, and evaluative elements, as we will see here in examining children's sense of wonder and what adults can do to encourage (and not discourage) it. Since cognitive development advances when second-order representations of experience are available, a key question is what forms of representation facilitate the sense of connection? Finally, I speculate that intelligence in relation to the natural world, and to animals in particular, constitutes a special kind of cognitive-affective skill.

One of the hallmarks of children's interactions with an optimally discrepant animal is the emotion of wonder. Animals present ambiguous and challenging properties for children to interact with and understand. To the young child, they must appear as beings with somewhat mysterious inner qualities and as frustrating but also gratifying interactants. Perhaps, Toby best expressed the feeling the time he exclaimed he was "amazed" by "you funny birds." Behavior or physical appearance can spark wonder:

> Ms. Collins brings out the other ferret, which is a lighter color. Chris: "He's *different*." Ms. Collins: "Yeah, see he's a different color." Dawn: "Yeah, that's what I was saying . . . Hey, but they are two different eye colors."

Toby exemplified the attitude of wonder. Consider some of his remarks about the turtle:

> "I, I got a chance to touch his shell. . . . That feels so funny. . . . I just touched, I got to feel one of his claws. . . . Hey, do ya wanta feel his shell?" Toby touches the turtle, pulls his hand away very quickly. . . . "Hey, this feels very funny, feel it. Feel this part right there. . . . Hey, look-it, he has a tail! Tail! Can you believe it? There's his tail." He puts his hand by the turtle, pointing. He, Rosa, and Mindy look closely. Toby: "I didn't know a turtle has a tail." Toby lies on his stomach, looking closely at the turtle.

In this case, the adults simply listened and helped him sustain safe interactions without overshadowing the animal with their own input. Toby showed he had benefited from such opportunities when he stopped Mindy from chasing pigeons:

> Mindy moves toward them a step or two, and suggests they chase or scare them. Toby, a bit behind her, reaches forward, grabs her coat, and says, "No, let's just watch."

Toby had learned to restrain even Mindy's urge to provoke a reaction, valuing more the chance to observe.

The teacher supported this attitude by encouraging appreciation. She did so by modeling, near the end of the tarantula visit:

> Mrs. Ray raises her hand to talk: "I thought they were ugly, and I thought they were scary, and I thought they were frightening, and I thought they felt wonderful, and I liked them after I knew them, so another animal that I didn't know about at first, and when I knew it, I really liked it."

Other times, she directly encouraged the children to observe:

Joe continues to look at the monkey more closely: "Hey, he got three fingers and um, one thumb." Mrs. Ray: "Look carefully Joe, look carefully." Joe and Dawn continue close inspection of feet, hands, fingers. Joe: "One thumb, one thumb—oh, that's his pinkie?"

Less directly but with equal effect, the teachers used questions:

Cassia shows Ms. Tanner what the visiting rabbit was doing: "This is what he was doing"—she puts her tongue out and makes a lapping noise, then lifts her foot up. "He was licking his shoe—yuk!" Ms. Tanner: "Does he have shoes?"

More open-ended questions do not verbally select a focus of the child's attention. Another practice was offering information about animals that highlighted the discrepancy between expectation and actuality. The tarantulas had a number of surprising features:

Mr. Dean: "Who thinks they have more than three eyes?" Toby exclaims: "Three eyes!?" He bends over to look with surprise into Billy's face.

Its ability to molt was another new thing:

Ms. Dean: "They have a skeleton on their outside, and what they do, is they actually walk right out of their skeleton. Now this [showing an old exoskeleton] is from this guy. . . . That's a spider skeleton." Billy: "He just walks out of his old skin?"

Stories about animal behavior also had the capacity to reveal the divergent subjective world of the animal:

Mr. Lloyd: "One winter . . . my wife was making a sweater. . . . And this turtle thought that that yarn was a worm, it was green, and it went over and it started to eat the end of the piece of yarn. And when we found him he had eaten over ten feet—that's almost as long as this wall—of yarn. We had to carefully pull it out again, because if it would have continued to eat, it would have eaten about a hundred feet. And it wasn't bothered by the fact it didn't taste it."

Several children mentioned this story to parents later.

Given some near-at-hand animals, children express their interest in various ways: Joe, for example, in his ability to focus on animals, ask questions, and spin ideas about them; Toby, in his intense desire to watch animals without disturbing them and his concern for their autonomy; Yasmin, in her vivid bodily identifications; Drew, in wanting to see what unconfined animals do; Ivy, in her closely attuned nurturant attitude; and Solly, in his style of observing closely and quietly. For each, cognitive and affective factors enhanced each other.

What larger social factors or attitudes affect this developmental potential? Some of our habitual attitudes to animals do not help. A list of possible candidates includes the belief that animals are okay for children but unimportant to serious adults; overly sentimental feelings toward pets, coupled with dismissal of animals we exploit and indifference toward other wild species; utter skepticism about attribution of subjective states to animals; insistence on clinical sterility in talking about the bodies and reproduction; and unreflective rejection of moral reactions to events in nature.

Some of our actual practices with animals objectify them or turn them into mere spectacles for detached observation and entertainment or crass curiosity. These include confining animals; training them to perform on command (especially for mere entertainment value); restricting their agency, interactivity, and access to fulfilling evolved-in environmental needs; reducing them to mere means (especially for nonessential human aims); and explaining them via reductionistic scientific doctrines to the exclusion of other ways of representing life processes. Each of these attitudes and practices prejudicially devalues some element of the child's (and adult's) total reaction to the animal world. Awareness of the tendency to sentimentalize animals too often leads to off-handed or willful ignorance of this devaluation.

There may be no great economic gain to be had by an appreciation of other species, but they are arguably some of the most intriguing and complex phenomena on this planet, and noneconomic values are clearly at stake. Ironically, since animals are considered part of the child's domain, they are an area where children can be the relative experts. This is good, but we also need to build support and acceptance for animals being a lifelong passion for more people. Several things can help. Observation, as encouraged by traditional natural history, stresses pattern detection and sympathy with the subject of study. There is certainly a fine line between objectification and critical yet appreciative observation, but science lessons can strike a balance. In the school I observed, most of the teachers' talk about animals reflected a very respectful attitude and was pitched right at the children's level.

Continuity of interest is encouraged by respecting children's expression of wonder at animals and helping them explore how the meanings they discover can be conveyed. Finding ways to re-present animate relatedness on a higher-order symbolic level without distorting the experience is a challenge but also facilitates continuity. One medium is the body. In the previous chapter, we saw that mimetic or theatrical representation of animals can be culturally supported. Teachers' appreciation of artistic expression and of children's own symbolic meanings fosters the conscious realization of connection.

A related problem is how we talk about animals so as to honor the interest children have. These children used the word *real* with a special emphasis when they meant an actual, living animal, as opposed to a dead or artificial one. Abeo, her older sister Ifama, and their mother talked about chicks they had recently hatched at home:

Mother: Abeo, do you like the chicks?

Abeo: *Yes!* I *did.* . . .

Mother: How come?

Abeo: Because! I got to pet one of them. . . .

Mother: Oh, Abeo's jumping up and down at the thought of the chicks! You really like the chicks then.

Abeo: *Yes.*

Mother: Is it because they're really nice and cuddly?

Ifama: They're real.

Mother: Because they're real.

Abeo, interrupting: *Yeess!*

Real carried an affective load far beyond its dry logical meanings. Can this be merely a cultural construction? Haraway (1989) deconstructed cultural notions of "encounter" with wild nature, and J. Berger (1980) said that modern experience makes it impossible to "centralize" animals' alterity. Yet, for young children, encountering living animals has a compelling, centralizing quality that shapes thought and culture.

Real animals interrupt easy anthropomorphism; they are familiar but also unknown. Too often, humans' (including social theorists') level of understanding of animals stops at particular symbolic meanings and misses the complexity and ambiguity that made these possible. Also missed are the affective dimensions of what a *living* animal means.

Interestingly, understanding animals may tap—and contribute to—what the psychologist Howard Gardner (1983) has called "interpersonal" intelligence. Relating with animals fits Gardner's framework for an intelligence in these respects: (1) It probably uses specific brain areas (used also by interpersonal intelligence), which would be those associated with processing of information about movement, including proprioceptive sensation, and about the expression of arousal and affect, perhaps associated with the limbic system. New evidence also suggests that other aspects of biological concepts may have innate bases. (2) It can be selectively spared when other faculties are absent or deficient, as in authenticated cases of feral children who adopted the social behaviors of their animal foster parents. Some syndromes show a related specific deficit having to do with a discrete mental module serving empathic and theory-of-mind functions. (3) It can be developed to a high degree of virtuosity, as shown in human-animal partnerships of various sorts.

Whether knowing animals is a subset of interpersonal intelligence or its own unique area of mental excellence, many other capacities contribute to the sense of connection. Language is probably essential for grasping the intentionality of animal action. Connection itself is metaphorical for intelligence, as suggested by a character in a story by Ursula K. Le Guin (1990): "I know that sentience or intelligence isn't a thing, you can't find it in, or analyze it out from, the cells of a brain. It's a function of the connected cells. It is, in a sense, the connection: the connectedness. It doesn't exist. I'm not trying to say it exists. I'm only guessing that Osden might be able to describe it" (p. 142). Animate relatedness retains a central place among our capacities throughout life. The richer the field of other entities it integrates, the greater our potential for locating the self and acting appropriately within that field.

Animals in Socialization

What is "human"—in the sense of sharply and preferentially divided off from the "nonhuman"—is a matter of cultural definition carried out in language, evaluative attitudes, and action. Such socially constructed distinctions cut across the human self, across body and mind. They function differently from the developmentally earlier connection-within-difference. When meanings become reified around a particular contrast between humans and animals; when the human becomes a discrete, separate category, the metaphoric movement between human self and animal other may be curtailed. In the previous chapter, we saw pathological examples of the breakdown of metaphorical ability in which the human self is mistaken for an animal. Far more common and normative are ideological and affective capture of "human" to mean emphatically "*not* animal."

At stake here is *continuity of community*—the sense that one's identity bonds one with others in an interspecies community sharing a common fate. Although the children's capacities, including language, inclined them to experience such identification, the nursery school reflected both wider human-animal boundary disputes and emotionally laden and culturally specific evaluations of "proper" behavior. What were these disputes and evaluations, and how did the children respond to them? I found that they did not just automatically fit in with these schemes. Nor was the result a simple additive acquisition of arbitrary and otherwise equal cultural attitudes. Nonetheless, some children displayed a discontinuity with animate relatedness and the formation of a more rigidly categorical human self.

The Contested Human-Nonhuman Boundary

We have observed the use of animal contrasts to mark the human boundary across cultures and, indeed, in developmental theory. So it should be no surprise to find them in everyday life, too. Language makes categorical distinctions across what are continua on the preverbal level. These distinctions can be treated as set in reality, making pretend, metaphorical comparison and linguistic expression of similarity more difficult. The instances of talk about animals we will see now reveal the presence of old cultural traditions. Through them, the categorically human self's specific similarities and differences with other species are negotiated.

Animals have long been key benchmarks for surveying the human-nonhuman boundary. The exact location of that boundary is a preoccupation of Western culture, and these debates even entered the nursery school classroom I observed. Broadly, humans and animals are in the same group:

> Mrs. Ray: "There are lots of animals in the class. Some are human animals—the people. Others are little animals like Toad." As she feeds the toad she notes how he wipes grass off his mouth, just like a person would wipe some food.

Continuity is recognized, but part of her statement begs the question because larger size does not set a clear boundary. But what does? Taxonomy seems to simplify the matter. Recently, biologists have pushed it to somewhere between humans and nonhuman primates; this has reached five-year-olds:

> Ms. Dean calls on Joe. Joe: "Are people related to monkeys?" Ms. Dean echoes the question back: "[Do] you think people are related to monkeys?" Ten children raise their hands; seven feel people are not.

We adults want to know, can apes talk, use tools, plan, remember, have culture?—all key criteria of humanity. Children focus on other features. Joe had one idea, evidently obtained by comparison:

> Joe: "Hey, I know why they're related to people." Ms. Dean: "Why?" Joe: "'Cause they have the same nose."

But of course the adult picks differences that relate to more profound philosophies:

> Joe: "His hands are his feet." Dawn: "And . . . he only has four fingers." Mr. Dean: "And how many do we have?" Dawn and Joe reply: "Five, five." Joe: "No, we have— no, we have eight and two thumbs." Joe holds his hands up, turning toward Mrs. Ray, behind him. Mr. Dean: "So what is he missing?" Dawn: "Two thumbs." Joe: "A thumb." Mrs. Ray: "[Remember what] we talked about—[he] cannot do this"—she pinches thumb and forefinger together several times. Joe, Chris, Dawn do the same.

Mrs. Ray did not explain the rationale for pointing out *this* feature instead of, say, having fur all over one's body. But the opposable thumb is the paradigmatic anatomical characteristic (and thus symbol) of *Homo faber* and his or her technology. Stressing it calls on the popular belief that human inventiveness makes us what we are.

What happened next was revealing. Joe transformed this abstractly important anatomical fact into a concrete and intentionally communicative gesture. He made an "okay" sign with thumb and forefinger and proclaimed, "[He] can't do this!" Joe's interest in categorical differences gravitated toward the interactively and communicatively relevant!

We know Joe had a theory that animal languages are like human languages. But adults went out of their way to be sure the kids were not thinking animals talk or understand language:

Drew: "Why is the turtle talk[ing] in the microphone?!" Mr. Lloyd: "Do turtles talk?" Kids: "No." Drew: "What if it just made noise in the mike?" Mr. Lloyd, interrupting: "No, turtles don't talk."

Joe contested this philosophically critical categorical boundary also, even against adult incredulity:

Ms. Dean: "Can he understand English?" Chris and Dawn answer: "No." Joe: "Yes." Ms. Dean: "Yes?" . . . He repeats this, nodding for emphasis to Chris and Mrs. Ray behind him. Ms. Dean: "Do you think he can hear what we're saying and understand exactly what we're saying?" . . . Joe nods: "Uh-huh, because he's *related* to us." Ms. Dean: "Because he's related to us? So he would automatically know English—but how about Japanese people? Would he understand what Japanese people say?" Joe: "Nooo!" Chris: "Only Japanese monkeys." Mr. Dean: "You mean he'd have to be a Japanese monkey?" Chris nods. Ms. Dean: "He'd have to be a Japanese monkey to understand Japanese people?" Joe: "Uh huh." Chris: "Yes."

At a risk of overinterpreting this humorous exchange, the children's belief that, to the extent a monkey will understand, it will only understand the tongue it has already heard seems reasonable. But Joe's rationale would not wash. From the adult point of view, monkeys are not *closely enough* related to us to understand. For Joe, there is continuity of intentional, meaningful communication—a belief that comes from seeing animate activity in the light of assumptions of language use and a theory of mind.

Cultural assumptions of human-animal difference are subtly communicated; what we have seen are just the most obvious parts. But they are not merely communicated; as we saw, these categorical distinctions are negotiated. Joe articulated his own experience of human-primate *continuity*—an experience that emphasized interactively important features. A child need not, however, be exposed to explicit philosophical rationales. Human-animal difference is implicit in many practices, and it is conveyed in the form of judgments about what is desirable, admirable, and good versus what is unacceptable, despicable, and bad. As we shall see, this fault line runs through evaluations both of humanity and animality and of the mind and the body.

Animals in Cultural Evaluative Perspective

Another entire set of categorical features attributed to animals by words has great relevance for continuity of community with other species. Language makes possible the evaluative marking of behaviors as good and bad, and animals are appropriated as symbolic markers of desirable and undesirable—as exemplars and antiheroes. Antiheroes—deviants—are either physically or symbolically annihilated by being appropriated to serve in a culture's practical and symbolic universe. Exemplary animals are made to stand for good traits.

Children are quite well attuned to this dimension, as an earlier study showed (Myers, 1986). In that study, I found that children from five to eighteen years wished most often to "be like" animals whose cultural meanings were appropriate for the age and gender roles they occupied or were moving into, and not those whose meanings were inappropriate. Of six animal photographs, young children liked the vulnerable bunny, ten-year-olds picked gendered animals, and late adolescents valued the omniscience of the eagle. More generally, the human-nonhuman distinction itself is heavily value laden (cf. Midgley, 1988). We will look at two more nursery school issues: unruly behavior and bodily taboos.

Animals stand ambiguously outside the social order; many of their behaviors set bad examples to be corrected. The teacher went so far as to censure aggressive bird behavior:

> Mrs. Ray notes that one bird is pecking another: "That bird needs to learn to be gentle"; she adds that some people are like that and need to learn also. Birds are like people sometimes, "or is it people are like birds?"

Ms. Wick once asked some rambunctious children, "Did a wild beast get you?" She may have mistakenly thought they were pretending to be animals, or else she saw children as roughly like wild beasts at times—certainly a familiar cultural theme!

Children do identify with animals' freedom from socializers like mothers and school. Perhaps in response, adults sometimes remarked on animal actions that are disallowed to children. For example, the monkey crawled over to the table and ate cracker crumbs off the rug:

Ivy: "He's eating the crumbs." Drew: "He's eating the crumbs." Ms. Dean: "He's eating the crumbs . . . Those must be good crumbs, do you think those crumbs are pretty good?" Several kids: "Yeah." Ms. Dean: "How come, would you guys eat those crumbs?!" Some kids: "Yeah." Solly: "No!" Ms. Dean: "You eat those crumbs before?!"

Ms. Dean's tone of voice and repetition conveyed a good-humored disapproval. The analogy between child and monkey socialization was even made explicit:

Drew: "Does he break your stuff, in your house?" Ms. Dean: "We can't really tell him 'Koko, don't break that because I like that, I like that plate, or I like that special glass or that special vase.'" Joe: "You have to train him." Ms. Dean: "We have to make sure that we keep a very close eye on him." Joe: "Why don't you train him?" Ms. Dean: "Well, that's the thing about monkeys is they're not very easy to train. They decide what they want to do because they have their own mind to think about what they want to do, so if I tell Koko, 'No,' sometimes he'll listen to me, but sometimes he's not too happy, just like when you guys, when your Mom says, 'No, I don't want you to do that,' sometimes you listen and sometimes you don't? Is that true?" Mr. Dean: "Because if you don't want to do something, sometimes you just don't want to do it, right? Same with a monkey." Ms. Dean: "Same with a monkey."

Monkey as child: disobedient, willful, unsocialized. Independence must be tolerated, but both creatures would ideally be tame. This analogy was exhibited in practice. On the one hand, children witnessed adults controlling animals' behaviors, physically or by command; on the other, children were the recipients of adult dictate:

Billy complains about not having enough blocks, or particular ones which others have. Mrs. Ray tells him: "Look around you!" He does so and sees that there are plenty. She says his behavior: "Tells me you need a nap so you can be in control."

Caregivers enforce behaviors and justify doing so with such appeals to the child's own good, and they use animal keeping as a metaphor for explaining such child-rearing strictures.

Thus, not surprisingly, adults are not alone in aiming for socialized outcomes. It was Joe who offered the obvious socialization procedure for Koko, training. Here is an additional alliance, not between the children and the animal but between the children and the adults, on the side of socialization. Children generally do not want the disapproval that misbehavior brings, even if they cannot control the behavior. And they may be given some responsibility for disorderly animals. Thus, it is not surprising that in the end children side with the social world. And to the extent that they see the animal world as opposite to that world, their sense of a categorically human self may exclude the animal.

A second evaluated issue is the body. Besides misbehavior, animals openly use and display their bodies in ways not allowed to humans. In the classroom, animals are used as didactic tools, particularly for nonverbalized issues or for feelings to which caregivers do not attune—that is, that are private. Among humans in Western culture (and many other cultures), such functions as defecation, urination, masturbation, intercourse, and childbirth are considered private. Parents socialize these functions as private by not attuning to the subjective experiences that go with them. Earlier, I suggested that this may make such bodily experiences more subjectively shared between children and animals.

But adults' intention is the opposite: Eventually children must identify with the socialized position. The practice of using animals' behaviors as examples of what is undesirable, messy, and private hastens this. The teacher of this classroom used animals as a vehicle for modern, open talk about functions that are less "appropriate" to talk about (or certainly to observe) in people. Dogs were a vehicle for discussing male and female anatomy; so were some other animals:

> Mrs. Ray says that with a guinea pig you can press its belly, and if it's a male you can see its penis show. Does that mean it's a boy or a girl? Kids: "Boy." She says that if it's a girl it has a vagina. Mrs. Ray explains it's the same on birds, though the parts are inside where you can't see them, and there's no way to tell about the toad.

Animals are clearly safe and public for talking about what is problematic between humans. Steps toward embracing this distinction can be traced in a series of examples involving animal excreta. Toby delighted in rubbing his hands on pigeon droppings; Mindy only admitted to a past in which such delights were acceptable:

> Mindy and I are at the guinea pig cage. She wants to touch its "poops," but says they're "yucky."

Her fascination was a step more restrained than Toby's. In the following case, three boys discussed the guinea pig's droppings:

> Drew advises Joe that the thing Joe is handling is a "BM." Joe denies it. Joe and Solly talk about whether it's guinea pig food or guinea pig "BM." Joe holds it in his fingers, firmly disagreeing. Solly tells him it's a "BM"; again he denies it.

In either account, a "BM" (Mrs. Ray's term) was obviously repulsive; the debate was only over whether the object was one. These boys seem to have fully accepted the social messages about excreta; the next step might be aversion to anything even resembling it.

In her talk, Mrs. Ray used animals as a safe way to talk about body functions and was careful to not be too loaded in what she said:

> Mrs. Ray: "Well, did you ever notice that our guinea eats a whole lot? And some of the food that all creatures [eat] becomes part of what your body needs for growing and some of it is extra and it's called waste, and it comes out of your body like a BM, and that—we use toilets but animals don't. I never saw a dog go to the toilet, did you?" Solly: "I have on TV." Mrs. Ray: "Really?" Solly: "Yeah." Mrs. Ray: "Well, I never have. And so, if our guinea pig is down on the rug, then he's, she's liable to leave droppings on the rug."

Although animals and humans are biologically similar, and no strong value judgments were made about body functions, the socialization message was clear.

Children of course grasp that growing up involves control over bodily functions, and they draw parallels between maturing humans and animals. For example, when the turtle's and toad's ways of urinating spontaneously were discussed, Dawn was reminded of how her baby brother sprinkled on her. Thus, children again are in alliance with adults over the issue of their own socialization. After all, they want to grow up, and be on the human side of the boundary, if a boundary there must be.

Thus, accompanying the moral and practical dismissal of animals and the ideological reification of the human-animal divide discussed previously, highly motivating affective valences are communicated by cultural agents. It would be no surprise if a felt connection to the nonhuman succumbed to these captures of preverbal meaning.

The Categorically Human Self

We have discussed two sorts of cultural discourses and practices. One is the setting of conceptual human-nonhuman animal boundaries. The second involves evaluative exclusion of animals by aligning them with negatively valued behaviors or with publicly unacceptable aspects of body and feeling. These cultural influences eventuate in a strong force against close identification with animals. They provide content and motivation for the formation of a categorically human self. Preverbal interactions and pretend-mediated senses of self simply entail degrees of difference within continuities. Little exists there to inform or motivate such a strict division. But when differences are discretely marked and preferentially ranked and an evaluation of certain differences is communicated by selective or misattunements and language, fluid identification becomes problematic to the self. The categorical self is an experiential integration like the other senses of self, but it is based on an abstraction from the full set of features of the self. The categorical human self is unequivocally *not* an animal self.

Toward the end of each small group session with five of the animals in the spring, each child was asked whether he or she would like to be that animal.[1] Most children said they would like to be a number of the animals; only ferrets were significantly less popular than monkeys, the most popular. But some girls responded quite differently. The data show a sex difference in identification with these animals, but most of the statistical weight changes when age is considered also. The *older* girls account for much of the difference.[2] Three of the four oldest girls in the class, Cassia (5 years, 8 months in the spring), Ivy (5 years, 8 months), and Adrienne (5 years, 6 months), showed an interesting pattern suggestive of a categorically human self.

Cassia answered, yes, she would like to be the animal, to *none* of the five—she gave an ambivalent response to the monkey and said no to the other four. Ivy said yes to the monkey, although qualifying her answer with "only for a day," a weak yes for the ferret, and no to the turtle; she was ambivalent about the others. Adrienne said yes to the monkey and no to the tarantula; she was ambivalent toward the thought of being a turtle, a snake, or a ferret. Interestingly, these girls enjoyed interacting with animals, and each of them readily pretended to be a dog during the dog small group sessions. But they showed markedly less self-other continuity with the animals than did the other children.

What might be causing this? These were the three we saw earlier intently discussing meat eating; perhaps some moral distancing and superiority is working as a defense against this discomfort. Ivy was exemplary in the taking of nurturant, motherlike roles in relation to the animals. Such roles are complementary rather than reciprocal and, although quite positive, are thus less conducive to a sense of shared experience. Gender socialization might be reflected here to the extent that it encourages this kind of role. Perhaps most likely, misbehaviors typically associated with being "animal-like" (aggressiveness, rough-and-tumble, dirtiness, the "grotesque" body, and so on) are more at odds with young girls' developing gender identities than boys'. "Don't be an animal!" carries a greater warning to one gender than the other. Although these data constitute no proof, they strongly suggest that toward the end of the age group studied, at least for girls, a sense of categorically human self is developing.

An instructive exception, however, was Dawn, who at 5 years, 6 months was the third-oldest girl. Dawn said, yes, she would like to be four of the five animals; she was only ambivalent about such identification with the snake. Dawn even found it strange that Cassia, who was in her small group, was so hesitant to express identification with animals:

> Mr. Myers: "I'm asking Cassia a question—did you want to be a ferret?" Cassia shakes her head. Mr. Myers: "No. How come?" Dawn: "You didn't want to be a dog, turtle, ferret." Mr. Myers: "It's okay not to want to be one. I'm just wondering why."

As we saw, Dawn often felt that the animals "liked" her, something she read from their approach behavior; and it was she who took her baby brother around the class, introducing him to its animal members. She was also the only child to imitate all the animals brought to the class, an indication that this activity encourages a child's continued sense of connection on terms that do not threaten animate relatedness. To generalize from imitation and pretend play, perhaps the wider class of favorable activities are ones that encourage metaphors and analogies and affective expressions of commonalties, gradient (not categorical) differences, and animate relatedness.

Another factor that differentiated Dawn from the other older girls was that her father took a keen interest in animals. The other girls' parents expressed mild interest or indifference about animals and their role in the children's lives. Asked "What, in your opinion are the benefits your child derives from the real or fictional animals in his or her life?" Dawn's father stressed concrete contact and letting the child discover how the animal felt—revealing his sense of the importance of core connection with the animal. In contrast, the other girls' parents stressed abstract socialization goals couched in terms of the animals, such as: "[through stories] develop sensitivity to the needs of the animals" or "love, caring for another." Adrienne's mother simply wrote, "I don't see many [benefits]; as a result we don't have many pets."

Probably no deficit in normal development would be detected with these girls; A. H. Kidd and R. M. Kidd (1987b) have said a lack of interest in animals can be normal. But this does not negate the possibility of unrecognized (or theoretically unformulated) developmental potentials. Cognitive developmental researchers note that young children put humans in a different category from animals. But if we look at pretend play and identification in most of these young subjects, we do not find a rigid separation. Categories can work in different ways in relation to felt, preverbal meanings—we need this way of thinking about concepts, too, in addition to their logical meaning or cultural referents. In particular, word meanings may be reified and function as if literal when we lose track of the fact that words are *about* meanings, not identical with the preverbal contents to which they refer. The younger children's sense of being a human self does not have this static quality; they take their bearings in a fluid continuity with a community of other animate subjectivities. But the older girls do have such clarity—perhaps rather rigidity—of self-concept, echoing Western culture's high evaluation of the mind and of the human over the body and the animal. Considering the multiple encouragements in this direction surveyed in this chapter, this result is hardly a surprise. The alternative, a developmental goal of a human self connected by concern, interest, and community to the other living beings of this planet, is a possibility we desperately need to better understand.

8 Conclusion

Our species evolved not only in the social environment of other humans but also in the nonhuman natural environment in which we continue—uneasily—to exist. Although this ancient history has left its enduring marks and various individuals and cultures demonstrate the human capacity for a finely attuned relation with the elements of this environment, a capacity for connection is not treated by the social sciences as a fundamental dimension of human potential or development. Rather, to the extent it is even considered, this capacity has too often been seen as an epiphenomenon of various putatively more basic processes. But the children in this book have demonstrated a constellation of developmental processes that account for animals being central to their sense of self. Far from these dimensions of animate relatedness being secondary, there is a strong case that they shape and constrain psychological, social, and cultural phenomena. Thus, basic issues about what makes us who we are come up for reexamination when we take children's relations to animals seriously.

Writing of feral children, Malson (Malson & Itard, 1799/1964) asked, "Now that it is generally recognized that the dominant, fundamental role in the shaping of man's personality is played by his social environment, should one be surprised that a non-human environment produces semi-human children?" (pp. 35–36). In turn, we can now ask, can a child, provided with a human social environment but deprived of nonhuman others, develop her or his full humanity? Thinking back over what we have learned, I can suggest a number of things that would be lacking in such a scenario. There would be no rich sense of different interactive styles, no quasi-social domain free of the pressures and deceptions of the human realm. There would also be a sense of isolation rather than of being in the company of other creatures who confirm one's sense of going-on-being, agency, affectivity, coherence, and history; fewer perceptions of other ways of being, of seeing-oneself-as, and of pretending to be in alternative concrete and subjective realities. The possibilities of the self-reflective self are reduced to the extent the community of animal others is impoverished in diversity.

The great social psychologist George Herbert Mead (1913) felt that ethical choice and action were possible when the person could represent internally every perspective in the situation. In his theory, these perspectives were limited to other humans'. But children themselves show that a much wider inner theater of moral deliberation is developmentally probable. Moving away from social psychology's fixation on language as the privileged route for knowing others, we can see that the more analogical and imitative modes of identification can include every element—every species! This has important implications for the possibilities of a society-wide ecological ethics.

The sense of connection to the animal and by extension to a subjective ecology is a *telos*, or end, of development. It is a prepotent potential, and we might do more to recognize its value. Its value derives from our experience of the animal and its ecological world as something more than human. Just as for children animals offer patterns of optimally discrepant social responsiveness, so, too, the natural world has value to us because we sense that it connects with but stretches beyond what is humanly identical, controlled, or created. That value is realized though our sense of connection to this realm. Thus, the sense of self is clarified and deepened by engagement with animals and thereby might ultimately extend to be a truly "ecological" self.

A sense of connection to the nonhuman also serves values beyond quality of immediate experience. Across the life span and across cultures, we must choose to make the changes that are required of us by ecological constraints. Choice and desire stem partly from our sense of self. *To the extent the self is experienced as connected with the systems by which it is in fact constituted, so much the likelier the needed changes.* Environmental problems are quintessential human problems, yet the sciences of the social have not striven greatly to contribute to adaptive change. Especially, they have not examined how their own foundations might be part of the problem. Like any other value that has such intrinsic and extrinsic appeal, we should seek to cultivate this one, although we have a long way to go.

To cultivate this value means first to understand it. Helping children develop to care about animals and their local habitats and wider ecologies is not straightforward. This is because as children draw animals into their developing selves, important cognitive, emotional, and moral responses to the welfare of animals develop also. These bonds have inherent dynamics that must be respected if continuity of interest, concern, and community are to be possible.

To the extent an ecological self is developed and inclusive, it enables the person to maintain a sense of connection despite loss and necessity. Hunter-gatherer cultures maintained continuity of connection despite exploiting animals because they believed in a spiritual realm that continued after death and that made it imperative to respect their prey. We have no such meaning system intact, but we still have the psychology of the sensitive carnivore who experiences the animal as a social other.

Children need acknowledgment and support of their feelings about harm to animals. A sense of connection creates psychological and spiritual challenges in dealing with loss and violence to those to whom one is connected—and those one opposes. If society were to really grasp what is at stake in child development, we might well reduce exploitation of animals to a minimum dictated by a stricter sense of necessity. But the aim of development cannot be the elimination of all conflicted relations and feelings. Vulnerability, loss, the taking of life are constants. Rather, the aim is continuity of openness and inclusion.

Such emotional support is needed even more for the extension of concern for animals beyond the familiar, near-at-hand, tame mammals children readily directly encounter. With development, care can extend to wild animals and to those far from human scale that play vital roles in ecosystems. This may require greater imaginative reach. An integral extension of care is to realize that animals' environments are important to them and that in some cases the protection of species must take precedence over individuals. These are not trivial challenges psychologically or intellectually, but we have created these choices and must decide them.

On the societal level, continuity depends on complex feedback relations between our representations of ourselves (are we separate from or part of nature?), our forms of thought (do we value artistic and metaphorical ways of affirming our connection?), and our practical action (do we care for, respect, and preserve other life forms?). Our "rationality" needs to be expanded to embrace the inherent values that we learn from the sense of connection. The philosopher David Rothenberg (1991) urged a conception of "a nature which includes us, which *we only understand to the extent which we can find a home* in the enveloping flow of forces which is only ever partially in our control" (p. 245, emphasis added). Finding a *home*—and our place in the family of creatures living there—is at once a cognitive and an affective task. Without this, our unalloyed instrumental rationality—our pursuit of efficiency to the exclusion of higher ends—will ruin the very conditions of our self-in-relation to other species in a defeating feedback of ecological and cultural-psychological destruction. Ultimately, no "transcendent" mind can lift us away from our body or the earthly world from whence both grow. This in turn suggests we should reconsider our self-image as a species, as a separate "humanity."

Appendix:
Methods, Setting, and Subjects

Much of this book relies on my research in one nursery school classroom. This design was the result of my search for optimal conditions in which to explore the patterns in children's relations to animals. By taking an ethnographic and interpretive approach to a single group, I gained a depth of understanding of child and context that would be hard to match any other way (see the work of the childhood ethnographers Thomas Rizzo, William Corsaro, & John Bates, 1992). My research involved an extended series of interactions of many kinds, which I sought to structure so as to answer an evolving set of hunches and to test out an emerging pattern, which this book presents. This appendix gives a more concrete sense of the settings, the actors, and my techniques for readers who want to know more about my methods.

The nursery school classroom where I spent a year in the early 1990s was part of a figure-eight-shaped complex of gray stone buildings serving multiple school grades. The class regularly used the inner play yards and occasionally portions of the neighborhood. The classroom itself was divided into three large areas for different activities: a rug-covered area used for meetings and block and other sorts of play; an area with tables for art, activities, and lunch; and, furthest from the entrance, an area furnished with tables and shelves stocked with materials for carpentry, fantasy play, games, puzzles, books, and so on. This area had the most open feeling because of windows and glass doors to the outside.

The teacher, Mrs. Ray, was a tall, vivacious woman who has been teaching young children for over twenty-five years. She brought tremendous experience, energy, insight, and affection to her relationships with the children. She was equally welcoming to me, willing to throw the doors open and let me get to know her children. Mrs. Ray encouraged science activities and equipped the room richly, including many things from nature. Among these were the resident animals—goldfish, Toad, Snowflake the guinea pig, and the diamond doves.

The classroom housed a two-year preschool program, after which the children go on to kindergarten. The children's ages in the fall ranged from three years, five months, to five years, four months. Of the twenty-five children, fourteen were boys and eleven were girls, but because two half-year children were boys, the ratio was always thirteen to eleven. Facts including age, sex, ethnic background, and whether the child was in the class for his or her first or second year are given in Table A.1. Although few patterns related to ethnicity arose in my analysis, the classroom was diverse, reflecting the international draw of the associated univer-

TABLE A.1   Basic Information on the Subjects (by age)

Name	Sex	Parent's Race/ Ethnicity	1st/2ndYear?	Age in Fall (Years:Months)
Chris	m	F: African-Amer.	1	5:4
Kevin	m	Caucasian	2	5:2
Cassia	f	Jewish-Amer.	2	5:1
Ivy	f	Caucasian	2	5:1
Dawn	f	M: Mexican	2	4:11
Adrienne	f	Caucasian	2	4:11
Joe	m	Caucasian	2	4:9
Benson	m	Caucasian	1	4:8
Drew	m	Caucasian	2	4:7
Abeo	f	Nigerian	2	4:5
Angela	f	Caucasian	2	4:4
Solly	m	Jewish-Amer.	1	4:4
Irvin	m	Chinese	2	4:4
Sam	m	Chinese	2	4:4
Yasmin	f	M: Middle Eastern	2	4:2
Chen	m	Taiwanese	1	not in class (4:9 in May)
Dimitri	m	F: Middle Eastern	2	4:2
Laura	f	Caucasian	1	3:10
Katra	f	Slavic	1	3:10
Mindy	f	Caucasian	1	3:9
Toby	m	Caucasian	1	3:8
Reuben	m	African-Amer.	1	3:8
Billy	m	Jewish-Amer.	1	3:8
Rosa	f	F: Mexican	1	3:6
Scott	m	Middle-Eastern	1	3:5 (in class Fall only)

sity. As a result of high tuition cost and modest financial aid, there was only moderate variation in socioeconomic status. Most parents were in (or preparing for) the professions or business; a few were working class or tradespeople. In many families, both parents were busy full-time.

My activities in the room were varied, but I avoided taking some adult responsibilities. After a period of observing and "gradual field entry" (Rizzo et al., 1992), I began to partake in play, ask questions, and learn from the relationships I developed. I obtained school and parental permission for the research and have preserved the anonymity of all subjects in this book. Whenever I conducted a special activity (such as individual play-interviews), I let each child know what we would do and allowed him or her to choose whether to do it then, later, or not at all.

I used many strategies to learn about the children. I observed all activities with animals, and I observed a subset of children systematically (focal-child sampling). I organized joint play sessions and interviews, and I collected children's stories. All parents completed a questionnaire and parents of focal children kept home journals recording animal-related comments and activities. Mrs. Ray provided further family background information. Finally, I arranged visits by the animals listed in Chapter 1. All animal presenters were expert animal keepers (except for Mr. Grier, a graduate student). Time was spent with each animal as a class and then in groups of four children, all videotaped. These small group sessions allowed the maximum permissible free interaction between child and animal, followed by questions designed to tap the children's perceptions of, and identification with, the animals. My transcriptions of these tapes serve as a major basis of actions and quotes I discuss in this book.

This book, then, works from a thickly contextualized understanding of animals in particular young children's development toward broader patterns that are informed by knowledge of development. It is my hope that the patterns I describe will be both rich enough to be convincing and general enough to be provocative. I hope others will find here departure points for investigation as well as convincing reasons to believe children's involvement with animals is worthy of such attention.

Notes

Chapter 1

1. See, e.g., the work of the cognitive scientist Francisco Varela, the philosopher Evan Thompson, and the psychologist Eleanor Rosch (1991).

2. For a philosophical discussion of the field of self and of a subjectively attuned biology, see the work of the philosopher Neil Evernden (1993).

Chapter 2

1. Although something we cannot yet answer, the exact nature of this process is an important question and a venerable one in anthropology. Many cultures have elaborate systems of *totemism*, often identifying a social group with an animal. Anthropologists report that the Amazonian Bororo claim to *be* red macaws—or, at least, to be metaphorically like them—as opposed to the totem species of other groups (J. Christopher Crocker, 1985; Lucien Levy-Bruhl, 1966). Another anthropologist, Claude Lévi-Strauss, described totemism as a manner of thinking based on a parallel between "*two systems of differences*, one of which occurs in nature and the other in culture" (1966, p. 115). But in which direction does the parallel making move? Some theorists, such as the early French sociologists Emile Durkheim and Marcel Mauss (1903/1963) and the anthropologist A. Irving Hallowell (1960/1975), argue that social or psychological distinctions are extended to the natural realm of species. Another possibility receiving attention recently is that the human mind has a proclivity to create biological species categories of an especially rigid or "essentialist" sort and that these are then extended by analogy to human social groups, thus partly accounting for prejudice (see Hirschfeld & Gelman, 1994). In either case, animal analogies employ the diversity of local fauna to interpret the particular social order.

2. See works by the cultural critic Donna Haraway (1989) and the cultural historian Harriet Ritvo (1995).

3. On feral children, see Chapter 5, Note 2. Robert Kidd (1986) has discussed other themes connecting animals and children in culture.

4. Johnson (1995) discusses primitivism in Hall's recapitulation theory.

5. For other early works by psychologists on children and animals, see W. Fowler Bucke (1903); C. F. Hodge (1902); Susan Isaacs (1930); Arthur Jersild and Frances Holmes (1935); and Mabel Marsh (1902).

6. See Chapter 4 for a further discussion of recent work by Carey and others.

7. Key questions here have been developed by the psychologist Eugene T. Gendlin (1962, 1992).

Chapter 3

1. Preference for interacting with animals was clearly demonstrated by kindergartners studied by the psychologist Barry Brucklacher (1992); these children made significantly more and longer visits to a live guinea pig than to a stuffed one.

2. My procedure was to observe any animal-related activity by the children, but my sampling was not sufficiently focused to catch all guinea pig/child interactions. Thus, the data must be taken as merely suggestive. I also cannot rule out an age explanation, since the average age of the "new" group was seven months less than the "last year" children.

3. Other psychologists have argued that increased empathy or role-taking skills are possible outcomes of children's involvement with animals (Cindee Bailey, 1987; Vanessa Malcarne, 1983; Robert Poresky & Charles Hendrix, 1990). Notably, Martin Hoffman (1987) and Ervin Staub (1986) have linked empathy with moral development.

4. Stern also describes one earlier stage of not-yet-gelled self, the "emergent self."

Chapter 4

1. Alternate parsings are suggested by Watzlawick, Beavin, and Jackson (1967, pp. 54–56).

2. In the following sections, I will discuss children's experience of subjective properties of animals on the assumption this is valid, even if children (or adults) may be wrong on the specifics. Thus, I affirm that agency and so forth *are* attributes of animals (indeed, Stern, 1985, also notes some animals may have "core" selves). The questions of anthropomorphism, and animal consciousness, feeling, and thought are being discussed in many forums, and a full treatment is beyond the scope of this book. Indeed, it constitutes both an urgent social issue and a frontier of science and practice. Provisionally, I take this fairly cautious position: At a minimum, all animals can be described as what the philosopher Daniel Dennett (1987) has called "first-order Intentional systems," that is, they can be validly regarded as agents with beliefs, desires, feelings, and other mental predicates. In science, the idea of animals' subjective worlds goes back at least to founders of ethology such as Jacob von Uexküll. The philosopher Gareth Matthews (1978) and the animal experimentalist Jerry Garcia (1981) have even avowed the strategic employment of such assumptions by behaviorists! Second-order intentionality (e.g., beliefs *about* beliefs) is a much harder question (related issues, such as the child's explicit belief in animal mental states, are discussed in the next chapter). But I disagree with assertions like that of the philosopher Donald Davidson (1985) that "a crea-

ture cannot have thoughts unless it is the interpreter of the speech of another" (p. 25). In an excellent discussion of Davidson's position, the philosopher John Fisher (1987) provides this paraphrase: "Beliefs only arise in the process of interpreting the utterances of a linguistic community." This confuses first- and second-order systems. In a milder version of his argument, Davidson said it is inaccurate to attribute to animals thoughts containing distinctions embodied in our linguistic expressions, but that there are thoughts that cannot be formulated in words, and animals might have these (Fisher, 1987), I would leave even more open, on methodological grounds. Sentiments such as those just cited seem overly concerned with marking boundaries based on ignorance. We have yet to test the limits of our own capacities to understand others, and even to appreciate the difficulties involved. On these issues, see the philosophers Harvey Sarles (1977), Richard Routley (1981), and Mary Midgley (1983); the Dutch human-animal writer Noske (1989, 1992); the philosopher Deborah Moore and the sociologist James Hannon (1993); and the sociologists Clinton Sanders and Arnold Arluke (1993). Also consider the difficulties surmounted by the chimpanzee and Bonobo language researcher E. Sue Savage-Rumbaugh (1986) and other animal researchers. Imaginative possibilities are pioneered by the animal trainer and writer Vicki Hearne (1986), the ethologist Robert Mitchell (1987), and the writer Elizabeth Marshall Thomas (1993). No mental predicates should be dismissed without contemplating such compendia of research on animal sensation, perception, cognition, and emotion as those by the Harvard cognitive ethologist Donald Griffin (1992) and the writers Jeffrey Masson and Susan McCarthy (1995). Such authors call for shifting the burden of proof to those who deny animal subjectivity in the face of the evidence available. Finally, much work remains to be done to understand species-specific semiotics (see the comment by the sociobiologist Robert Trivers, 1991).

3. The French animal behaviorists Jean-Louis Millot and Jean-Claude Filiatre (1986) noted that children avoid getting close to a dog's muzzle.

4. But the roles are not necessarily evenly shared. In a study of children and their dogs, Millot and Filiatre (1986) found that although 70 percent of the dog's actions were followed by a modification in the child's behavior, only 40 percent of the child's actions produced a response in the dog.

5. The Dutch educator Margadant-van Arcken (1984, 1989) noted touching (and the passion for knowing animals' names) in her early observations of children and live animals. Millot and Filiatre (1986) observed that young children touched their pet dogs in 68 percent of interactions.

6. The perception of animal vitality affect and its effects on the person may be unconscious. It might explain a number of findings, e.g., why aquaria of fish, dogs, or other animals lower adults' and children's blood pressure readings, even in stressful situations; see, e.g., the work of the researchers Aaron Katcher, Erika Friedmann, Alan Beck, and James Lynch (1983).

7. Note that we are considering near-human-scale nonwild animals. But those who sensitively watch even very small creatures under the microscope may also

respond to evident agency, coherence, etc.—see an example provided by the Norwegian philosopher Arne Naess (1986/1988) for an example. Wild animals show all animate properties, but with much less opportunity for relationships to develop; on children's attitudes to wildlife, see the work of the Yale researchers Stephen Kellert and Miriam Westervelt (1983).

8. This book is unusual in dealing with human-animal interactions across a range of phyla, orders, and species, as well as across stereotypical pet and nonpet species, but others have called for such study also, including the psychologists Timothy Eddy (1995); Aline Kidd, Hellen Kelley, and Robert Kidd (1983); and Julia Nielsen and Lloyd Delude (1989).

9. The psychologists James Hillman (1991) and Stephen Kellert (1993) have listed several factors behind the radical "otherness" of insects: they have differing spatial-temporal ecological survival strategies; they have a "multiplicity" that affronts selfhood; they have "monstrous" forms; they are associated with mindlessness and absence of feeling; and they demonstrate radical "autonomy" from human will and control.

10. How the child's cognitive categories (of animals, and in the child's theory of mind) relate to interactional variation is a topic ripe for future research based on findings presented here.

11. Similarly, Millot and Filiatre (1986) observed that interactions with dogs necessarily differ from those with other children, because the rates of response differ.

12. See, e.g., the psychologists Bruno Bettelheim (1976); Marcel Heiman (1956); Kerstin Kupferman (1977); Ivan Sherick (1981); and Robert Van de Castle (1983).

13. The implications of attachment for the study of child-pet relations have been definitively described by the psychologist Gail Melson (1990), who discusses four dimensions: time with pet, affect, knowledge, and responsiveness to the pet.

14. Our discussion here omits interpretation of the animal's side of the bond, though it is surely real and important—companion animals are attached to their owners.

15. An important early report on unresponsive psychiatric patients' successes with dogs is by the psychiatrists Samuel Corson, Elizabeth Corson, Peter Gwynne, and Eugene Arnold (1977). The psychologists Laurel Redefer and Joan Goodman (1989) found autistic children's social exchanges were dramatically increased during and immediately after animal intervention; other studies have since confirmed this effect. The child therapist Gerald Mallon (1992) reviews animals in child therapy. For more on how pets contribute to social development, see Bryant (1986); A. H. Kidd and R. M. Kidd (1990a, 1990b); Melson (1990, 1991); Melson and the developmental psychologist Alan Fogel (1988); Myers (1986, 1994); Poresky and Hendrix (1990); the German psychologists Detlef Rost and Anette Hartmann (1994); and several authors in the volume edited by the family researcher Marvin Sussman (1985), among others.

16. See the work of the historian Gerald Carson (1972); Diamond (1993); the psychologist Harold Herzog and the animal behaviorist Gordon Burghardt (1987);

the anthropologist of human-animal relations Elizabeth Lawrence (1982); Menninger (1951); Tuan (1984).

17. The perspective I am developing here is in line with theorists who stressed the social self. New concepts about how we understand others are required. For instance, the social psychologist James Youniss (1983) criticizes the concept that "taking the role of the other" equals "understanding" the other, because it assumes there is not the communication requisite to knowing the other in the first place. Similarly, the philosopher Lawrence Blum (1987) argues that the idea that "projection" entails imagining how one would feel and attributing that feeling to the other assumes too sharp a self-other boundary, one too cognitively demanding for very young children who, counterfactually, *do* understand others. Instead, he claims, "Our ability to grasp another's condition is a more fundamental cognitive process that more specialized uses of inference can only build upon but not replace." One attempt to describe such a process is the philosopher Nel Noddings's (1984) suggestion that it is not by projection but by receptivity or "taking in" the other that the child opens himself or herself to the differences and feelings of the other. Blum (1987) characterizes such responsiveness to others as an "immediate and non-inferential grasp of another's feelings" (p. 315). New work stemming from the psychologist James Gibson's (1979) ecological theory of perception and from the previously mentioned area of infants' perceptual abilities strengthens such assertions. This study of children with different animals contributes to this direction in contemporary psychology.

18. On children and animal abuse, see Ascione (1993) and Felthous and Kellert (1987). Corson et al (1977, p. 72) discuss "security by rank," perhaps a kindred phenomenon.

Chapter 5

1. See Chapter 4, note 2.

2. We might be more certain that it *only* arises within human relationships had the few authentic cases of "feral children" raised by nonhuman animals been studied for the possibility that the child's interaffective abilities can work within other species' repertoires of mood and signal. On feral children, see Lucien Malson's assessment and reprinting of Jean Itard's (1799/1964/1972) *The wild boy of Aveyron*; the work of the psychologists Mary McNeil, Edward Polloway and David Smith (1984); and the work of the Indian Reverend J. A. L. Singh and author R. M. Zingg (1939), who cared for the "wolf children" Amala and Kamala. Noske (1989) proposed studying such cases to better understand animals.

3. Selective attunement specifies a nonpsychoanalytic account of feelings similar to those discussed in Freud's (1913/1950) statement that opened Chapter 2.

4. Sure examples are in Savage-Rumbaugh's (1986, Savage-Rumbaugh et al., 1993) chimpanzee and bonobo language studies.

5. The psychologist Ken Shapiro (1989) has described precisely this process in "keep-away" with a dog.

6. Ricard and Allard's (1993) research documents an early step in this development.

7. Research to date on the child's theory of mind has not dealt extensively with attribution of mental properties to nonhuman animals. Other work on children's biological reasoning shows their strong tendency to think of animal properties according to innate potentials and maintenance-of-identity components of an essentialist view (Gelman et al., 1994). An interesting inquiry at the intersection of these domains would be whether and when young children think different species have different traitlike mental qualities. Their tendency to see immanent causes behind animate action, together with their ability to register differences in interactive qualities reported here, suggests they might.

8. It could be argued that children are in a favorable position to discover whatever shared communication *is* possible with animals, because they regard animal action as communicative. Even if one lowers the threshold of what is considered conventional and reversible, however, animals in the naturalistic setting of this study did not qualify. This is not to say that under no circumstances *could* they. See Sanders and Arluke (1993) for a consideration of the possibilities for enhancing communication with animals. See Dennett (1995) for a more qualified appraisal of our potential for understanding animal consciousness.

9. This expectation was also shown by the children in Millot and Filiatre's (1986) study, who gestured more to their dogs when in front of the dogs and used physical contact more when positioned behind them.

10. In my work, I did not examine attribution of second-order intentionality (such as communicative intent) according to species. But the psychologists Timothy Eddy and Gordon Gallup and the anthropologist Daniel Povinelli (1993) found that adults attribute more higher-order intentionality the more they perceive the animal as similar to humans.

11. Indeed, classical ethology was able to proceed in cataloguing animal behavior partly because its methodology assumed behavior is transparent. The functions of behavior may not be apparent at first, but the behaviors themselves are relied on as unproblematic data. Only recently has a challenge been raised (Griffin, 1976, 1992).

12. Mallon (1994) found that seven- to sixteen-year-olds in a treatment center spoke to farm animals because they were sure their words would not be repeated.

13. For example, Sanders (1990, 1993) brilliantly describes owner-dog behavior in public, following the sociologist Erving Goffman's (1959) perspective of social impression management.

Chapter 6

1. This and the following are indebted to Hanson (1986, especially chap. 3).

2. The probability of the relationship I found occurring by chance alone is given by the Fisher exacta test as 0.048, or less than one in twenty.

3. One commonality between Chen, Billy, Yasmin, and Rosa is that they are younger than average. Drew, a few months to a year older than these four, liked to pretend to be "baby animals, after his bath . . . [a] different one each time." But "Drew hasn't been playing this game in the last few months." One might be tempted to suppose that age is a factor here, but older children accounted for more of the animal-pretend episodes in school. And some of these kids were not reported to pretend at home, i.e., Ivy, Dawn, and Benson (of these, only Ivy had no pets at home). Thus, the context—home or school—may interact with age and exposure to pets, but the question awaits more focused study.

4. The human ecologist Paul Shepard (1978) was among the first to draw attention to animals in children's pretend play and in cognitive development. I hope that this book will substantiate cognate insights for a broader community of psychologists.

5. Analogous pairs of terms are the sociologist Anthony Giddens's (1979) discursive versus practical consciousness, Grice's (1957) nonnatural meanings versus natural meanings, and Bruner's (1986) paradigmatic versus narrative thought.

6. See, e.g., works by the psychologist Eugene Gendlin (1962, 1992).

7. Some argue this is "intersubjectivity," but I have followed Stern's (1985) stricter criteria.

8. Thus, de Gramont argues that confusion about language (not egocentrism) leads to the phenomena Piaget (1929/1960) termed realism and animism.

9. For a thorough discussion, see de Gramont (1990, chaps. 1 and 6).

10. See, e.g., the historian Sabine Baring-Gould (1865/1995), and the psychiatrists Aaron Kulick, Harrison Pope, and Paul Keck (1990).

11. Arluke and Sax's important 1992 study places this evidence in the context of multiple blurrings of the meaning of human and animal, all of which served Nazi ends.

Chapter 7

1. This question was not asked about the dog.

2. Each of these three was in a separate small group, so they probably did not influence each other's immediate responses.

References

Alibali, M. W., & Goldin-Meadow, S. (1993). Gesture-speech mismatch and mechanisms of learning: What the hands reveal about a child's state of mind. *Cognitive Psychology 24*(4), 468–523.

Aristotle (1984). "Rhetoric." In J. Barnes (Ed.), *The Complete Works of Aristotle* Vol. 2 (Revised Oxford Translation). Princeton, NJ: Princeton Univ. Press.

Arluke, A., & Sax, B. (1992). Understanding Nazi animal protection and the holocaust. *Anthrozoös, 5*(1), 6–31.

Ascione, F. R. (1993). Children who are cruel to animals: A review of research and implications for developmental psychopathology. *Anthrozoös 6*(4), 226–247.

Ashcraft, R. (1972). Leviathan triumphant: Thomas Hobbes and the politics of wild men. In E. Dudley & M. E. Novak (Eds.), *The wild man within: An image in Western thought from the Renaissance to Romanticism* (pp. 141–181). Pittsburgh, PA: University of Pittsburgh.

Ashley-Montagu, M. F. (1937). *Coming into being among the Australian Aborigines: A study of procreative beliefs of the native tribes of Australia.* London: George Routledge.

Astington, J. W. (1993). *The child's discovery of the mind.* Cambridge, MA: Harvard University.

Avis, J., & Harris, P. L. (1991). Belief-desire reasoning among Baka children: Evidence for a universal conception of mind. *Child Development, 62,* 460–467.

Bailey, C. (1987). Exposure of preschool children to companion animals: Impact on role-taking skills. *Dissertation Abstracts International, 48*(08), 1976A.

Barba, B. E. (1995). A critical review of research on the human/companion animal relationship: 1988 to 1993. *Anthrozoös, 8*(1), 9–15.

Baring-Gould, S. (1995). *The book of werewolves.* London: Senate/Studio. (Original work published 1865)

Bates, E. (1976). *Language and context: The acquisition of pragmatics.* New York: Academic Press.

Bates, E. (1979). Intentions, conventions and symbols. In E. Bates (Ed.), *The emergence of symbols: Cognition and communication in infancy* (pp. 33–68). New York: Academic Press.

Bateson, G. (1972). *Steps to an ecology of mind.* New York: Ballantine.

Bateson, G., Jackson, D., Haley, J., & Weakland, J. (1956). Toward a theory of schizophrenia. *Behavioral Science, 1,* 251–264.

Beck, A. H., & Katcher, A. H. (1983). *Between pets and people.* New York: Putnam.

Berger, J. (1980). Why look at animals? In *About looking.* New York: Pantheon.

Berger, P. L., & Luckmann, T. (1966). *The social construction of reality*. Garden City, NY: Doubleday.

Bertenthal, B. (1993). Infants' perception of biomechanical motions: Intrinsic image and knowledge-based constraints. In C. Granrud (Ed.), *Visual perception and cognition in infancy* (pp. 175–214). Hillsdale, NJ: Lawrence Erlbaum.

Bettelheim, B. (1976). *The uses of enchantment*. New York: Vintage.

Blount, M. (1974). *Animal land: The creatures of children's fiction*. London: Hutchinson.

Blum, L. (1987). Particularity and responsiveness. In J. Kagan & S. Lamb (Eds.), *The emergence of morality in young children* (pp. 306–337). Chicago: University of Chicago Press.

Borges, J. L., & Guerrero, M. (1974). *The book of imaginary beings* (N. T. di Giovanni, Trans.). Middlesex, UK: Penguin. (Original work published 1967)

Borstelmann, L. J. (1983). Children before psychology: Ideas about children from late antiquity to the late 1800s. In P. Mussen & W. Kessen (Eds.), *Handbook of child psychology: Vol. 1. History, theory and methods* (4th ed., pp. 1–40). New York: Wiley.

Bowlby, J. (1969). *Attachment and loss: Vol. 1: Attachment*. New York: Basic Books.

Brazelton, T. B., Tronick, E., & Main, M. (1974). The origins of reciprocity. In M. Lewis & L. Rosenblum (Eds.), *The effect of the infant on its caregiver* (pp. 49–76). New York: Wiley.

Bregman, E. (1934). An attempt to modify emotional attitude of infants by the conditioned response technique. *Journal of Genetic Psychology, 45,* 169–198.

Brucklacher, B. (1992). The effects of live- and stuffed-animal displays on the behaviors and attitudes of kindergarten students. *Dissertation Abstracts International, 53*(05), 1392A.

Bruner, J. (1969). Modalities of memory. In G. Talland & N. Waugh (Eds.), *The pathology of memory*. New York: Academic Press.

Bruner, J. (1986). *Actual minds, possible worlds*. Cambridge, MA: Harvard University.

Bryant, B. K. (1986, August). *The relevance of family and neighborhood animals to social-emotional development in middle childhood*. Abstract of paper presented at meeting of the Delta Society, Boston.

Bucke, W. F. (1903). Children's thoughts, reactions and feelings toward pet dogs. *Pedagogical Seminary (Journal of Genetic Psychology), 10,* 459–513.

Carey, S. (1985). *Conceptual change in childhood*. Cambridge: MIT Press.

Carroll, L. (1946). *Through the looking glass*. New York: Random House. (Original work published 1871)

Carson, G. 1972. *Men, beasts and gods: A history of cruelty and kindness to animals*. New York: Scribner.

Carson, H. (1917). The trial of animals and insects: A little known chapter of medieval jurisprudence. *American Philosophy, 56,* 410–415.

Cirillo, L., & Wapner, S. (Eds.). (1986). *Value presuppositions in theories of human development*. Hillsdale, NJ: Lawrence Erlbaum.

Cohen, E. (1994). Animals in medieval perceptions: The image of the ubiquitous other. In A. Manning & J. Serpell (Eds.), *Animals and society: Changing perspectives* (pp. 59–80). New York: Routledge.

Clark, E. (1979). Building a vocabulary: Words for objects, actions, and relations. In P. Fletcher & M. Garmon (Eds.), *Language acquisition: Studies in first language development* (pp. 149–160). Cambridge, UK: Cambridge University Press.

Coley, J. D. (1995). Emerging differentiation of folkbiology and folkpsychology: Attributions of biological and psychological properties to living things. *Child Development, 66*(6), 1856–1874.

Corsaro, W. A. (1985). *Friendship and peer culture in the early years.* Norwood, NJ: Ablex.

Corson, S. A., Corson, E. O'L., Gwynne, P. H., & Arnold, L. E. (1977). Pet dogs as nonverbal communication links in hospital psychiatry. *Comprehensive Psychiatry, 18*, 61–72.

Crocker, J. C. (1985). My brother the parrot. In G. Urton (Ed.), *Animal myths and metaphors in South America* (pp. 13–47). Salt Lake City, UT: University of Utah Press.

Csikszentmihalyi, M. (1990). *Flow: The psychology of optimal experience.* New York: Harper & Row.

Damon, W., & Hart, D. (1988). *Self-understanding in childhood and adolescence.* Cambridge, UK: Cambridge University Press.

Darwin, C. (1874). *The descent of man and selection in relation to sex* (2nd ed.). New York: Appleton. (Original work published 1871)

Darwin, C. (1965). *The expression of emotion in man and animals.* Chicago: University of Chicago Press. (Original work published 1872)

Davidson, D. (1985). *Inquiries into truth and interpretation.* Oxford, UK: Clarendon.

Davis, H., & Balfour, D. (Eds.). (1992). *The inevitable bond: Examining scientist-animal interaction.* Cambridge, UK: Cambridge University Press.

de Gramont, P. (1990). *Language and the distortion of meaning.* New York: New York University Press.

Dennett, D. C. (1978). Beliefs about beliefs. *Behavioral and Brain Sciences, 1,* 568–570.

Dennett, D. C. (1987). *The intentional stance.* Cambridge: MIT Press.

Dennett, D. C. (1995). Animal consciousness: What matters and why. *Social Research, 62*(3), 691–710.

de Saussure, F. (1959). *Course in general linguistics.* New York: Philosophical Library.

Descartes, R. (1971). Discourse on method. In *Descartes philosophical writings* (E. Anscombe & P. T. Geech, Trans. & Ed.). Indianapolis, IN: Bobbs-Merrill. (Original work published 1637)

Descartes, R. (1972). *Treatise of man.* (T. S. Hall, Trans.). Cambridge, UK: Harvard University Press. (Original work published 1632)

Diamond, J. (1992). *The third chimpanzee.* New York: HarperCollins.

Diamond, J. (1993). New Guineans and their natural world. In S. R. Kellert & E. O. Wilson (Eds.), *The biophilia hypothesis* (pp. 251–271). San Francisco: Island Press.

Douglas, M. (1975). *Implicit meanings: Essays in anthropology*. Boston: Routledge & Kegan Paul.

Durkheim, E., & Mauss, M. (1963). *Primitive classification*. Chicago: University of Chicago Press. (Original work published 1903)

Eddy, T. J. (1995). Human cardiac responses to familiar young chimpanzees. *Anthrozoös, 8*(4), 235–243.

Eddy, T. J., Gallup, G., & Povinelli, D. (1993). Attribution of cognitive states to animals: Anthropomorphism in comparative perspective. *Journal of Social Issues, 49*(1), 87–101.

Erikson, E. H. (1958). *Young man Luther: A study in psychoanalysis and history*. New York: Norton.

Evans-Pritchard, E. E. (1940). *The Nuer*. Oxford, UK: Oxford University Press.

Evernden, N. (1993). *The natural alien: Humankind and environment* (2nd ed.). Toronto: University of Toronto Press.

Felthous, A. R., & Kellert, S. R. (1987). Childhood cruelty to animals and later aggression against people: A review. *American Journal of Psychiatry, 144*(7), 10–17.

Fernandez, J. W. (1986). *Persuasions and performances: The play of tropes in culture*. Bloomington, IN: Indiana University Press.

Fisher, J. A. (1987). Taking sympathy seriously: A defense of our moral psychology toward animals. *Environmental Ethics, 9,* 197–215.

Flavell, J. H., Green, F. L., & Flavell, E. R. (1986). Development of knowledge about the appearance-reality distinction. *Monographs of the Society for Research in Child Development, 51*(1, Serial No. 212).

Freud, S. (1950). *Totem and taboo: Some points of agreement between the mental lives of savages and neurotics* (J. Strachey, Trans.). New York: Norton. (Original work published 1913)

Freud, S. (1955). Analysis of a phobia in a five-year-old boy "Little Hans." In J. Strachey (Ed. & Trans.), *Case histories* (Vol. 1, pp. 165–312). Middlesex, UK: Pelican. (Original work published 1909)

Freud, S. (1965). *The interpretation of dreams* (J. Strachey, Trans.). New York: Avon/Basic. (Original work published 1900)

Frith, U. (1989). *Autism: Explaining the Enigma*. Oxford: Basil Blackwell.

Garcia, J. (1981). Tilting at the paper mills of academe. *American Psychologist, 36*(2), 149–158.

Gardner, H. (1983). *Frames of mind*. New York: Basic Books.

Gelman, S. A., Coley, J. D., & Gottfried, G. M. (1994). Essentialist beliefs in children: The acquisition of concepts and theories. In L. A. Hirschfeld & S. A. Gelman (Eds.), *Mapping the mind: Domain specificity in cognition and culture* (pp. 341–365). Cambridge, UK: Cambridge University Press.

Gendlin, E. T. (1962). *Experiencing and the creation of meaning: A philosophical and psychological approach to the subjective*. New York: Macmillan.

Gendlin, E. T. (1992). The primacy of the body, not the primacy of perception. *Man and World, 25*(3–4), 341–353.

Gibson, J. J. (1979). *The ecological approach to visual perception.* Boston: Houghton Mifflin.

Giddens, A. (1979). *Central problems in social theory.* London: Macmillan.

Gillberg, C., & Rasmussen, P. (1994). Brief report: Four case histories and a literature review of Williams syndrome and autistic behavior. *Journal of Autism and Developmental Disorders, 24* (3), 381–393.

Gilligan, C., & Wiggins, G. (1987). The origins of morality in early childhood relationships. In J. Kagan & S. Lamb (Eds.), *The emergence of morality in young children* (pp. 277–305). Chicago: University of Chicago Press.

Goffman, E. (1959). *The presentation of self in everyday life.* Garden City, NY: Doubleday.

Golinkoff, R. M., & Halperin, M. S. (1983). The concept of animal: One infant's view. *Infant Behavior and Development, 6,* 229–233.

Gopnik, A. (1982). Words and plans: Early language and the development of intelligent action. *Journal of Child Language, 9,* 303–318.

Gopnik, A., & Astington, J. W. (1988). Children's understanding of representational change and its relation to their understanding of false belief and the appearance-reality distinction. *Child Development, 58,* 26–37.

Gould, S. J. (1977). *Ontogeny and phylogeny.* Cambridge, MA: Harvard University Press.

Grene, M. (1968). *Approaches to a philosophical biology.* New York: Basic Books.

Grice, H. P. (1957). Meaning. *Philosophical Review, 66,* 377–388.

Grice, H. P. (1975). Logic and conversation. In P. Cole & J. L. Morgan (Eds.), *Syntax and semantics: 3. Speech acts* (pp. 43–58). New York: Academic Press.

Griffin, D. R. (1976). *The question of animal awareness: Evolutionary continuity of mental experience.* New York: Rockefeller University Press.

Griffin, D. R. (1992). *Animal minds.* Chicago: University of Chicago Press.

Hall, G. S. (1897). A study of fears. *American Journal of Psychology, 8,* 147–249.

Hall, G. S., & Browne, C. E. (1904). The cat and the child. *Pedagogical Seminary (Journal of Genetic Psychology), 11,* 3–29.

Hallowell, A. I. (1975). Ojibwa ontology, behavior, and world view. In D. Tedlock & B. Tedlock (Eds.), *Teachings from the American earth* (pp. 141–178). New York: Liveright. (Original work published 1960)

Hanson, K. (1986). *The self imagined: Philosophical reflections on the social character of the psyche.* New York: Routledge & Kegan Paul.

Haraway, D. (1989). *Primate visions: Gender, race and nature in the world of modern science.* New York: Routledge.

Hearne, V. (1986). *Adam's task: Calling animals by name.* New York: Vintage.

Heidegger, M. (1962). *Being and time.* New York: Harper & Row.

Heiman, M. (1956). The relationship between man and dog. *Psychoanalytic Quarterly, 25,* 568–585.

Herzog, H. A., & Burghardt, G. M. (1987). Attitudes toward animals: Origins and diversity. *Anthrozoös, 1*(4), 214–222.

Hillman, J. (1991). *Going bugs.* Gracie Sta., NY: Spring Audio.

Hinde, R. A. (1976). On describing relationships. *Journal of Child Psychology and Psychiatry, 17,* 1–19.

Hirschfeld, L., & Gelman, S. (Eds.). (1994). *Mapping the mind: Domain specificity in cognition and culture.* Cambridge, UK: Cambridge University Press.

Hirsh-Pasek, K., & Treiman, R. (1982). Doggerel: Motherese in a new context. *Journal of Child Language, 9,* 229–237.

Hobbes, T. (1965). *Leviathan* (W. G. Pogson Smith, Ed.). Oxford, UK: Oxford University Press. (Original work published 1651)

Hodge, C. F. (1902). *Nature study and life.* Boston: Ginn.

Hoffman, M. (1987). The contribution of empathy to justice and moral judgment. In N. Eisenberg & J. Strayer (Eds.), *Empathy and its development* (pp. 47–80). Cambridge, UK: Cambridge University Press.

Ingold, T. (1988a). Introduction. In T. Ingold (Ed.), *What is an animal?* (pp. 1–16). London: Unwin Hyman.

Ingold, T. (1988b). The animal in the study of humanity. In T. Ingold (Ed.), *What is an animal?* (pp. 84–99). London: Unwin Hyman.

Isaacs, S. (1930). *Intellectual growth in young children.* New York: Harcourt, Brace.

James, W. (1890). *The principles of psychology.* New York: Dover.

James, W. (1961). *Psychology: The briefer course.* New York: Harper. (Original work published 1892)

Jersild, A., & Holmes, F. B. (1935). Children's fears. *Child Development Monographs, 20.* New York: Teachers College Press.

Johnson, A. (1995). Constructing the child in psychology: The child-as-primitive in Hall and Piaget. *Journal of Phenomenological Psychology, 26*(2), 35–57.

Jung, C. G. (1971). *The portable Jung.* (B. F. C. Hall, Trans., & J. Campbell, Ed.). New York: Viking.

Kagan, J. (1984). *The nature of the child.* New York: Basic Books.

Kagan, J. (1990). The concepts of self: A dialogue. In D. Cicchetti & M. Beeghly (Eds.), *The self in transition: Infancy to childhood* (pp. 363–383). Chicago: University of Chicago Press.

Katcher, A., Friedmann, E., Beck, A., & Lynch, J. (1983). Looking, talking and blood pressure: The physiological consequences of interaction with the living environment. In A. Katcher & A. Beck (Eds.), *New perspectives on our lives with companion animals* (pp. 351–359). Philadelphia: University of Pennsylvania Press.

Kaylor, M. A. (1909). Feelings, thought and conduct of children toward animal pets. *Journal of Genetic Psychology, 16,* 205–239.

Keil, F. C. (1990). *Concepts, kinds and cognitive development.* Cambridge: MIT Press.

Kellert, S. R. (1993). The biological basis for human values of nature. In S. R. Kellert & E. O. Wilson (Eds.), *The biophilia hypothesis* (pp. 42–69). Washington DC: Island Press.

Kellert, S. R., & Westervelt, M. O. (1983). *Children's attitudes, knowledge and behaviors toward animals (Phase 5)*. Washington DC: U.S. Fish and Wildlife Service.

Kessen, W. (1965). *The child*. New York: Wiley.

Kidd, A. H., Kelly, H., & Kidd, R. (1983). Personality characteristics of horse, turtle, snake and bird owners. *Psychological Reports, 52,* 719–729.

Kidd, A. H., & Kidd, R. M. (1987a). Reactions of infants and toddlers to live and toy animals. *Psychological Reports, 61,* 455–464.

Kidd, A. H., & Kidd, R. M. (1987b). Seeking a theory of the human/companion animal bond. *Anthrozoös, 1*(3), 140–157.

Kidd, A. H., & Kidd, R. M. (1990a). Factors in children's attitudes toward pets. *Psychological Reports, 66,* 775–786.

Kidd, A. H., & Kidd, R. M. (1990b). Social and environmental influences on children's attitudes toward pets. *Psychological Reports, 67,* 807–818.

Kidd, R. M. (1986, August). *Children and animals: Symbol and reality.* Abstract of paper presented at meeting of the Delta Society, Boston.

Kulick, A. R., Pope, H. G., Jr., & Keck, P. E., Jr. (1990). Lycanthropy and self-identification. *Journal of Nervous and Mental Disease, 178*(2), 134–137.

Kupferman, K. (1977). A latency boy's identity as a cat. *Psychoanalytic Study of the Child, 32,* 363–385.

Lakoff, G. (1987). *Women, fire and dangerous things*. Chicago: University of Chicago Press.

Langdon, T. (1975). *Food restrictions in the medical system of the Barasana and Taiwano Indians of the Colombian Northwest Amazon*. Doctoral dissertation, Tulane University, New Orleans, LA.

Lawrence, E. A. (1982). *Rodeo: An anthropologist looks at the wild and the tame*. Chicago: University of Chicago Press.

Le Guin, U. K. (1990). *Buffalo gals*. New York: Penguin.

Leslie, A. M. (1991). The theory of mind impairment in autism: Evidence for a modular mechanism of development? In A. Whiten (Ed.), *Natural theories of mind: Evolution, development and simulation of everyday mindreading* (pp. 63–78). Oxford, UK: Basil Blackwell.

Lévi-Strauss, C. (1966). *The savage mind*. Chicago: University of Chicago Press.

Levinson, B. M. (1969). *Pet-oriented child psychotherapy*. Springfield, IL: Charles C. Thomas.

Levy-Bruhl, L. (1966). *How natives think*. New York: Washington Square Press.

Linzey, A. (1990). For God so loved the world. *Between the Species, 6*(1), 12–16.

Lorenz, K. Z. (1962). *King Solomon's ring*. New York: Time. (Original work published 1952)

Lovejoy, A. (1961). *The great chain of being*. Cambridge, MA: Harvard University Press. (Original work published 1936)

Maccoby, E. (1980). *Social development: Psychological growth and the parent-child relationship.* New York: Harcourt, Brace, Jovanovich.

Malcarne, V. (1983). *North American Association for Humane Education special report: Empathy and humane education.* East Haddam, CT: North American Association for Humane Education.

Mallon, G. P. (1992). Utilization of animals as therapeutic adjuncts with children and youths: A review of the literature. *Child and Youth Care Forum, 21*(1), 53–67.

Mallon, G. P. (1994). Cow as co-therapist: Utilization of farm animals as therapeutic aides with children in residential treatment. *Child and Adolescent Social Work Journal, 11*(6), 455–474.

Malson, L., & Itard, J. M. G. (1972). *Wolf children and the problem of human nature* and *The wild boy of Aveyron* (E. Fawcett, P. Ayrton, & J. White, Trans.). New York: Monthly Review Press. (Malson's original work published in French 1964; Itard's original work published 1799)

Margadant-van Arcken, M. (1984). "There's a real dog in the classroom?": The relationship between young children and animals. *Children's Environment Quarterly, 1*(3), 13–16.

Margadant-van Arcken, M. (1989). Environmental education, children and animals. *Anthrozoös, 3*(1), 14–19.

Marsh, M. A. (1902). Children and animals. In E. Barnes (Ed.), *Studies in Education, 2* (pp. 83–99). New York: Stechert.

Masson, J. M., & McCarthy, S. (1995). *When elephants weep: The emotional lives of animals.* New York: Delacorte.

Matthews, G. B. (1978). Animals and the unity of psychology. *Philosophy, 53,* 437–454.

McNeil, M. C., Polloway, E. A., & Smith, J. D. (1984). Feral and isolated children: Historical review and analysis. *Education and Training of the Mentally Retarded, 19*(1), 70–79.

McNeill, D. (1992). *Hand and mind: What gestures reveal about thought.* Chicago: University of Chicago Press.

Mead, G. H. (1913). The social self. *The Journal of Philosophy, Psychology, and Scientific Methods, 10,* 374–380.

Mead, G. H. (1962). *Mind, self and society from the standpoint of a social behaviorist.* Chicago: University of Chicago Press. (Original work published 1934)

Melson, G. (1990). Studying children's attachment to their pets: A conceptual and methodological review. *Anthrozoös, 4*(2), 91–99.

Melson, G. (1991, April). *The relationship between children's attachment to pets and socioemotional development.* Paper presented at the biennial meeting of the Society for Research in Child Development, Seattle.

Melson, G. F., & Fogel, A. (1988). Children's ideas about animal young and their care: A reassessment of gender differences in the development of nurturance. *Anthrozoös, 2*(4), 265–273.

Meltzoff, A., & Gopnik, A. (1993). The role of imitation in understanding persons and developing a theory of mind. In S. Baron-Cohen, H. Tager-Flusberg, & D. Cohen (Eds.), *Understanding other minds: Perspectives from autism* (pp. 335–366). New York: Oxford University Press.

Menninger, K. A. (1951). Totemic aspects of contemporary attitudes toward animals. In G. B. Wilber & W. Muensterberger (Eds.), *Psychoanalysis and culture: Essays in honor of Géza Róheim* (pp. 42–74). New York: International Universities Press.

Merleau-Ponty, M. (1962). *Phenomenology of perception* (C. Smith, Trans.). London: Routledge. (Original work published 1945)

Midgley, M. (1983). *Animals and why they matter*. Athens, GA: University of Georgia Press.

Midgley, M. (1988). Beasts, brutes and monsters. In T. Ingold (Ed.), *What is an animal?* (pp. 35–46). London: Unwin Hyman.

Miller, P. J., & Hoogstra, L. (1989, November). *How to represent the native child's point of view: Methodological problems in language socialization*. Paper presented at the meeting of the American Anthropological Association, Washington, DC.

Millot, J.-L., & Filiatre, J.-C. (1986). The behavior sequences in the communication system between the child and his pet dog. *Applied Animal Behaviour Science, 16,* 383–390.

Mitchell, R. W. (1987). Projects, routines, and enticements in interspecies play between familiar and unfamiliar dogs and people. *Dissertation Abstracts International, 8*(07), 2136B.

Moore, D. E., & Hannon, J. T. (1993). Animal behavior science as a social science: The success of the empathic approach in research on apes. *Anthrozoös, 4*(3), 173–189.

Myers, O. E., Jr. (1986). *Symbolic ethology: The role of animal symbols in socialization*. Unpublished manuscript, University of Chicago, Chicago.

Myers, O. E., Jr. (1994). *Young children's sense of connection to animals: The developmental basis of an ecological self*. Doctoral dissertation, University of Chicago, Chicago.

Naess, A. (1988). Self realization: An ecological approach to being in the world. In J. Seed, J. Macy, P. Fleming, & N. Naess, *Thinking like a mountain* (pp. 19–30). Philadelphia: New Society Publishers. (Originally delivered as the Fourth Keith Roby Memorial Lecture, Murdoch University, Murdoch, Australia, March 12, 1986)

Nelson, K. A. (Ed.). (1989). *Narratives from the crib*. Cambridge, MA: Harvard University Press.

Nelson, R. K. (1983). *Make prayers to the raven: A Koyukan view of the northern forest*. Chicago: University of Chicago Press.

Nielsen, J. A., & Delude, L. A. (1989). Behavior of young children in the presence of different kinds of animals. *Anthrozoös, 3*(2), 119–129.

Noddings, N. (1984). *Caring: A feminine approach to ethics and moral education*. Berkeley: University of California Press.

Noske, B. (1989). *Humans and other animals: Beyond the boundaries of anthropology*. London: Pluto.

Noske, B. (1992). Deconstructing the animal image: Toward an anthropology of animals. *Anthrozoös, 5(4)*, 226–230.

Perner, J., Leekam, S., & Wimmer, H. (1987). Three-year-olds' difficulty with false belief: The case of a conceptual deficit. *British Journal of Developmental Psychology, 5*, 125–137.

Piaget, J. (1963). *The origins of intelligence in the child*. New York: Norton. (Original work published 1936)

Piaget, J. (1975). *The child's conception of the world*. (J. Tomlinson & A. Tomlinson, Trans.). Totowa, NJ: Littlefield, Adams. (Original work published 1929)

Plous, S. (1993). Psychological mechanisms in the human use of animals. *Journal of Social Issues, 49*(1), 11–52.

Poresky, R. H., & Hendrix, C. (1990). Differential effects of pet presences and pet-bonding on young children. *Psychological Reports, 67*, 51–54.

Redefer, L., & Goodman, J. (1989). Pet-facilitated therapy with autistic children. *Journal of Autism and Developmental Disorders, 19*(3), 461–467.

Ricard, M., & Allard, L. (1993). The reaction of 9- to 10-month-old infants to an unfamiliar animal. *Journal of Genetic Psychology, 154*(1), 5–16.

Richards, D. D., & Siegler, R. (1986). Children's understanding of the attributes of life. *Journal of Experimental Child Psychology, 42*, 1–22.

Ritvo, H. (1995). Border trouble: Shifting the line between people and other animals. *Social Research, 62*(3), 481–500.

Rizzo, T. A., Corsaro, W. A., & Bates, J. E. (1992). Ethnographic methods and interpretive analysis: Expanding the methodological options for psychologists. *Developmental Review, 12*, 101–123.

Roberts, K., & Cuff, M. D. (1989). Categorization studies of 9- to 15-month-old infants: Evidence for superordinate categorization? *Infant Behavior and Development, 12*, 265–288.

Rosengren, K. S., Gelman, S. A., Kalish, C. W., & McCormick, M. (1991). As time goes by: Children's early understanding of growth in animals. *Child Development, 62*, 1302–1320.

Ross, G. (1980). Categorization in 1- to 2-year-olds. *Developmental Psychology, 16*, 391–396.

Rost, D. H., & Hartmann, A. (1994). Children and their pets. *Anthrozoös, 7*(4), 242–254.

Rothenberg, D. (1991). The greenhouse from down deep: What can philosophy do for ecology? In M. S. Sontag, S. D. Wright, & G. L. Young (Eds.), *Human Ecology: Strategies for the future. Selected papers from the Fourth Conference of the Society for Human Ecology* (pp. 243–247). Fort Collins, CO: Society for Human Ecology.

Rousseau, J.-J. (1979). *Emile* (A. Bloom, Trans.). New York: Basic Books. (Original work published 1762)

Rousseau, J.-J. (1986). Discourse on the origins of inequality. In *The first and second discourses* and *Essay on the origins of languages* (V. Gourevitch, Trans. & Ed.). New York: Harper & Row. (Original work published 1755)

Routley, R. (1981). Alleged problems in attributing beliefs, and intentionality, to animals. *Inquiry, 24,* 385–417.

Rusca, G., & Tonucci, F. (1992). Development of the concepts of living and animal in the child. *European Journal of Psychology of Education, 7*(2), 151–176.

Sanders, C. R. (1990). The animal "Other": Self-definition, social identity and companion animals. *Advances in Consumer Research, 17,* 662–668.

Sanders, C. R. (1993). Excusing tactics: Social responses to the public misbehavior of companion animals. *Anthrozoös, 6*(2), 82–90.

Sanders, C. R., & Arluke, A. (1993). If lions could speak: Investigating the animal-human relationship and the perspectives of nonhuman others. *Sociological Quarterly, 34*(3), 377–390.

Sarles, H. (1977). *After metaphysics: Toward a grammar of interaction and discourse. (Studies in Semiotics, 13).* Lisse, The Netherlands: Peter De Ridder.

Savage-Rumbaugh E. S. (1986). *Ape language: From conditioned response to symbol.* New York: Columbia University Press.

Savage-Rumbaugh, E. S., Murphy, J. Sevcik, R. A., Brakke, K. Williams, S. L., & Rumbaugh, D. M. (1993). Language comprehension in ape and child. *Monographs of the Society for Research in Child Development, 58*(3–4, Serial No. 233).

Schutz, A. (1951). Making music together: A study in social relationship. *Social Research, 18*(1), 76–97.

Searle, J. R. (1983). *Intentionality: An essay in the philosophy of mind.* Cambridge, UK: Cambridge University Press.

Searles, H. F. (1960). The nonhuman environment in normal development and in schizophrenia. *Monograph Series on Schizophrenia, 5.* New York: International Universities Press.

Serpell, J. A. (1986). *In the company of animals: A study of human-animal relationships.* New York: Basil Blackwell.

Shapiro, K. (1985). *Bodily reflective modes: A phenomenological method for psychology.* Durham, NC: Duke University Press.

Shapiro, K. (1989). Understanding dogs through kinesthetic empathy, social construction, and history. *Anthrozoös, 3*(3),184–195.

Shepard, P. (1978). *Thinking animals: Animals and the development of human intelligence.* New York: Viking.

Sherick, I. (1981). The significance of pets for children: Illustrated by a latency-age girl's use of pets in her analysis. *Psychoanalytic Study of the Child, 36,* 193–215.

Sherrod, L. R. (1981). Issues in cognitive-perceptual development: The special case of social stimuli. In M. E. Lamb & L. R. Sherrod (Eds.), *Infant social cognition: Empirical and theoretical considerations* (pp. 11–36). Hillsdale, NJ: Lawrence Erlbaum.

Shweder, R. A. (1984). Anthropology's romantic rebellion against the enlighten-
ment, or there's more to thinking than reason and evidence. In R. A. Shweder &
R. A. LeVine (Eds.), *Culture theory* (pp. 27–66). Cambridge, UK: Cambridge
University Press.

Shweder, R. A., Mahapatra, M., & Miller, J. G. (1987). Culture and moral development. In J. Kagan & S. Lamb (Eds.), *The emergence of morality in young children*
(pp. 1–83). Chicago: University of Chicago Press.

Singer, P. (1975). *Animal liberation*. New York: Avon.

Singh, J. A. L., & Zingg, R. M. (1939). *Wolf children and feral man*. New York:
Harper & Brothers.

Soares, C. J. (1985). The companion animal in the context of the family system.
Marriage and the Family Review, 8, 49–62.

Spelke, E. (1979). Perceiving bimodally specified events in infancy. *Developmental
Psychology, 15,* 626–636.

Spelke, E., Phillips, A., & Woodward, A. (1995). Infants' knowledge of object motion and human action. In D. Sperber, D. Premack, & A. Premack (Eds.), *Causal
cognition: A multidisciplinary debate* (pp. 44–78). Oxford, UK: Clarendon.

Stallones, L. (1994). Pet loss and mental health. *Anthrozoös, 7*(1), 43–54.

Staub E. (1986). A conception of the determinants and development of altruism
and aggression: Motives, the self, and the environment." In C. Zahn-Waxler,
E. M. Cummings, & R. Iannotti (Eds.), *Altruism and aggression: Biological and social origins* (pp. 135–164). Cambridge, UK: Cambridge University Press.

Stern, D. (1985). *The interpersonal world of the infant*. New York: Basic Books.

Strayer, J. (1987). Affective and cognitive perspectives on empathy. In N. Eisenberg & J. Strayer (Eds.), *Empathy and its development* (pp. 218–244). Cambridge,
UK: Cambridge University Press.

Sullivan, H. S. (1953). *The interpersonal theory of psychiatry*. New York: Norton.

Sully, J. (1896). *Studies of childhood*. New York: D. Appleton.

Sussman M. (Ed.). (1985). Pets and the family [Special issue]. *Marriage & Family Review, 8*(3/4).

Symcox, G. (1972). The wild man's return: The enclosed vision of Rousseau's *Discourses*. In E. Dudley & M. E. Novak (Eds.), *The wild man within: An image in Western thought from the Renaissance to Romanticism* (pp. 223–247). Pittsburgh, PA:
University of Pittsburgh Press.

Tambiah, S. J. (1969). Animals are good to think and good to prohibit. *Ethnology 8,*
423–459.

Tester, K. (1991). *Animals and society: The humanity of animal rights*. New York: Routledge.

Thomas, E. M. (1993). *The hidden life of dogs*. Boston: Houghton Mifflin.

Thomas, K. (1983). *Man and the natural world: A history of the modern sensibility*. New
York: Pantheon.

Thorslev, P. L. (1972). The wild man's revenge. In E. Dudley & M. E. Novak (Eds.), *The wild man within: An image in Western thought from the Renaissance to Romanticism* (pp. 281–307). Pittsburgh, PA: University of Pittsburgh Press.

Tiedemann, D. (1927). Observations on the mental development of a child. (C. Murchisan & S. Langer, Trans.). *Journal of Genetic Psychology 35,* 205–230. (Original work published in 1787)

Trivers, R. (1991). Deceit and self-deception: The relation between communication and consciousness. In M. H. Robinson & L. Tiger (Eds.), *Man and beast revisited* (pp. 175–191). Washington DC: Smithsonian Institution.

Tuan, Y. F. (1984). *Dominance and affection: The making of pets.* New Haven, CT: Yale University Press.

von Uexküll, J. (1982). The theory of meaning (B. Stone & H. Weiner, Trans.). *Semiotics, 42*(1), 25–82. (Original work published 1940)

Van de Castle, R. (1983). Animal figures in fantasy and dreams. In A. H. Katcher & A. M. Beck (Eds.), *New perspectives on our lives with companion animals* (pp. 148–173). Philadelphia: University of Pennsylvania Press.

Varela, F. J., Thompson, E., & Rosch, E. (1991). *The embodied mind: Cognitive science and human experience.* Cambridge: MIT Press.

Watson, J. B., & Rayner, K. (1920). Conditioned emotional reactions. *Journal of Experimental Psychology, 3,* 1–14.

Watzlawick, P., Beavin, J. H., & Jackson, D. D. (1967). *Pragmatics of human communication: A study of interactional patterns, pathologies and paradoxes.* New York: Norton.

Wellman, H. M. (1990). *The child's theory of mind.* Cambridge: MIT Press.

White, S. H. (1983). The idea of development in developmental psychology. In R. M. Lerner (Ed.), *Developmental Psychology: Historical and philosophical perspectives* (pp. 55–77). Hillsdale, NJ: Lawrence Erlbaum.

Wilson. E. O. (1994). *Naturalist.* San Francisco: Island Press.

Winnicott, D. W. (1989). *Playing and reality.* New York: Tavistock/Routledge. (Original work published 1971)

Youniss, J. (1983). Understanding differences within friendship. In R. L. Leahy (Ed.), *The child's construction of social inequality* (pp. 161–178). New York: Academic Press.

Zimmer, H. (1960). *The king and the corpse.* New York: Meridian.

About the Book and Author

What role does an animal play in a child's developing sense of self? Do children and animals interact in ways no longer recognizable to adults? *Children and Animals: Social Development and Our Connections to Other Species* addresses these and many other intriguing questions by revealing the interconnected lives of the inhabitants of the preschool classroom—an environment abounding in childish verbal and nonverbal interactions with birds, turtles, toads, snakes, bugs, and other creatures.

The child-animal interactions captured here suggest that the young child's developing sense of self and interactive skills are honed and enriched by the presence of nonhuman creatures. In touching and playing with animals, in talking to them or in silent presence, children reveal feelings and objectives they share with these important members of their daily lives. A privileged route by which these meanings are expressed and made conscious is pretend play, in which children translate the shapes and moods of the animal body into their own. As adults, we tend to marginalize the role of the animal body and animals' presence in our lives. In contrast, children see "*real* animals" (as they put it) as co-conspirators, as creatures to contend with, as fascinatingly different yet similar other beings. Children's sense of connection to animals provides insights into social development—and into our ideas about what it means to become human.

Based on Gene Myers's study of two dozen children and containing excerpts from children's dialogues with their nonhuman playroom cohabitants, this book is a delightful and rewarding opportunity to learn how children craft a sense of self that differentiates them from the animal world. It captures in children's own words and acts the importance of animals, birds, and reptiles to the child's growing social self.

Parents, educators, and students of early childhood social development, as well as those intrigued by the intersection of human experience and the natural environment, will find this book to be a rewarding reading experience.

Gene Myers teaches human development, environmental education, and human ecology at Huxley College of Environmental Studies at Western Washington University.

Index